D0169074

George F. Will

Twayne's United States Authors Series

Frank Day, Editor
Clemson University

TUSAS 675

GEORGE F. WILL
Steve Fenn/ABC

George F. Will

Larry W. Chappell

Mississippi Valley State University

Twayne Publishers
An Imprint of Simon & Schuster Macmillan
New York

Prentice Hall International
London • Mexico City • New Delhi • Singapore • Sydney • Toronto

Twayne's United States Authors Series No. 675

George F. Will
Larry W. Chappell

Copyright © 1997 by Twayne Publishers
All rights reserved. No part of this book may be reproduced or transmitted in any form
or by any means, electronic or mechanical, including photocopying, recording, or by
any information storage and retrieval system, without permission in writing from the
Publisher.

Twayne Publishers
An Imprint of Simon & Schuster Macmillan
1633 Broadway
New York, NY 10019

Library of Congress Cataloging-in-Publication Data

Chappell, Larry W.
  George F. Will / Larry W. Chappell.
    p.   cm. — (Twayne's United States authors series ; TUSAS 675)
  Includes bibliographical references and index.
  ISBN 0-8057-4001-5 (alk. paper)
  1. Will, George F.   2. Journalists—United States—Biography.
  I. Title.   II. Series.
  PN4874.W62C43   1997
  070'.92—dc20
  [B]   96-38640
                                                                        CIP

The paper used in this publication meets the minimum requirements of American
National Standard for Information Sciences—Permanence of Paper for Printed Library
Materials. ANSI Z39.48-1984. ∞ ™

10 9 8 7 6 5 4 3 2 1 (hc)
Printed in the United States of America

For Bernie and Carle, partners in criminalities and leavings.

Contents

Preface

The preacher warns that there is no end to making books, and indeed authors find it difficult to stop writing. One reason stopping is so difficult concerns the quest for fairness. There is always less time than we need for doing justice to a weighty subject or a serious author.

George F. Will, as a good writer and a reflective thinker, presents a problem of selection. His work is richer than any summary can capture. I have chosen to focus on some major themes in his writing. I am comfortable in calling them major but would be hard-pressed to call them central or defining. Can a short list of themes capture a life's work? I can only hope to snare a few issues that are repeated concerns for Will and that also match my expertise and interests.

The study focuses on debates that have been at the forefront among political philosophers during the '80s and '90s. Political philosophy has centered on critiques of liberalism, especially by those representing communitarian and republican traditions. George Will has been a significant part of these debates, representing both republican and communitarian ideas in his writings. Unfortunately, his work has not received the attention it deserves among political philosophers and legal theorists. This book is an effort to rectify that oversight.

My efforts benefited considerably when Mr. Will graciously consented to a rather lengthy interview. The interview allowed me to sharpen my understanding of his political and legal philosophy. It also aided me in gauging some changing directions in his thought.

The reader will learn rather quickly that my sentiments and thoughts are favorable to the liberal tradition broadly construed. I also hope to have demonstrated that Will does not depart from the American liberal tradition so sharply as some might suppose. The disagreements I have with Will are crevasses rather than canyons, but they are serious enough. Where agreement exists, I have attempted to show that Will supports his positions with well-reasoned arguments and distinctions. Where disagreement exists, I have attempted to suggest nuances that may cast the issues in a different light.

Political arguments in America have tended to reflect a fairly high degree of consensus when compared with, say, Weimar Germany or

Northern Ireland. That does not mean that our disagreements are trivial. What liberal life demands is civil and thoughtful discussion. My hope is that this book makes a small contribution to sustaining our tradition of liberal discussion while recommending the work of someone who has made a notable contribution to it.

Acknowledgments

Good readers of manuscripts help us avoid sins of both commission and omission. I would be guilty of the latter were I not to mention the people who read and commented on all or part of my manuscript. Bernard Bray, Frank Day, Carle Jackson, Elen Singh, and Rob Waters read and commented on drafts of this book. Their efforts have made my work less prone to intellectual sins than it would have been otherwise.

Michael Franz and Ed Wheat served as discussants for conference papers from which substantial portions of this text were drawn. Their comments were incisive and helpful.

I am thankful to Glen Erickson for suggesting that I write this book. My long discussions with him of philosophical issues have decisively shaped my thinking.

I am grateful to the National Endowment for the Humanities for sponsoring several summer seminars and institutes from which I have learned much of what has gone into this book. The directors of these programs deserve mention for their outstanding efforts to foster careful thought. Stephen Holmes's seminar on the history of European liberalism was especially helpful in exposing the intellectualist fallacy of comparing liberal societies with nonliberal societies—maintaining that the fair comparison is theories with theories and societies with societies. Richard Schacht's seminar helped me understand that liberal societies need no metaphysical warrant for their existence. Edwin Curley's seminar deepened my appreciation of Hobbes's and Spinoza's contributions to liberal thought and of the distance between authentic liberalism and flabby optimism. George Lucas's institute helped me understand the importance of tradition for sustaining regimes that allow for deep questions concerning tradition.

George F. Will and his staff were most gracious in hosting my interview with Mr. Will. Dusa Gyllensvard was especially patient and cooperative in answering my requests for information. Throughout the process of writing the book, Mr. Will and his staff demonstrated the qualities of respect and courtesy without which intellectual and moral life cannot flourish.

I owe an entirely unpayable debt to the people who taught me how to do political philosophy: Walter H. Bennett, Cecil Eubanks, and Ellis

Sandoz. I can only hope to approximate the unapproachable standards they set.

I gratefully acknowledge permission to quote from several sources:

The Morning After: American Successes and Excesses, 1981–1986 by George F. Will. Copyright © 1986 by The Washington Post Company. Reprinted with permission of the Free Press, a division of Simon & Schuster.

Suddenly: The American Idea at Home and Abroad, 1986–1990 by George F. Will. Copyright © 1990 by the Washington Post Company. Reprinted with permission of the Free Press, a division of Simon & Schuster.

Restoration: Congress, Term Limits, and the Recovery of Deliberative Democracy by George F. Will. Copyright © 1992 by George F. Will. Reprinted with the permission of the Free Press, a division of Simon & Schuster.

Statecraft as Soulcraft: What Government Does by George F. Will. Copyright © 1983 by G.F.W., Inc. Reprinted with the permission of Simon & Schuster.

The New Season: A Spectator's Guide to the 1988 Election by George F. Will. Copyright © 1987 by G.F.W., Inc. Reprinted with the permission of Simon & Schuster.

The Leveling Wind: Politics, the Culture, and Other News, 1990–1994 by George F. Will. Copyright © 1994 by George F. Will. Reprinted with the permission of Viking Penguin, a division of Penguin Books USA Inc.

The Pursuit of Happiness and Other Sobering Thoughts by George F. Will. Copyright © 1979 by George F. Will. Reprinted with the permission of George F. Will.

The Pursuit of Virtue and Other Tory Notions by George F. Will. Copyright © 1982 by George F. Will. Reprinted with the permission of George F. Will.

"Beyond the Reach of Majorities: Closed Questions in the Open Society," a Ph.D. dissertation by George F. Will. Copyright © 1968 by George F. Will. Reprinted with the permission of George F. Will.

Interview conducted by Larry W. Chappell with George F. Will, June 1994. Reprinted with the permission of George F. Will.

Book review by Larry W. Chappell of *Restoration: Congress, Term Limits and the Recovery of Deliberative Democracy* by George F. Will, reviewed in *The American Review of Politics*, Autumn 1993, 420–22. Reprinted with the permission of *The American Review of Politics*.

I would also like to express gratitude to Capital Cities/ABC, Inc. for allowing me to use Steve Fenn's picture of George Will for the book.

Chronology

1941   George F. Will born in Champaign, Illinois, child of Mr. and Mrs. Frederick L. Will. His father was professor of philosophy at the University of Illinois.

1962   Received B.A. from Trinity College in Hartford, Connecticut.

1964   Received B.A. in politics, philosophy, and economics from Magdalen College of Oxford University.

1967   Received M.A. and Ph.D. from Princeton University.

1967   Taught political philosophy at Michigan State University (1967 to 1968).

1968   Taught political philosophy at the University of Toronto (1968 to 1970).

1970   Served on the staff of Senator Gordon Allott, Republican from Colorado (1970 to 1972).

1973   Washington editor for *National Review* magazine (1973 to 1976).

1974   Began writing a syndicated column for the *Washington Post*.

1977   Won Pulitzer Prize for commentary in his columns. Served for seven years as a regular panelist on *Agronsky and Company*.

1978   *The Pursuit of Happiness and Other Sobering Thoughts*.

1981   Became a founding member of the panel of ABC's *This Week with David Brinkley*.

1982   *The Pursuit of Virtue and Other Tory Notions*.

1983   *Statecraft as Soulcraft: What Government Does*.

1986   *The Morning After: American Successes and Excesses, 1981–1986*.

1987   *The New Season: A Spectator's Guide to the 1988 Election*.

1990   *Men at Work: The Craft of Baseball*.

1995 Appointed commissioner of the Texas-Louisiana Baseball League. Visiting lecturer at the School of Government, Harvard University.

Chapter One
Introduction

Frequently, studies of an author involve a book-by-book review of the major works by the author. Such a format is not particularly appropriate for a study of George F. Will. Will is a working journalist who earned his Pulitzer Prize by writing short weekly columns. He does not usually write books as books. Rather, he collects his columns to be published later as books.

I am not suggesting that Will's books lack the unity that would allow us to appreciate them as "works." Instead, I want to highlight the manner in which they acquire their unity. Will, like other good writers, has a limited range of concerns (and obsessions) around which his thoughts and writings revolve. From these concerns his work develops a thematic unity. I want to focus on his variations and refinements of a few central themes. These are highlighted and expressed in some books more fully than others. But I want to retain the freedom to explore Will's development regarding ideas that have recurred in a variety of works. In some cases, a single book explores a theme with sustained concentration. In those instances, I use the book as a point of departure and introduce comments on other books as the narrative requires.

In reviewing an author's writings, I do not want to assume that there is a single standard for a "good book." Good books are usually good examples of their kind (assuming they are not sui generis). What kind of writer is George Will? He is (among other things) a journalist, a conservative, and an ethical, political, and legal thinker. Consequently I evaluate his merits as a journalistic essay writer and his contributions to conservative thought in particular and ethical, legal, and political philosophy in general. I devote full chapters to Will's contribution to conservative thought and legal theory. Discussion of his ethical and political thought runs through several chapters. Some comments on his role as a journalist are appropriate now.

Political Ethics and the Task of Journalism

The principal focus of my study is Will's ethical and political thought. That focus creates an immediate problem. George Will is a journalist.

1

Although his education was in political philosophy, his chosen profession as a journalist seems to separate him from the world of philosophical thought. There is a common conviction that ethics and political thought are the province of a tribe of specialists known as ethicists, political philosophers, and political scientists, but this conviction serves us poorly on two counts. First, it places reflection in the hands of a few when action is expected from all. Second, the segregation of thought from journalism invites irresponsibility from those who are instrumental in shaping our public consciousness. Will believes that journalists (especially those who style themselves commentators) must rise to the challenge of thinking through our obligations as citizens and the conditions for the good life.

Will is aware that the task of ethical and political thinking is formidable. After all, philosophers have proposed numerous theories and systems purporting to reveal our station and its duties. The most obvious thing about these systems and theories is that most, if not all, have been contradicted by able thinkers. This is not to counsel despair. The disagreements among the specialists may liberate nonspecialists to think about ethics and politics. An awareness of the insecurity of ethical and political theories frees us from the anxieties of professionalism. An educated general public appears no worse off than professional theorists— neither has produced a measure of certainty that allows easy dismissal of competing claims. Nevertheless, the act of writing about moral and political issues embodies a claim to some sort of expertise. Why write for an audience that already knows what you know?

If we concede the existence of some degree of ethical expertise, there is still a role for reflection among nonprofessionals. If thought is to have public significance, it must be possible to translate it into action. Thinking may require complexity and sophistication, but when it comes time to convert thought to practice, it must be presented as what Bergson calls "high-level popularization." The ethical insights of professionals must be converted to usable form. Ordinary citizens lack the time, and in some cases the skills, to appropriate insights by evaluating complex lines of argument. Will studied as a political philosopher, served as a member of a legislative staff, and spent many years writing popular essays. He seems well suited to mediate between professionals and a larger public.[1]

There are two fairly obvious, though incompatible, objections to what I have written. First, a radical egalitarian could object that I should concede no role whatsoever for ethical expertise.[2] An egalitarian critic would argue that whatever standards or principles we adopt should be accessible to and capable of discussion by any ordinary citizen. Ethics, especially in a democratic society, is not the domain of experts in morality. A contemporary critic of moral expertise would likely claim that moral elites rely on some version of "foundationalism," believing that moral principles are guaranteed by a higher principle that is discoverable by some procedure inaccessible to the common person. Give up the belief that moral principles are subject to demonstration, and you will abandon the belief in moral expertise, or so the critique might conclude.[3]

Second, a staunch defender of moral expertise might object that I underestimate the rarity, nobility, and difficulty of ethical thinking. Ethics requires rigor, and rigor requires both concentration and skill. Popularization, a specialist might argue, tends to distort by simplifying. It may be as important to understand how we arrive at a moral standard as what the standard is. In any case, we will want to understand how a principle applies or fails to apply to varied circumstances. In some cases, the principles governing action may be so complex as to require delegation of judgment, allowing another to act for us.

I think there is enough truth in both of these stances to give pause, but not enough to lead us to reject the role of the popularizer. I am sympathetic with the repudiation of foundationalism and metaphysics, but that does not lead me to accept a moral nihilism that claims equal moral knowledge for all. Moral nihilism entails the conviction that no moral judgment is superior to another. If there are no correct moral judgments, surely we are all equal, and moral expertise is impossible.[4] I want to retain the possibility of moral debate, inquiry, and instruction. Moral discussion requires the conviction that there are considerations that may be unknown but relevant for someone seeking to form a judgment. If a person knows relevant considerations that another does not, that person has moral expertise. This conception of moral expertise is not abstruse or metaphysical. A moral expert could know the likely costs of garbage collection and be deemed a moral expert if the knowledge is relevant to a decision. What seems missing from this account is a more general expertise that we are likely to associate with moral theory. Are there general practitioners in moral discourse?

If we affirm moral expertise, we are vulnerable to a claim that moral expertise is distant enough from common understanding to negate the possibility or propriety of popularization. Surely some moral expertise is. There are bound to be relevant considerations that are not known, or even possible to be made known, to a well-educated general public. I suspect that the range of these issues is more narrow than an aspiring moral aristocrat might imagine. Even if we assume that the range of expertise is large, we should neither inflate the role of experts nor dismiss that of popularizers. Having moral expertise is not the same as being a moral expert on all matters. One's expertise may be formidable, yet relevant to only a small portion of issues. We cannot assume that any group of experts can address all the issues we face. Experts frequently find it difficult to arrive at consensus in their fields, much less in areas where expertise overlaps. Indeed, one's expertise is often incomprehensible to other experts. In any case, expertise can have moral relevance only when we credit it as expertise, and that requires at least some understanding by nonexperts of what the expert is doing. If expertise is so arcane that no one can popularize it, it derives whatever public significance it has from an act of faith for which no evidence is available. Is rule by an incomprehensible elite an ideal to which we (the inexpert public) want to subscribe? If not, the role of popular mediation seems indispensable.

A journalist making a serious contribution to the full range of our public debates would have to be a generalist. Is there a place in our public lives for ethical generalists? Why not accept Michel Foucault's view that there is no place for general political or ethical theories? Foucault would replace general commentary on public life with the work of "specific intellectuals" who share widely the results of their studies and leave it to the intellectual consumer to decide the proper use of the intellectual archive.[5] I share Foucault's suspicions of the tendency, inherited from the enlightenment, to construct philosophical systems that more often than not are transformed into prisons and gas chambers for millions. But writing is an inherently ethical activity if we understand ethics as seeking and prescribing right order. Effective writing selects for the reader a way of thinking that structures (intentionally or unintentionally) the way we live. Since acts are embedded in ways of life, they are not local. They web outward into a network of relations that are incapable of isolation. To say that important writing is not a narrowly localized set of relations is not to affirm that writing aims or should aim at a universal audience. Rejecting a crusading universalism does not, however, preclude reflection on the direction of the society in which we live or how it comports itself toward other societies.

If we are not to prescribe rules of conduct for all the world, what is the role of the generalist? What is the subject matter of ethical and political thought? We can conceive political ethics as reflection on the traditions we inherit and their connection to the choices we face. Conceiving political ethics this way has distinct advantages for a study of George Will. As a journalist, Will must reflect on the issues of the day, which are the stuff of politics. As a conservative, he assumes an obligation to connect his journalism to the broad traditions that sustain our political life. His obituary and tribute to Joseph Alsop eloquently captures a vision of journalism as a portal to larger considerations: "Journalists' lives are tethered to events. Their occupational hazard is depletion of intellectual capital. Their challenge to which none has arisen as well as Alsop did, is to irrigate their judgment with clear, cold waters from springs—history, literature, art—that flow far from the deadening everydayness of public life."[6] The challenge, then, is to maintain a dual awareness of both the flux of daily life and the deeper truths of the civilization. That is a tall task. It requires someone with tremendous energy and intellectual discipline. George Will has both, but keeping in touch with a broad range of philosophical, scholarly, and literary work while attending to the latest wrangles in Congress is a risky business. Deciding how well Will survives the risks is the key to evaluating his accomplishments.

On Criticism

In criticizing a journalist and political thinker, the temptation is to demand conformity with our views. Criticism as cheerleading, however, suffers from a major defect. If the author is so right, what is the point of criticism other than encouraging people to read the author and making additional observations in your own voice? That alone would not justify adding to the forest of secondary literature merely explicating the work of people who write clearly. Criticism as booing is more understandable. Critics need to exorcise demons, but most serious criticisms are about authors who are less than demonic or at least interesting demons. Criticism aims to preserve the memory of an author, not destroy it. The critic hopes to enrich our understanding of an authorship, not to bury it in invective.

What, then, is a critic looking for? For me, an author worth writing about must be serious. What do I mean by serious? A serious author causes arrests in our judgments.[7] We normally rock along, confident in the views we offer to willing and unwilling audiences. A good author will force us to pause and either admit that we may be wrong or at least realize that our cherished positions need reformulating. The obligation of a critic toward a serious writer is to produce serious criticism that causes one to revise one's own views, acknowledge worthy insights, introduce qualifications that strengthen a position an author has weakened, or admit that it is difficult to decide between one's position and that of the author. These responses build on the awareness that we do not undertake criticism on blank slates. Critics do not have the luxury of objectivity or presuppositionless stances. That does not mean we cannot be fair. Serious views are revisable. The very act of criticism presupposes that the encounter between clashing perspectives can result in reasonable adjustments among civilized disputants.

Apart from evaluation, a critic can serve to connect an author and the readers to a larger literature. Will writes for a general audience, some of whom may be oblivious to the sometimes arcane debates in ethical, legal, and political theory upon which he touches and from which he draws. Many readers will know little of the disputes among republican, communitarian, and liberal thinkers or where Will stands in these debates. One of the aims of my book is to show how Will's work links us to important issues in contemporary thought and to point the way for the general reader to deepen his or her understanding of those issues. Consequently, I have included a fairly large number of notes—though these hardly exhaust the huge volume of works I could have cited. One mark of Will's seriousness is that his writing fits so well in many of the deepest debates of our time.

This book is about George Will. This is obviously not the place to extensively elaborate my approach to political philosophy. Nevertheless, I do owe the reader some idea of the perspective from which my criticism derives.

Augustinian Counterpoint

The general attitude from which I approach political affairs I term "Augustinian liberalism."[8] I articulate my notion of liberalism throughout the text. It is appropriate here to consider in what sense my liberalism is Augustinian.

It must certainly seem bizarre to invoke Augustine in praise of liberalism. How could I dream of associating a doctrine whose central value is freedom with such a staunch defender of governmental authority? Much of Augustine's case for authority hinges on biblical exegesis, but if we bypass those arguments, the connection is perhaps less strange. I am not proposing to abstract purely "philosophical" elements from Augustine's writings, since I doubt these exist. I am simply making the eclectic use I make of any writer—choosing what I find appealing or interesting or useful and leaving the rest. What I find most interesting are those aspects of Augustine's thought that serve to undermine authority. Paul Ricoeur associates the "hermeneutics of suspicion" with Marx, Freud, and Nietzsche. These writers call into radical suspicion claims to truth, beauty, and goodness and undermine the rhetoric of justice by revealing it as naked power. Augustine too was willing to subvert the authoritative logos that undergirded Greek and Roman claims to right order. Is there anything in Nietzsche that destroys the appearance of justice more tellingly than Augustine's account of Alexander the Great and the pirate?

Justice being taken away, then what are kingdoms but great robberies? For what are robberies themselves, but little kingdoms? The band itself is made up of men; it is ruled by the authority of a prince, it is knit together by the fact of the confederacy; the booty is divided by the law agreed on. If, by the admittance of abandoned men, this evil increases to such a degree that it holds places, fixes abodes, takes possession of cities, and subdues peoples, it assumes the more plainly the name kingdom, not by the removal of covetousness, but by the addition of impunity. Indeed, that was an apt and true reply which was given to Alexander the Great by a pirate who had been seized. For when the king had asked the man what he meant by keeping hostile possession of the seas, he answered with bold pride "what thou meanest by seizing the whole earth; but because I do it with a petty ship, I am called a robber, while thou who doest it with a great fleet art styled emperor."[9]

Of course, Augustine appeals to authority as he undermines the authority of the "pagans." Christ is as authoritative as authority can get. Nevertheless, a critic can agree with Augustine's critique of authority without accepting Christian dogmatics. Furthermore, the authority of Christ may have marginal relevance for temporal affairs. The reign of justice is not for this world; true justice requires the transfiguring grace of Christ at the end of time. Transcendent justice might be as "wholly other" as the God who sustains it.[10]

To raise the banner of Augustinian liberalism, what do I need to borrow from the saint? I want to maintain Augustine's commitment to what Eliseo Vivas calls "axiological realism."[11] The right and the good have an ontological status independent of human wishes and will. The

right obligates us (inclines us toward the good), and both the right and
the good give direction to ethical questing. From this perspective, it is
possible to speak of evil regimes and policies across time and cultural
boundaries. Note that I read the axiologically real not as an object of
reason or experience, but rather as an experience of seeking order—a
"call forward" as John Cobb would have it.[12]

Another feature of Augustine's thought that I stress is moral finitude.
Human beings (as currently constituted) cannot accomplish what is
right with anything near complete perfection. A rationalist might object
that what is missing from our present moral constitution is the scientific
knowledge to remedy our situation. The Augustinian riposte, however,
stresses the radical character of our failings—failings that are not
reducible to intellectual inadequacies. I maintain this aspect of Augustinian thought because the single most effective complaint against some
liberal thought concerns naive optimism. Kant may be right that a
nation of intelligent devils could solve the problem of establishing public order.[13] We need to cultivate the cautious expectation that public
order without full justice (what Augustine calls "the peace of Babylon")
may be the best we can get.

The final aspect of Augustine's thought from which I draw concerns
the evil of moral perfectionism. Moral perfectionism is a moral mistake.
Attempts to eradicate evil and tragedy from the human condition frequently make matters worse. The effort to transfigure human experience into paradise is more than likely to accomplish the reverse. For
Augustine, we overrate our goodness and understanding when we set
out to remake the world. We do not have a God's-eye view of things,
and we tend to mistake our good for the common good. Consequently,
even when we have good intentions, our efforts to remake the world
reflect our flawed image.

The three aspects of Augustine's thought that I have appropriated
correspond to his doctrines of natural law, original sin, and pride. I do
not wish to carry all the baggage associated with these doctrines. There
is a kernel of meaning in each that corresponds well with my experience
of the human condition. More important, the doctrines set severe limits
on the possibilities for politics, discouraging optimistic glosses on political action.

The principal message I take from Augustine is: Avoid evil. Fre-
quently, that means: Do not attempt to do good.[14] Augustine (as
Hobbes would do later) converts the golden rule into a negative maxim:
Do not unto others that which you would not have done unto you. Since

doing good frequently entails prideful harm, Augustine enjoins us to restrain ourselves even from our most sincere acts of doing good. That requires a willingness to release others from our care and supervision. Thus freedom, the center of any genuinely liberal thought, relies less on confidence in human capacity than in mistrust of ourselves and our government.

I teach classes in constitutional law. In those classes, I ask my students to learn "Chappell's laws of constitutional interpretation." The first law is: You can't trust anyone. The second is: You have to trust someone. The third is: You must watch those you can't trust. I illustrate throughout two semesters how these laws help us understand the design of the U.S. Constitution. These principles are distinctly Augustinian, and they are also compatible with liberalism. Liberalism is about freedom, and freedom often appears in the social interstices created by mistrust.

The Plan of the Book

As I have stated, the focus of the book is Will's ethical and political thought. The central themes of his political philosophy are community and virtue. These themes I explicate and evaluate in chapter 2. I ask whether a commitment to community and virtue provides the basis for a fundamental critique of the American political order.

For Will, the basis for community and virtue is a sound system of laws. Chapter 3 discusses his approach to legal issues and his approach to interpreting the Constitution. I focus on three issues to illustrate and evaluate his legal theory: (1) his commitment to a theory of judicial interpretation known as "original intent," (2) his promotion of law as a tool to provide training in virtue, and (3) his theory of "constructive repression" as an alternative to liberal theories concerning the First Amendment.

One test for the adequacy of a political theory is its applicability. Can we apply the insights in the theory to the world of concrete political disputes? Chapters 4 and 5 explore the ways Will applies his theory to practical politics. I connect a variety of issues including abortion, affirmative action, political correctness, and gay rights to central themes in Will's political philosophy.

Chapter 6 examines the applicability of Will's search for a virtuous community to electoral politics and theories of representation. Here the theme of virtue introduced in earlier chapters expands to encompass the

notion of civic virtue. I connect the idea of civic virtue to Will's affirmation of "classical republicanism."

Chapter 7 discusses Will's contributions to conservative thought.
There are many strands of conservative thought in America, and they do
not easily weave into a single tapestry. I explore the tensions among
Will's variety of conservatism and other conservatisms. I also consider
the value of adding a disparate voice to the conservative conversation
and how that conversation fits into the panoply of American thought.

Chapter 8 concludes the book by exploring the theme of tension. As I
shall argue, there is little room to introduce a robust conception of
virtue into the American order. Consequently, much of what Will has to
offer to our moral and political life is, to use his phrase, "more tension."[15] Indeed, I think the main strength of his work is helping to
maintain tension. That is why readers along the political spectrum owe
him serious attention.

The most obvious omission that Will's readers will notice is a discussion of baseball. Will's book on baseball is *Men at Work: The Craft of
Baseball*.[16] As the subtitle indicates, the book is about the craft of one
sport. Unfortunately, I know little about this sport and next to nothing
about the technical aspects of it. Consequently, readers seeking an evaluation of that book will have to look elsewhere.[17]

The other obvious omission is international relations—about which
Will has written extensively. I plead two reasons for the exclusion. For-
eign affairs is not my strongest area. I do not think it is Will's either.[18]
In any case, the most prominent feature of Will's writings on foreign
affairs was his firm advocacy for vigorously prosecuting the cold war.
Those writings have less relevance than they once had.

Chapter Two

In Search of the Virtuous Republic: George Will's Critique of the American Political Tradition

Do thyself no harm: for we are all here.

Acts 16:28

You can't shut out the risk and the pain
Without losing the love that remains.
We're all riders on this train.

Bruce Springsteen

Statecraft as Soulcraft

Much debate over the character of the American regime has stemmed from a classic study by Louis Hartz.[1] Hartz maintained that the American political tradition involves a Lockean, liberal consensus. There have been challenges to the Hartz thesis, claiming a place of honor for republican thought, Biblical faith, classical philosophy, radical egalitarianism, and natural law, among others. Furthermore, there is serious doubt that liberalism is a single, unified tradition.[2] Hartz's thesis that liberalism has been the dominant tradition in America has received substantial criticism but not refutation. At best, critics have demonstrated that other traditions are important parts of our liberal tradition, not that they have displaced or seriously challenged the liberal reign. We can, with Robert Bellah and his associates, plausibly conceive America as a liberal culture with submerged "second languages" weakly competing for our allegiance.[3]

American liberalism is best described as classical liberalism, stemming from practical experience as well as from the theories of Hobbes, Locke, and Spinoza. Classical liberalism is, in the American context, a conservative force seeking to preserve the basic traditions of a Lockean republic. Classical liberalism is, like all liberalisms, a defense of freedom.

11

Liberals defend freedom either with an appeal to natural rights or, more plausibly for many Americans, with a plea for its utility.

When I use the term "classical liberalism," I do not connote a theory of laissez faire political economy—a common but mistaken association. Adam Smith, who is frequently associated with both classical liberalism and laissez faire, was willing to sanction considerably more intervention in economic affairs than, say, Herbert Spencer, who is, in my conception, a progressive liberal. Liberalism should not be confused with the narrow connotations it has assumed in America. In America we use the term "liberal" to refer to staunch defenders of the welfare state and contrast them with conservative critics. Our ideological divisions are much more complicated than this stark contrast. Liberalism includes those committed to freedom as the primary political good and who believe in government limited by constitutional constraints. Considered broadly, liberalism includes Bill Clinton, Ted Kennedy, Daniel Patrick Moynihan, Newt Gingrich, Bob Dole, and William Weld—along with almost anyone whom we take seriously in the American political arena. This is not to doubt that the differences among us are serious but rather to maintain that the fidelity to the liberal tradition by a wide range of our political and intellectual figures is genuine.

George Will shares the belief that America's principal tradition is liberalism broadly understood. He also believes that our political tradition is defective. In declaring the American tradition defective, Will faces a basic problem in American conservative thought. Conservatives cannot conserve tradition in general, since a tradition is always that of a concrete society. If liberalism is our basic tradition, a call to jettison it is radical rather than conservative.[4] Consequently, some conservatives have concluded that their primary obligation is to conserve liberalism.[5]

Will is far from being a radical critic of liberalism. Instead of being jettisoned, he believes liberalism needs tempering by forgotten resources within our tradition. Our liberal culture is an event within a longer tradition from which we can draw sustenance. Commenting on Solzhenitsyn, Will observes that "his ideas about the nature of man and the essential political problem are broadly congruent with the ideas of Cicero and other ancients, and those of Aquinas, Richard Hooker, Pascal, Thomas More, Burke, Hegel and others. Compared with the long and broad intellectual tradition in which Solzhenitsyn's views are rooted, the tradition of modernity, or liberalism, is short and thin."[6] Will attributes too much unity to his list of thinkers, but his general point is valid. There is a larger set of ideas about right order available in our culture than is incorporated into our practices. The question remains: What ideas have we ignored that would improve our regime? Will believes that the greatest need is to restore a robust conception of the common good. A liberal regime stresses the freedom of the individual to choose a way of life without coercion, or even guidance, from public authorities. When the individual is free, the conditions for abundance arise; but a life devoted to pursuit of private advantage carries costs. In a liberal society, we lose sight of the common good. As our sense of obligation to one another eclipses, we relinquish any idea of justice suitable to bind us. The result is what Will calls the "cuisinart theory of justice" where "the endless maelstrom of individuals pursuing private goods produces, magically, the public good."[7] According to Will, the magic is nothing more than the reduction of serious conceptions of the good to a semantic fiat.

Will argues that restoring a conception of the common good requires us to rekindle the notions of community and virtue. Will asserts that a community "consists of people held together by a broad deep consensus about justice under a common sovereignty" (SUD, 85). This Ciceronian conception of community contrasts sharply with the liberalism portrayed in *Statecraft as Soulcraft*. There, Will portrays the American regime as increasingly devoid of any shared conception of the common good, much less a deep one.[8]

Will bemoans our failure to inculcate the civic virtue necessary for devotion to the public good. Early in his career as a journalist, Will acknowledged the need for leaders willing to call for public virtue. "There is something missing in the conservatism that marches beneath the DISPOSABLE INCOME! banner. In my mind's ear, I hear Peggy Lee singing, 'Is that all there is?' What is missing is political leadership that summons individuals to citizenship, to the pursuit of something in addition to the expanded personal freedom that disposable income conveys. What is missing is a politics that appeals to what Lincoln called 'the better angels of our nature.' Lincoln, the fountain of Republicanism, is a reminder that even a muddy stream can have snow at its source."[9]

Will has defined civic virtue as "a steady predisposition to prefer the public good to private advantage when they conflict."[10] He maintains that civic virtue is unwelcome in our regime because it demands sacrifice (RES, 156). Our sense of civic obligation has thinned to an unbearable minimum: "The sole publicly relevant . . . character traits—self-interestedness and tolerance—are suddenly within the reach of virtually everybody" (SS, 44).

For Will, the key to fostering virtue is statecraft, and statecraft must be soulcraft. Soulcraft is inescapable because all societies educate their citizens, and "all education is moral education because learning conditions conduct" (SS, 19). Will does not believe the state can shape people in any direction it chooses. Human nature limits the possibility for molding conduct.[11]

Will protests James Madison's largely Hobbesian vision of human nature as too "stark" (SS, 67). Will concedes we are self-interested, prone to faction, and liable to threaten the rightful interests of others, but he thinks we can supply some of the better motives for which Madison's institutional arrangements were to provide auxiliary precautions. Will sees himself as occupying a middle ground between the ancients who overestimated the power of civic education and the moderns who hold our capacity for disinterested action in too little esteem (SS, 72–79). He maintains a philosophical anthropology thought consonant with Christianity. "Christianity's assessment of man, at once high and severe, is about right for political philosophy: Man can be magnificent [sic], but is magnificent [sic] rarely and never spontaneously—without help from nurturing institutions" (MA, 223). Creating nurturing institutions is the proper business of soulcraft.

Will denies that soulcraft involves an extensive training in civic virtue on the order of, say, the Spartan republic. "The aim is not to make society inhospitable to pluralism, but to make pluralism safe for society" (SS, 94). Preserving pluralism requires only a modicum of civic virtue and devotion to the common good. "To say that statecraft is soulcraft is not to say the government should be incandescent with ardor for excellence in everything at all times. That would be tiresome. Statecraft as soulcraft should mean only a steady inclination generally unfelt and unthought. It should mean a disposition in the weighing of political persons and measures to include consideration of whether they accord with worthy ends for the polity" (SS, 94). This does not make clear how we are to reshape our language and practices to comport with the public interest, but a lack of clarity is endemic to initial formulations of principles.

As a practicing journalist, Will has the advantage over many contemporary political philosophers of regularly applying his principles to the issues of the day.[12] Nevertheless, some initial clarification of his key terms is desirable. Critically evaluating Will's contribution to contemporary political theory involves clarifying three key concepts that appear to distinguish his thought from American liberalism: the good, community, and virtue. After addressing these terms, I turn to two questions. First, does the liberal tradition lack the resources to answer the challenges Will poses to its authority and viability? Second, does Will offer usable suggestions on how to mend ruptures in our political tradition? I address the first question in this chapter. The second question is the focus of chapters 4 and 5.

Goodness, Community, and Virtue

The Good

Affirming the common good is central to Will's critique of the American political order. The affirmation raises three questions. First, how are we to define the good? Second, can we secure agreement on its meaning? Third, can we attain the good we have agreed to seek? Will does not offer a detailed theory of the good. Does that mean his appeal to the common good is no more than empty rhetoric? Not at all.[13]

We ought not assume that a usable term requires either a definition or a theory before we can put it to work. Many of our most serviceable terms are undefined but subject to explication. We learn what we mean by them as we use them.[14] Regarding the common good, we can begin with a vague contrast between private interests and the public good and explicate through examples. We can also follow the *via negativa* by showing cases of what the public weal is not—a procedure Will uses quite well.

Will adopts an approach to the good that is largely deliberative. The good is something we ought to talk about.[15] Will confirmed the centrality of discussion for seeking the good in an interview with me during June of 1994. When I asked him how we achieve agreement on the meaning of the common good in a pluralist society, he replied: "We talk about it" (Will interview). He insisted, however, that we maintain more confidence than philosophers such as John Rawls, Bruce Ackerman, and Stuart Hampshire about our ability to answer questions about the good. In any event, there is no way of knowing the good independent of our deliberations about it. An adequate knowledge of the good requires a satisfactory deliberative process. I discuss Will's approach to deliberation in chapter 6. Here I mark problems key to evaluating his approach—problems that will figure into my analysis later.

First, Will needs not only to distinguish the public from the private good, he must also establish when the common good should take precedence. When does my good contribute to our good? Can we assume that what is good for the community is always preferable to that which benefits only some of us? If not, we need to decide when the common good takes priority. Second, Will should assure us that the claim to commonalty is not merely domination. How can we distinguish what is truly good for all of us from what is merely good for General Motors? Third, Will would be well-advised to weigh the costs of an education in virtue. Busybodies may know best, but that alone does not make them admirable. Even when moral instruction produces good results, it may have unintended, negative consequences. Instructing others to do good may produce resentment and discord. It may also produce moral infancy among people who never learn to reflect on the limits and dangers of doing good.

Community

Contemporary discussions of togetherness deploy the term "community."[16] The term is deeply contested, perhaps "essentially contested."[17] I doubt that a general definition will produce much assent or attain much utility. We understand "community" best when we examine and analyze "communities." Identifying the general property of being in community with another is not initially very informative.[18] I begin with a very general notion of community and work my way toward more concrete embodiments. Generally, the term describes any state where two or more things regularly relate to one another. Community involves all ways of being together. Within this general conception are innumerable ways to instantiate community.

Unfortunately, much contemporary debate in political philosophy frames a contest between communitarians and liberals.[19] The debate builds on a false contrast—as if communitarians were simply for and liberals against community. Liberal societies are one type of community among others. Any form of association requires ongoing patterns of belief and behavior that connect people, and liberal communities certainly have those. The illusion of starting fresh is one pattern of belief that sustains and invigorates liberal politics. In any case, I use the term "community" to refer broadly to ongoing ways of being together and differentiate types of communities within the broad category.

What kinds of communities are liberal? No answer can avoid controversy, but I focus on a few features of liberal polities that help to provide a framework for analyzing Will's work.

Liberal regimes, if they are viable, federate communities—communities of communities as Horace Kallen (who coined the term "cultural pluralism") puts it.[20] National liberal communities are distinguishable from local communities and neither are coextensive with governments. What distinguishes one community from another is the degree of "thickness" each embodies. Thickness requires analysis along a variety of dimensions.[21] Among these are intensity, pervasiveness, exitability, presence, contiguity, and level of demands. Using these variables, a complex typology of communities can emerge—some very thick, others very thin.

The thickest community would be one in which relations among members are quite intense; the community pervades all aspects of one's life; no exit is possible; other members of the community are constantly present; all members live in the same area; and demands by other members are constant. A monastery from which one could not exit or a prison that engenders strong emotional bonds would qualify as maximally thick communities. The thinnest community would be one in which relations are not very intense; the community concerns only one aspect of existence; exit is easy; other members are rarely present and live at a distance; and demands are few and sporadic. A chess club connected by modems sans the intensity would qualify as a minimally thin community.

Using the notions of thickness and thinness helps us avoid a Manichaean contrast. It will not do to allege that liberal societies are thin, communitarian societies, thick. The contrast is too stark. No functioning political association is maximally thick or minimally thin. A communitarian critic of liberalism would have to qualify criticisms in two ways. First, the critic needs to specify what dimension (e.g., pervasiveness) needs thickening. Second, the critic needs to specify the level (national or local) at which the thickening is to occur.

The second specification creates two serious difficulties for communitarian thought. First, the idea of a "locality" is indefinite. I can consider my city a locale, or I can think of a neighborhood within a city as the locality to which my greatest loyalty is due. I can even consider my family and friends the most local (and intense) object of my affections. Indeed, there is no single community to which I belong. My loyalties are multifederal.[22] Second, thickening one level of community may thin another. Tocqueville worried that Americans would draw into a small circle of family and friends, weakening loyalty to the nation. He also worried that the national community would thicken its hold on us, and urged the development of intermediate loyalties that would thin our ties to the larger community.

A critic cannot demand thickening of community ties in general. The critic should say where (and how) ties need strengthening and assess the costs of thinning ties elsewhere. Consequently, a successful communitarian critique would be quite detailed—an area in which Will excels over other communitarian critics.

Virtue

Virtue has a long and honorable career as a concept in political philosophy. Aristotle made virtue (*arete*) the centerpiece of his ethics, and most western ethical theorists have produced some version of virtue ethics. The notion of virtue has not been a term of choice among 20th-century liberal thinkers. Most liberal theories have stressed rights, rules, or duties rather than building character. For some liberals, the neglect is a matter of principle because efforts to build character limit the freedom of agents. As I will argue shortly, liberalism is compatible with virtue, but critics such as George Will and Alasdair MacIntyre have rightfully stressed the absence of virtue in much liberal theory.

What is virtue? Any answer will occasion controversy, but a sketch is necessary.[23] Virtues are those qualities necessary to be a good person, live a good life, or both. The qualities we count as virtue may be inborn, but they assume their full moral and political significance if they develop through teaching or personal effort. The lists of virtues required for living well vary from thinker to thinker, and some suspect that what counts as virtuous is radically culture-bound. We do not need to enter the debates on the naturalness or universality of virtue to understand Will's work. Rather, three things need stressing.

First, there is a tension in virtue ethics between civic virtue and personal excellences. What fulfills me may not assist my community and vice versa. Resolving (or successfully maintaining) this tension seems far more important than deciding the issues of nature and universality.

Second, one does not have to be a "relativist" to believe that virtues function differently in different settings. Some virtues may even be vices in some regimes or cultures. For instance, the "best" soldiers under the tutelage of an aggressive tyrant are the least brave. We have to evaluate virtues in two ways. Do they help to sustain a way of life? Is the way of life worth sustaining?

Third, the political significance of virtues depends on whether they are teachable. In politics, we want to encourage, extinguish, or manage action. If we can teach habits and dispositions that produce right action, understanding virtue has political significance. If we cannot, virtue has no political uses. I do not prejudge what might fall under the heading of "teaching" virtue. It could range from role modeling to behavioral modification to genetic engineering. I only wish to stress the continuing significance of Aristotle's claim that ethics and politics are about that which is changeable (*Nicomachean Ethics*, bk. 6).

Is Liberalism Dead?

Is Will's portrait of liberal thought and practice accurate? Is liberalism insufficiently committed to the public good and virtue? Will reproaches Justice Oliver Wendell Holmes for his famous statement that our constitution is for people with "fundamentally differing views." Will claims that Holmes's view is radically false. "A constitution not only presupposes a consensus of 'views' on fundamentals; it also presupposes concern for its own continuance. Therefore, it presupposes efforts to predispose rising generations to the 'views' and habits and dispositions that underlie institutional arrangements. In this sense, a constitution is not only an allocator of powers: it is also the polity's frame of mind" (SS, 79).

What Will has to say about the function of a constitution is persuasive; however, it does not necessarily contradict Justice Holmes's statement. Surely there must be some agreement on fundamentals if we are to have a constitution. At a minimum, we must agree that the constitution is fundamental law to which we may appeal in settling disputes. How much agreement we need is open to debate, but one of the defining features of a liberal regime is the wide latitude it allows for deep, yes fundamental, disagreement.

Will sometimes misreads the history of liberal thought and practice by reducing it to the extreme expressions of a few contemporary liberals. Will accurately describes the extremes of subjectivism toward which liberalism can drift in his analysis of the Supreme Court's use of the "market of ideas" metaphor on free speech litigation, but these expressions do not exhaust the liberal tradition.[24] His reading of Hobbes and Locke especially diminishes the richness of the liberal tradition. Will believes that both writers reduce the essence of the state to coercion. He thinks that both commit a non sequitur by saying "that because the state has a monopoly on legitimate coercion, its essence is coercion, actual or latent" (SS, 95). This seems a strange reading of Locke. How can the celebrated defender of the theses that all government rests on consent and that the people have a right to revolution be reduced to a panegyrist for raw force? The reading of Hobbes is plausible but badly in need of qualification. Hobbes does believe that coercion can create authority—as his famous discussion of the robber demanding money in exchange for life amply illustrates (*Leviathan*, ch. 14).[25] However, Hobbes does not believe that coercion is sufficient to sustain a regime. No prudent ruler would rely solely on threats. The much neglected 30th book of *Leviathan* is a sustained argument for the necessity of civil teachings designed to reinforce the authority of the sovereign by teaching the wisdom of obedience.[26]

Hobbes, Locke, and the other great, early liberal thinkers do not shrink from the task of seeking agreement on fundamentals. Indeed, they teach the necessity of a civil theology that roots our allegiance in a sense of duty that transcends fear, wealth, or honor. What distinguishes the liberal commitment to civil theology from nonliberal versions is its thinness. Liberal civil theology posits a minimal set of teachings deemed necessary to sustain the polity. A thin civil theology allows room for a wide range of disagreement. Fundamental disagreements must be privatized, however.[27] Liberal civil theology reconciles the danger of intense warring faiths with the inevitability that we will base our judgments on passionately held articles of faith.[28]

Recognizing the role of liberal civil theology allows us to reconcile two passages from Jefferson that bother Will. Will notes that Jefferson, in defense of toleration, wrote

> something quoted and admired today: ". . . it does me no injury for my neighbor to say that there are twenty gods, or no God. It neither picks my pocket nor breaks my leg." . . . Yet in the same essay . . . he wrote: "And can liberties be thought secure when we have removed their only firm basis, a conviction in the minds of the people that these liberties are a gift of God? That they are not violated but with his wrath?" . . . How can religious convictions, or their absence be a matter of indifference if the liberty of the nation—and hence the safety of his pocketbook and even his limbs—depends on a particular conviction? Whether Jefferson is correct about the connection between the security of liberty and the prevalence of a particular conviction is an empirical question, and perhaps still an open one. But the logic of his position is awkward, as is the logic of modern politics generally. (SS, 71–72)

There is a tension here, but no necessary contradiction. I can tolerate someone who refuses to believe things necessary to sustain the polity. I can worry that enough people will emulate a social apostate to threaten our continued existence. Indeed, if the apostate begins to proselytize, I may watch warily with the thought of withdrawing my tolerance if the threat begins to grow. My wariness is quite consistent with a commitment to toleration.

The hope that sustains a liberal regime is that enough people will share the civil faith to preclude the necessity of withdrawing tolerance. Will understands the point: "A democratic society presupposes only a minimal consensus; but it presupposes consensus nonetheless" (SS, 142). What is lacking is a "unifying culture" of the sort he thinks Homer brought to Greece, and the Bible and Shakespeare once provided for English-speaking people. Was there ever as much unity in the golden ages as Will thinks? Does a common culture require noble paradigms to replace those (*Star Wars* and *M*A*S*H*) that Will dismisses (MA, 394–96)? Have we expended our cultural capital and become incapable of fresh expressions of our heritage?

However we answer these questions, the prospects of creating or restoring the one great masterwork that would let us all get along are remote. One important difference between the ancients and us involves our media of expression. Masterworks play better in oral cultures. They tend not to thrive in sprawling, urban regimes with widely accessible multimedia. Homer did not fare that well under the withering competition of written work in varying genres. Recall that Plato's most pointed criticisms were against Homer. Sharing the Bible and Shakespeare has not always secured harmony either, considering the great religious wars that ravaged Europe. We cannot rest our hopes on a unifying work. We can, however, appeal to some fundamental symbols of our national unity (the Constitution, citizen loyalty, a common commitment to freedom) to cement a political culture that allows a wide diversity of cultural expression.

If the liberal tradition allows for a common, teachable commitment to public order, the question remains: Can liberalism teach and sustain the necessary virtues? Several liberals have vigorously challenged the claim that liberalism leaves no room for virtue.[29] Entering too deeply into the debates over the appropriate list of liberal virtues would carry us too far afield. Rather I take a closer look at the short list Will provides: tolerance and self-interestedness—those virtues he believes us to have merely because they are within the reach of everybody (SS, 44). Will has underestimated both the difficulty and value of these virtues.

Tolerance is central to a liberal regime. Liberal societies came into existence in large part as attempts to subdue the war of faiths ravaging

Europe. Tolerance is pivotal for those who value domestic peace, security, and liberty. Contrary to Will's assertion, it is not an easy virtue. Recognizing deflections from tolerance in ourselves is difficult; convincing others of the propriety of it is more so. We rub against the grain of our normal tendencies when we ask ourselves to permit others to be different, nay, even repulsive by the standards we apply to ourselves. Nevertheless, the blessings of tolerance are great. We secure what Hobbes and his successors wanted most—the opportunity to lead peaceful and productive lives without constant threat to our security. We also gain the possibility, cherished by Mill, of learning from various experiments in living and improving our own lives. Of course, diversity carries costs as well. Many ways of living seem threatening to "our" way of life; some are threatening. Knowing the difference between genuine and ersatz threats is a matter of great difficulty and greater urgency.

In any event, tolerance is a virtue, perhaps the key virtue, in a liberal society. It can be and is taught. Teaching it may lead students to produce inelegant and theoretically problematic formulations such as: "One should never impose one's values on another." In any case, the purpose of training in virtue is not to produce logicians and scholars. Rather, an education in virtue fits us for living in a concrete regime.[30] We may decide that the regime is flawed and seek to transform or abandon it, but the threshold question is whether the virtues taught in a polity sustain it. Will has not shown that most of our students are unfit for their way of life.

Will's most sustained discussion of tolerance occurs in his dissertation. There he repudiates subjectivist defenses of tolerance in favor of "constructive repression" (409–77). Will is surely correct that tolerance must have limits and that many liberal theories of tolerance are self-refuting. Nevertheless, Will's commitment to an "open society" entails some affirmation of tolerance. Will's critique of optimistic versions of tolerance seems well directed. The more effective pleas for tolerance are more Augustinian. We tolerate because it would be disastrous not to. There are also positive benefits stemming from tolerance that we can defend without recourse to subjectivism.[31]

What of self-interest?[32] Reading self-interest as a virtue will seem odd to many, especially those enamored with the "republican" tradition of thought that stresses sacrifice and civic virtue. It can be read as a virtue if Mandeville's thesis (known best from Adam Smith's invisible hand metaphor) that private "vices" can produce public virtues is correct. Mechanist notions that private interests always (or even usually) aggregate into the public good are most difficult to defend. I merely maintain that they can. When they do, self-interest appears as a form of civic virtue. If someone finds the idea that self-interest is civic virtue too hard to swallow, we may consider it merely as a private virtue—a habit or disposition that contributes to private flourishing or well-being. Only a radical republican such as Rousseau could reject all contributions of virtue to private happiness.

Tocqueville correctly observed that the American order gambled on self-interest rightly understood. The anguish comes in determining the rightness of the understanding. This is no place to assemble a theory of self-interest, but an adumbration is in order. A liberal regime need only foster a minimal self fit for liberal citizenship. Liberal societies should allow more robust selves to emerge if they are to flourish, but they cannot mandate them. What minimal self does a liberal regime need to encourage?

If anything is integral enough to be called a self, it will have a hierarchy of aims. Selves are not reducible to momentary impulses. Our hierarchy of aims conflicts with our impulses. Resisting impulses is necessary for a self-sustaining hierarchy. Self-interest secures our aims even at the expense of our impulses.[33]

Do we have the same hierarchy of aims? Hobbes thought not. Do we share enough aims to sustain a social order? Hobbes thought so. Whatever our aims, we require a common commitment (obtained through a combination of coercion, habituation, and edifying discourse) to sustain peace and security in our way of life. A liberal order assumes that a variety of hierarchies are permissible. The variety has limits because some hierarchies are destructive of liberal order; therefore, some ways of life are not tolerable. On this interpretation, liberalism requires impartiality— but hardly neutrality—toward a number of conceptions of the good.[34]

If we strip a strong conception of the good from self-interest, can we still regard it as a positive, teachable conception of virtue? Yes, but there is a problem. Liberal societies require abundance to sustain them, and abundance undermines the teaching of necessary virtues. Will laments the course of modern learning: "Education to inform discretion has often seemed less important than the sort of education encouraged by the political philosophy of modernity: that is, education for a republic in which passions are absorbed by commerce; education to equip the individual for efficacious self-interestedness" (SS, 75).

Will tempers his lamentation by his awareness that such education is vital for a liberal republic. He realizes that the pursuit of commercial

virtues is both vital and difficult. Plato long ago analyzed the tendency
of a commercial regime to undermine itself (*The Republic,* bk. 8). Will
illustrates that Plato's concerns are no less troubling today:

> Democracy and capitalism are compatible only as long as habits of polit-
> ical and economic self-restraint (deferral of gratification; industriousness;
> thrift) reinforce one another. The question is what happens when the
> ethics of commercial civilization—the relentless manufacturing of
> appetites, and the incitement to gratify them on credit—undermines
> self-restraint in political and economic behavior? The essence of childish-
> ness is an inability to imagine an incompatibility between one's appetites
> and the world. Growing up involves, above all, a conscious effort to con-
> form one's appetites to a crowded world. By so thoroughly taking our
> political, hence our moral bearings from low but strong and steady pas-
> sions, are we in danger of lingering in perpetual childishness? (SS,
> 136–37)

I have not a single quarrel with these powerful questions and observations. What they serve to highlight is that self-interest in a commercial
regime requires liberal virtues (deferral of gratification, thrift, industri-
ousness) and we do not always do a good job of cultivating them. Since
Will does not want to jettison capitalism, or any other major aspect of
our tradition, the only serious question is: How can liberals do a better
job of teaching liberal virtues? That is an awfully good question. Like
me, Will does not have many concrete and reliable answers.[35]
    Beyond cultivating liberal virtues, what does Will propose to add to
our repertoire? His summary statement is general to say the least: "By
virtue I mean nothing arcane or obscure. I mean good citizenship,
whose principal components are moderation, social sympathy and willingness to sacrifice private desires for public ends" (SS, 134). Leaving
aside the vagueness of the terms, there seems little to offend liberal sensibilities. On closer inspection, Will's call for sacrifice requires discussion. Will's demand to sacrifice private desires is unobjectionable. What
is objectionable is his request for us to "sacrifice some self-interest for the
common good" (RES, 156). Will wrongly traces the demand to Aristotle, who conceives virtue as a source of fulfillment rather than sacrifice.[36]
The demand is surely out of line with Hobbes, for whom sacrifice of
desires is acceptable precisely because it allows us to achieve our interests (common and private).
    Will is not content with self-interest. He wants to revive some
aspects of "classical republicanism" that yield a deeper sense of public

obligation than a liberal regime engenders (RES, 148–68).[37] He seems to assume that there is a public interest greater than the intersection of our private interests. Will is right to criticize the pluralist assumption that the cuisinart will produce justice or goodness through the artless blending of various pressure groups. That criticism disturbs neither the claim that the public good must be thinly defined, nor the contention that our common interests are fewer than our private interests. Will is aware of the dangers of public spiritedness, but he does not always temper his call to republican virtue. The people most disruptive of public order are not those who would advance their interests, but those burning with zeal calling for all of us to sacrifice. A revival of republicanism entails the danger of either exacerbating the tensions within a pluralist culture, or reducing the pluralist culture to a monolith.

None of these concerns should make us lose sight of what is surely correct in Will's observations. There are times when sacrifice is necessary. The existence of a regime may require such sacrifice, and private happiness depends on maintaining a public order. Since we do not want to be "tiresome," what kind of sacrifice can a liberal regime inculcate?

The major virtue we need is loyalty. I want to make a somewhat strained distinction between loyalty and patriotism.[38] Patriotism is a consuming passion for the res publica. The main energies of the patriot belong to the commonwealth. The patriot devotes every waking moment to answering President Kennedy's call to ask what we can do for our country. The patriot will also demand the same level of commitment from other citizens.

Loyalty is a form of civic virtue differing from patriotism.[39] The loyalist does not burn with zeal for public matters, but waits instead for the country to call. When the country calls, the loyalist is willing to sacrifice life itself. The virtue of loyalty will transcend self-interest, but there is no reason why a loyalist cannot devote the bulk of living to private pursuits. The virtue calls for an intermittent but intense expression. Without intermittence, loyalty would wreck the possibility for liberal living, no matter how exhilarating classical republicans might find it. Liberal regimes have been quite successful in sustaining a reservoir of loyalty. Similarly, our citizens have maintained enough attention to public affairs to arouse sufficient watchfulness and enough indignation to regulate the worst abuses of power and to overcome lethargy in government, frequently as the result of great sacrifice. Sporadic virtues may not satisfy civic humanists or populists, but they are virtues nonetheless. We may question their adequacy but not their existence.[40]

If we admit that liberal regimes promote virtues that help us secure private and public goods while sustaining some degree of togetherness at both the national and local levels, there is still room for debate. The key issue becomes adequacy. Do we have the right virtues? Are we inculcating them properly? Do they secure sufficient togetherness? We can best assess Will's critique of the liberal republic by analyzing the issues that absorb our political lives. That is the concern of chapter 4 and chapter 5. Before turning to Will's views on public issues, I need to note some changes in the direction of his thought—changes that temper his call for a virtuous republic.

Second Thoughts and Changing Directions

In a perceptive article, Tim Ferguson welcomed what he regarded as Will's move toward the mainstream of conservative thought.[41] Will used to describe himself as a "big government conservative." His celebration of government stemmed from two sources. First, Will read the "Reagan revolution" as confirming America's nearly ineffaceable attachment to our middle-class welfare state (SUD, 141–50).[42] Second, and more important, Will insisted that government has a positive role in shaping character. A weak government would lack the wherewithal to practice soulcraft. Government must consciously choose how to shape the character of its citizens.

Will has become more suspicious of government. In the interview with me, Will described his growing mistrust of government as a "new bleakness." He mentioned two books that illustrate and reinforce his doubts: Jonathan Rauch's *Demosclerosis: The Silent Killer of American Government* and David Frum's *Dead Right*.[43]

Rauch argues that American government has become incapable of making decisions about its priorities. American politics has lately seen the growth of interest groups. These groups have attained a rough parity so that they function somewhat like John C. Calhoun's "concurrent majority." In Calhoun's vision, each major segment of American society would have a veto over the actions of the national government.[44] According to Rauch, American politics today works like Calhoun's political theory—something to be decried if one believes in democratic deliberation. Each group today mobilizes to defend its interests from governmental action. Since much of the budget goes for entrenched outlays, especially entitlements, there is no opportunity to experiment with new programs. A coalition of entrenched interests will defeat intrusions by newcomers.

Rauch does not picture a small cabal of "special" interests working against the vast majority of ordinary citizens. Almost everybody is represented by a group, and even small, "public interest" organizations can work with other groups to freeze the public agenda. Under conditions of perpetual gridlock, the power of democratic deliberation atrophies. Will carries from Rauch's book a key message: Energetic action to solve serious problems cannot rely on government.

Will takes a slightly different message from Frum's study. Frum argues that the Republican party has fractured into three factions: optimists, moralists, and nationalists. Each brings a message that Frum thinks will augur failure for conservative politics.

Jack Kemp personifies the optimist whose central cliché is: "A rising tide lifts all boats." The optimist's faith centers on the promise of prosperity. Seek ye first a high GNP and all else will be added unto you. Frum complains that optimism ignores the prevalence of what he regards as social pathologies. There is an underclass that resists inclusion in the mainstream economy—an underclass that shows signs of growing. Kemp touts quasimarket solutions such as enterprise zones and transferring housing projects to private ownership. Frum doubts that these will work because they do not address, and may encourage, underlying pathologies. Optimists continue the "failure of the Reagan gambit" because they do not create the restraints on vice that are necessary to sustain a prosperous and healthy republic. Optimists succumb to the illusion that tax cuts without spending restraints can ensure stable growth (*Dead Right*, 34–99).

Moralists, personified by William Bennett, recognize the connection between character and prosperity, but they wrongly attempt to shape character from above.[45] Frum wonders what government can do to instill "values."[46] More important, Frum believes that the reliance on and intervention from government is the source of moral decay. By dreaming of turning government into a moral nanny, moralists risk more than ineffectiveness. They miss the possibility of serious remedies (*Dead Right*, 99–123).

Pat Buchanan personifies the nationalists who try an end run around the problem of virtue by practicing a politics that divides the world into us and them. Frum charges Buchanan and his friends with importing the "identity politics" of the left into a new setting. The world is divided among incompatible groups whose ways of thought and living cannot be melted into one big pot. The solution is to separate the groups and preserve "our" way of life against the threat "they" pose. If you can't shape 'em, exclude 'em. Frum does not think that America can unite or sustain a vibrant economy on these principles (*Dead Right*, 124–58).

Frum believes that each branch of contemporary conservative thought has foundered on a common error. They all fail to see the source of our current malaise. Frum believes that our social pathologies stem from our addiction to government. Government is pathogenic for two reasons. First, good character requires self-reliance and the welfare state fosters dependency. Second, centralizing government shelters people from social disapprobation. Were we to devolve more responsibilities to states, localities, and private organizations, there would be more chance to enforce morals. As matters stand, the government protects people from local sanctions by enforcing restrictions against discrimination, thereby weakening stigmas. For instance, by banning housing discrimination against unmarried couples, the government weakens the moral force of marriage (*Dead Right*, 174–205).

Frum's analysis, if correct, contains major implications for Will's thinking. Perhaps less statecraft is better soulcraft. If public action distorts character, we need less public action. We can best gauge how the antigovernment turn in Will's thought will play out by turning to the issues that have absorbed his attention over the years. Before turning to policy issues, however, we need to discuss Will's conception of law, since law provides the framework for practicing statecraft. That is the subject of the following chapter.

Chapter Three

The Path of Law

Oh how I love thy law! It is my meditation all the day.

Psalms 119:97

Woe unto you also you lawyers for ye lade men with burdens grievous to be borne, and ye yourselves touch not the burdens with one of your fingers.

Luke 11:46

The nexus between morals and politics is maintained through law. The nature and importance of law is regularly featured in George Will's work. Throughout his career, he has followed the key cases that have shaped the Supreme Court's interpretation of the Constitution.

The Constitution is our basic law, the framework for our governance. Its fate is inextricably tied to the fate of our statecraft. From Will's point of view, the Court has not always guarded our legal heritage with sufficient care. Its failure is particularly notable in three areas: an insufficient regard for the original intentions of the founders, an inadequate understanding of the educative role of legal penalties, and an insecure theory of legal tolerance. Looking at these concerns allows us to envision how Will thinks law should work. Understanding Will's approach to legal thought requires outlining the basic features of the legal tradition from which he is working and some of the problems it involves. That outline will provide background for the somewhat narrower issues to which he has devoted attention. The basic tradition from which Will draws sustenance is constitutionalism.

On Constitutionalism

The central idea in the western constitutional tradition is that the authority to act (by a group or an individual) ought to be limited.[1] Simply because someone wants to act does not imply that he or she ought to be allowed to act. Just action requires authority that derives from reason rather than desire or will. In the tradition of constitutionalism, the greatest sin is to be arbitrary. Indeed, the fundamental purpose of a constitution is to prohibit arbitrary acts. It is not enough, however, for law to restrain our will to act. The restraints themselves should not be arbitrary. Law that honors the principles of constitutionalism is based on settled principles that serve the interests of justice. The basic law must be known to the people and respected by them. It cannot be changed at will. Everyone must know and abide by "the rules of the game."

Many theorists stop with the notion that a constitution establishes the rules of the game. These theorists want the Constitution to be neutral among competing visions of the good, merely establishing the rules under which competition will occur. Will, as one might expect from the discussion in the previous chapter, is quite critical of proceduralism. He thinks that the Constitution, in its preamble and in a variety of specific provisions, chooses sides advocating one vision of the good to the exclusion of another (Will, interview). Nevertheless, Will agrees with the proceduralists in viewing the Constitution as a restraint on arbitrary decisions. Will argues that a constitution must put some matters "beyond the reach of majorities" as the title of his dissertation asserts. He thinks that a constitution not only restrains temporary majorities, but also restricts supermajorities that would presumably have the power to amend the Constitution (BM, 294–98).[2] Thus there is real convergence among contending parties in debates on the Constitution: A constitution restrains arbitrary decisions.

A basic law that restrains our will and desires must be, in some sense, "above" our will and desires. From where can such a law come? There are at least three purported sources for the basic law: tradition, democracy, and the "higher law."

When the constitution is based on tradition, the limits under which we live are set by beliefs and rituals that are accepted without question. A constitution based on tradition is accepted simply because it has been there so long; its antiquity gives it authority. The notion that long settled customs lend authority is well expressed in Edmund Burke's famous description of the "prescriptive constitution." For Burke, the British constitution is one "whose sole authority is, that it has existed time out of mind." Its authority comes from prescription, which "is the most solid of all titles, not only to property but, which is to secure that property, government."[3]

A democratic constitution derives its authority from popular sovereignty. Restraints are set by the people at the founding of the republic. The people set for themselves difficult democratic procedures (e.g., constitutional amendments) for changing the rules under which they live.

At any time the people can decide to change the rules, but no authority is legitimate unless it is sanctioned by the consent of the people.[4] The constitution restrains majorities because it expresses the binding will of a supermajority.

The higher law tradition in American constitutionalism has deep roots in Western thought.[5] It is based on the idea that restraints are set by what is "reasonable," and our ability to act is limited by rational deliberation. Higher law or, to use the most enduring terminology, natural law, is the most basic tradition of western constitutionalism. It holds that no one can act both arbitrarily and lawfully, and that what is reasonable can be universally understood to be both reasonable and binding. Law, in this tradition, cannot be made but must be discovered by reasoning. Cicero captured the conception of the higher law in one of his dialogues.

> There is in fact a true law—namely right reason—which is in accordance with nature, applies to all men, and is unchangeable and eternal. By its commands this law summons men to the performance of their duties; by its prohibitions it restrains them from doing wrong. . . . To invalidate this law by human legislation is never morally right, nor is it permissible to ever restrict its operation, and to annul it wholly is impossible. . . . It will not lay down one rule at Rome and another at Athens; nor will it be one rule today and another tomorrow. But there will be one law, eternal and unchangeable, binding at all times upon all peoples; and there will be, as it were, one common master and ruler of all men, namely God, who is the author of the law, its interpreter and its sponsor.[6]

Natural law is higher than any human enactment, and ordinances that violate it are not binding. As Augustine says, "a law that is unjust does not seem to me to be a law at all."[7] The principles of higher law have been openly championed, attacked, and surreptitiously incorporated into legal reasoning throughout our constitutional history.

Natural law contrasts with positive law—law as the product of human will. Most modern theories of law emphasize its human origins, rejecting any divine sanction.[8] The connection between higher law and religion is more complicated than these comments suggest. One can think that there is something "higher" than human will without appealing to a divine lawgiver. Will observes that "classical natural law theory holds that there is a characterizing excellence of which man is capable. This end toward which he should strive is knowable through reason. It is not, in fact, universally understood. But it is, in theory, universally understandable" (SS, 70). Will's version of natural law actually departs significantly from classical doctrines. He writes that the law of which he speaks is a "norm." For it to attain the status of law as ancient and Christian philosophers understood the term, there would need to be a theory of obligation that Will's version lacks. Will straddles the divide Hobbes identifies between law strictly understood as binding authority and law as "counsel" (*Leviathan,* ch. 25). Will never develops a full theory of universal obligation.

Most modern theories stress the variability of law from culture to culture, denying to human reason any common knowledge of what is right or wrong in all places at all times. In other words, most modern theories accept some form of moral and legal relativism. Neither traditionalism nor allegiance to the voice of the people can escape the charge of relativism; a pure traditionalism and unbridled popular sovereignty are inconsistent with higher law. Neither tradition nor popular will creates a standard valid for all times and places. Defenders of natural law maintain that "a government of laws, not of men," must appeal to a law higher than tradition or the will of the people.[9]

Upholding tradition and democratic restraints as opposed to higher law, as most contemporary legal theorists are inclined to do, poses serious problems for defenders of constitutionalism. For traditionalists, the problem is this: What if, as is the case in our society, respect for tradition has lapsed? How then are limits set? The defender of popular sovereignty faces different problems. Why are present majorities constrained by the decisions of past generations? The idea of constitutionalism implies a restraint on the will and that includes the will of even supermajorities. What if the founding majority got things wrong? Can we not just jettison what Paine calls the dead hand of the past? If so, how does the Constitution restrain us? "Consent" does not help here, although consent may be a condition for having a legitimate government. The people can consent to, as well as will, unlimited government. Will insists that "the notion of democratic power as self-legitimizing is just another version of the might makes right doctrine, and it is just as morally squalid as all the other versions" (BM, 279).

My sketch of basic options in constitutional theory frames many of the key legal issues Will has addressed. He wants a government vigorous enough to promote virtue, but he also wants to protect against the abuse of power through arbitrary enactment. Maintaining the balance between impotence and tyranny is the central aim of constitutionalism. Will's stance on law can be best appreciated by turning to the three issues important for understanding his political theory: original intent, law-as-education, and the limits of tolerance.

The Politics of Original Intent

For Will, a valid constitution restrains our political will. He fears that law no longer functions as a restraint on a political life but rather as a particularly contentious manifestation of it. Consequently, he defends a jurisprudence that emphasizes judicial restraint and a constitutionalism based on the "original intent" of the framers. In advocating originalism as an interpretive theory, Will follows the lead of Judge Robert Bork, though Will endorses Bork's theory with reservations (Will, interview).[10]

Originalism is the view that the Constitution should be interpreted in light of the original intentions of the founders. Understanding this theory requires comprehending what the Constitution is trying to accomplish and the competing theories of interpretation it rejects.

Originalism attempts to address the key problem I identified earlier—avoiding arbitrary government. There are at least two sources of arbitrariness we ought to fear: popular will and willful judges. These twin fears give rise to what Judge Bork calls "the Madisonian dilemma." The dilemma is that "neither majorities nor minorities can be trusted to define the proper spheres of democratic authority and individual liberty. To place the power in one or the other would risk either tyranny by the majority or tyranny by the minority" (*Tempting,* 139). For Bork, a valid constitutional interpretation must rely on neutral application of neutral principles that force judges to eschew personal preferences. Will doubts that original intent is a fully satisfactory way of restraining arbitrary power, but he agrees with Bork that some means of restraint is necessary. Will notes that he does not go as far as Bork: "There's a little more room in my jurisprudence for judicial assertiveness. But I go right down the path of Bork when he says that if you sever yourself entirely from original intent, in what sense do you have a constitution? Because when you are severed entirely—and I stress the word 'entirely,' and I stress the word 'severed'—. . . you are cast unavoidably on the tides of contemporary judicial preferences" (Will, interview). Will's comments imply what Bork asserts quite vigorously—that relying on original intent is necessary to avoid arbitrary constitutional interpretation. If that is true, we would need to reject competing theories of interpretation. What are they, and what is wrong with them?

One of the oldest theories of judicial restraint is strict construction. Strict constructionists argue that judicial arbitrariness can be avoided only if judges refuse to stray from the strict meaning of the words contained in the Constitution. There are at least two fatal problems with this theory. First, few important clauses in the Constitution have precise and uncontroversial meanings. For instance, few constitutional provisions have occasioned more controversy than the Due Process Clause of the 14th Amendment.[11] What exactly does it mean to say that life, liberty, and property may not be taken without due process of law? There are a number of plausible interpretations around, which jurists and legal scholars have harangued endlessly. That there are plausible interpretations lends no comfort to strict constructionists. Two plausible interpretations are one too many. The Due Process Clause is not unusual. Numerous provisions operate at its level of generality and ambiguity. The vagueness of the Constitution is, to use a phrase Trotskyists love, no accident. The vagueness is in the very nature of a functioning constitution. A constitution differs from a legal code insofar as it must give general rules to guide a nation through the ages. A constitution burdened by too much specificity would soon be discarded as an unreasonable weight for people facing unforeseen circumstances. In any case, judicial literalism cannot provide a basis for a theory of judicial review (the power of the courts to declare acts of the other branches and the states unconstitutional) because judicial review is never mentioned in the Constitution.

Second, following the language of the Constitution literally would constitute a disaster in some instances. Justice Hugo Black was eternally fond of reminding his colleagues that the First Amendment says that Congress shall make no law abridging the freedoms of speech, press, religion, and assembly. For Black, "no law" meant no law. Black's view has been shared by exactly one other Supreme Court Justice (though Justice Douglas would have had us go further than Black by adding unwritten but absolute restrictions to the Bill of Rights). Will sensibly observes that "no law" cannot mean no law. Were we to adopt Black's position, the nation would be helpless to protect us from the serious abuses to which freedom lends itself (BM, 104–87).

Another competing theory of judicial interpretation has already been mentioned: natural law. Defenders of natural law are willing to enforce the specific provisions of the Constitution, but they argue that there is more to constitutional government than any document can codify. Natural law restrains arbitrary action in two ways. First, any written provisions of the Constitution that violated God's laws would be unenforceable. I know of no cases in which this principle has been invoked, but it is clearly implied in natural law doctrine. Second, and more important, powers, duties, and rights not mentioned in the Constitution are nonetheless enforceable as valid rules of reason. Prior to 1937, a large number of state and federal statutes were invalidated on natural law grounds. The Roosevelt Court turned the tide, preaching a theory of judicial restraint and deference to the legislature on economic legislation. Some critics have charged that many liberal jurists' repudiation of natural law has been duplicitous.[12] Liberals preach restraint on economic legislation and the rule of reason on other civil liberties. For instance, privacy is not mentioned in the Constitution, but the Supreme Court discovered it emanating as a penumbra from provisions that are mentioned. Advocates of judicial restraint charge that discovering unenumerated rights is nothing more than natural law smuggled in with a new packaging. The charge begs the key question: What is wrong with natural law as a theory of interpretation?

Judge Bork repudiates natural law partly because it lends itself to serving as a disguise for arbitrary preferences. More important, he appeals to a democratic ethos to create skepticism about natural law reasoning. Bork does not deny the existence of natural law, but rather denies that judges are entitled to enforce it and that they have any special access to it (*Tempting,* 66). His argument is not dispositive. Aquinas and other natural law theorists argue that the primary principles of natural law are comprehensible to all but that the application of principles derived from the natural law requires careful study and thought. Jurists would be among those most likely to have the opportunity and skills to make the necessary inquiries. Furthermore, if we accept the doctrine of judicial review, judges would be qualified to enforce any binding law, including the natural law. Bork's rejection of natural law seems to hinge on his fear that appeals to natural law will simply mask a results-oriented jurisprudence (*Tempting,* 209–10). Surely judges sometimes wear the mask of judicial impartiality to disguise ideological commitments, but could not a judge claiming to read original intent wear it as well? The major problem with natural law involves the unwillingness of most jurists to treat it as a credible doctrine. It has indeed lent itself to arbitrary (or at least discredited) readings of the Constitution, and most parties to our debates are committed to excluding it from discussion.

A major alternative to literalism and natural law in contemporary debates is articulated by Ronald Dworkin. Dworkin argues that the

Constitution was never meant to serve as a legal code that specifically restrains or empowers. A constitution must be written at a level of generality that will allow it to survive for a long time, which requires considerable flexibility. To ensure the requisite flexibility, Dworkin insists that we distinguish between rules and principles. Rules are specific enough to rigidly constrain interpretation, while principles serve to guide our decisions without unduly limiting our adaptability. For Dworkin, constitutional interpretation requires the jurist to ask how a particular decision will direct us toward the principles that ought govern our lives. How do we determine which principles should rule? For Dworkin, the answer is, of necessity, philosophical. The constitution is not self-enacting, and judges must find the principles that it represents. The analysis and articulation of principles is inherently philosophical. Good judges must be able to do moral and political philosophy. Dworkin the philosopher assists our judges in their deliberations, concluding that the key principle that ought govern our legal decisions is equality.[13]

As one might expect, Judge Bork does not accept Dworkin's analysis. From Bork's perspective, Dworkin has not solved the Madisonian dilemma. Bork thinks Dworkin leaves too much room for judicial arbitrariness. Bork agrees with Dworkin's claim that the choice of a philosophy of interpretation is, of necessity, a political choice. However, with originalism, "that choice is not made by a judge; it was made long ago by those who designed and enacted the Constitution" (*Tempting,* 177). Consequently, Bork contends that originalism constrains arbitrariness, whereas Dworkin's theory is just another version of the claim that the Constitution is merely what judges say it is.

Bork's case against Dworkin rests on the presumption that philosophy is inherently arbitrary. In establishing this point, Bork invokes the philosopher Alasdair MacIntyre who notes the wide variety of seemingly intractable positions in philosophy (*Tempting,* 254). Bork misreads both MacIntyre and the grounds for his own case. MacIntyre does not rest content with exposing our current moral impasse; he attempts to diagnose and overcome what he perceives to be an unfortunate fall into ethical and legal Babel. Regardless of how closely Bork reads the texts he uses and criticizes, he does not seem aware of his own reliance on philosophical commitments. The case against arbitrariness derives from a legal tradition that is keenly informed by philosophy. Can one imagine Roman law without stoic philosophy? Are Bork's commitments to democracy and constitutional government simply self-evident with respect to either their meanings or validity? Eric Voegelin forcefully argues that the very diversity of legal theories and claims forces us to turn to philosophical considerations.[14] If Bork persists in dismissing philosophical claims as arbitrary, he loses the capacity to defend his legal philosophy as anything other than arbitrary.

Bork's claim that legal philosophies such as Dworkin's are inherently arbitrary rests on observations concerning the proper "level of abstraction" at which interpretation should occur. Dean Paul Brest argues that originalism will not work because intentions function at various levels of meaning—some quite abstract, others concrete. Brest believes that a judge is forced to choose the level of abstraction at which a clause will be interpreted and that the choice cannot be determined by the intent. Bork, arguing against Dean Brest, remarks that judges committed to originalism should not "choose" a level of abstraction; rather, they should find a meaning for a text.

Stephen Carter notes the inconsistency with which Bork applies his principle. Bork defends the Supreme Court's decision in *Brown v. Board of Education,* which outlawed segregation in public education. Bork realizes that the framers of the Fourteenth Amendment did not intend for its Equal Protection Clause to prohibit segregated education. Nevertheless he accepts the Court's decision to outlaw legally imposed segregation. Bork argues that the Warren Court was faced with the choice of upholding two contradictory intentions: "to abandon the quest for equality by allowing segregation or to forbid segregation in order to achieve equality" (*Tempting,* 82). Carter notes that Bork has made a choice and that the choice is to defend the principle rather than the specific intention. Carter then observes that Bork's choice of defending principles that the Constitution seeks to enact puts him quite close to Dworkin.[15]

Will appears to stand with Dworkin on the question of how to decide *Brown.* He told me that *Brown* is an excellent example of a case in which the time had come to jettison precedent. I observed that the precedent had been eroded by previous decisions, to which Will replied that "even if it had not been tested and eroded, [I] would say it touched values so central to American life you just say: 'sorry, we made a wrong turn—that happens' " (Will, interview).

A final competitor to originalism is the "balancing" approach to interpretation. This is an approach that Will has employed from the beginning of his writing career (BM, 103). The balancing test builds on the notion that a constitution embodies competing values. There is no

clear hierarchy among these values; they have to be weighed against one
another in particular cases. The key values that must be weighed are the
interests of society and the rights of the individual. A judge must ask in
each case whether the balance has drifted too far in favor of one or the
other. Will, like many conservatives, thinks the balance has tilted too far
toward the individual, especially in free speech cases, and needs to be
tipped back toward allowing society the means to promote and preserve
itself.

Judge Bork does not comment specifically on the balancing test, but
we can reasonably infer his response from his claim that none of originalism's competitors can solve the Madisonian dilemma. Does the balancing approach rule out arbitrary decisions? Its imprecision seems to
invite them. It may serve as a rule of thumb, but it can hardly generate
binding rules of interpretation.[16] When I discuss balancing doctrines
with my students, I ask them: How much do interests and rights weigh?
They respond eloquently with blank stares of puzzlement. Balancing is
probably necessary and wise in constitutional interpretation, but no one
benefits by confusing a useful metaphor with a precise rule of law.

The key question remains: Does originalism conquer its competitors
by offering the only alternative to judicial willfulness? Early in his writing career, Will cast doubt on the conclusiveness of original intent:
"Obviously it will not do to say that the beliefs enshrined in the Constitution are of special high moral value simply because they were
endorsed by some eighteenth century Americans. Edmond Cahn is right
to insist that being in agreement with the Founding Fathers 'is only a
comfort, not an obligation.' There is no reason why the intent of earlier
Americans should—merely as intent—bind subsequent generations.
Anyway, it is far from clear what was the intent of those who advocated
the Constitution. It is hard even to say whose intent we are talking
about" (BM, 308–9). Will thinks that there are ways to determine original intent. We can review "not only the language, but the structure of
the document and what it implies, and what we know the structure
implies, both the text and structure of the document from the ratifica-
tion debates *and* the Constitutional Convention debates and the political
literature of the time" (Will, interview). Nevertheless, Will notes that
"intention" could refer to the ratifiers of or the drafters of or the signatories to the Constitution. In any case, we are hard pressed to determine
what they believed. Even if we could, "they" (ratifiers, drafters, and signatories) constituted only a small percentage of the people at that time
(BM, 309–10). Will's criticisms of original intent do not lead him to

abandon it entirely. "These gray facts from history [concerning the minority status of the founders] do not undo Chief Justice John Marshall's vision of the Constitution as the nation's 'original and supreme will.' . . . What was originally the conscious, articulated will of a small minority can become—and in a sense can have been right along—the permanent will of the people organized as a nation" (BM, 310). And how does our permanent will express itself? Will avers that avoiding the "shifting winds of doctrine" entails fidelity to "some guiding ideals" (BM, 286–87). This puts him closer to Dworkin than Bork.

Of course, admitting the relevance of philosophy does not entirely sever us from considerations of the original meaning of the Constitution or the original intentions of the founders.[17] The founding generation were deeply informed by philosophical thought, and we can learn from their musings. But their philosophical importations are by no means binding because they sometimes did philosophy well, sometimes badly. We have to decide for ourselves when to follow and when to depart from their reasoning. We should not make the decision to depart freely, however. Will thanks God for the "dead hand of the past" (Will, interview). A document that allows too much room for rapid innovation is a periodical, not a constitution. A constitution worthy of the name must preserve continuity if it is to restrain arbitrariness and create security. Consequently, a constitution must conserve. But conserve what? Will answers like Dworkin: guiding ideals. Insisting on guiding ideals leaves much room for debate and arbitrary decisions.

Arbitrary decisions are probably unavoidable, but the courts have been less prone to "judicial legislation" than their critics assume. Our courts frequently offer good reasons for their decisions. We may find their reasons plausible even as we disagree with their decisions.[18] That the decisions leave room for sharp debate is no reason to brand them as arbitrary.

Even if we resign ourselves to a modicum of willfulness, the key question remains: What can our constitution conserve? From time to time Will mentions a variety of principles that need conservation and balancing. He frequently and plausibly recurs to the Preamble to discover the guiding aims of our binding document. From my perspective, we need to lift our jurisprudence to a higher level of abstraction than even the very general purposes listed in the Preamble. My view is that a constitution conserves a particular type of regime—what the Greeks called a *politea*. The fundamental unit of analysis in constitutional theory is nothing less than a way of life. If good constitutional interpretation helps preserve a way of life, what should be the fundamental aim of our jurists? My answer: To conserve liberalism. Recurring to our basic tradition yields no rules of interpretation, but it does yield a standard for evaluating the rules we adopt. Natural lawyers will demand that we take one step higher and yield to the will of God. Maybe they are right, but Judge Bork is probably correct that our society will not agree on either the content of the natural law or the propriety of using it. Defending a concrete liberal order is likely to produce greater assent.

Putting the liberal way of life at the center of jurisprudential debates brings us back to the central debates around which this book revolves. A critique of our legal order is necessarily connected to a critique of our political order. I explore details of Will's critique in the chapters that follow. Before turning to political issues, I consider Will's criticisms of liberal legal theory related to the use of law to instill virtue and the protection of free speech.

Crime and Punishment

Will was once an opponent of capital punishment, doubting its deterrent effects (PH, 57–60). He has not relinquished his doubts about the efficacy of the death penalty, but he has changed his mind in favor of applying it. Why?

At times, Will uses Kantian, retributivist arguments that those of us steeped in one or another form of consequentialist ethical theory find almost impossible to understand, much less approve (MA, 159). Consequentialist arguments are forward looking, stressing the future good (e.g., deterrence or rehabilitation) deriving from a punishment. Retributivist arguments rely exclusively on the notion that a criminal "deserves" punishment. They look back to the act to form a proper judgment about it at the time it occurred. I consider only Will's consequentialist arguments for punishment (including capital punishment) since these shed more light on his conception of statecraft as soulcraft.

Will insists that punishment is not justified primarily by its deterrent value. We must justify punishment through its civilizing effects. Like Lord Devlin and, more recently, Walter Berns, Will justifies punishment by its "expressive function" (MA, 157; SD, 183).[19] What do we express when we make law requiring the intentional infliction of pain? We express our outrage at the evil embodied in an act and demand that citizens act responsibly. We express our "justified anger" and desire for vengeance through the law (MA, 29–31; 153–59). What end do these expressions serve? For Will, laws prescribing punishment help sustain "the indignation that society needs for self-defense" (MA, 156). This is statecraft as soulcraft with a vengeance!

Will maintains that laws inevitably shape our dispositions. The issue is how well a particular law shapes virtue. Punitive laws are not very good at forming character. They are blunt instruments. There is little evidence to support the idea that punishment fosters virtue in those being punished, but that is not Will's concern.[20] Are we to believe that punishment vicariously ennobles ordinary citizens? We certainly do not need to invoke law to enhance our sense of indignation; a culture that lionizes Dirty Harry is bursting with indignation. What we need are ways of bearing ourselves that sustain a tolerable level of civility with only a minimally necessary degree of cruelty. If Will can show that our highly punitive culture engenders actions contributing to the good life, we have cause to praise the expressive function of law.[21]

There is a case for the educative role of punishment. James Q. Wilson has argued that the way people comport themselves in public sends a message about the community. If vagrant and threatening behavior is tolerated, citizens feel less secure and criminals feel free to claim a neighborhood.[22] Wilson has also argued that punishment deters "at the margins"; i.e., using hard-core criminals (whom punishment does not deter) as examples deters normally law-abiding citizens.[23] Wilson's claims, if true, do not establish that laws send messages capable of fine tuning behavior. Sometimes we need legal sanctions to create moral sanctions, but it usually works the other way around.

Americans use the notion of "sending a message" with unbridled confidence. We add highly punitive and extremely expensive laws to our vast catalogs of criminal law to create tough, new messages. We keep demonstrably ineffective and costly laws on the books to avoid sending a message of acceptance. Our punitive culture relies little on evidence, and frequently acts against the best evidence we have accumulated. In short, our soulcraft is more faith than measured evaluation of probable consequences. The issue, then, concerns whether we are more interested in satisfying our visceral responses to wrongdoing or in developing good character based on careful consideration of what works. At present the soulcraft of educational punishment is more faith than study.

Will's faith in punishment extends beyond "street crime." He would use law to restrain vices as well as violence. In the following chapter, I discuss two areas, pornography and censorship, where law can be used to shape our moral sensibilities. For now, it is necessary to turn to an issue intimately connected to law-as-education. What are the limits to tolerance?

Constructive Repression in a Liberal Regime

The First Amendment protects freedom of speech, press, religion, and assembly. Will, as a dedicated defender of our constitution, cherishes these liberties. Nevertheless, he questions the way our basic liberties have been interpreted and the breadth of protection they have received. He counterpoises an "economy of virtuous intolerance" to the strenuous civil libertarian ethos of many liberal jurists (BM, 349–477). In his dissertation, Will explains what he finds lacking in liberal jurisprudence and offers a program of constructive repression to remedy its deficiencies.

For Will, liberal legal thought suffers from two defects. First, it relies on a dubious metaphor to substitute for sound empirical knowledge. Liberal jurists in America frequently recur to the image of a "marketplace of ideas." If we allow free exchange in this market, the truth will emerge. The prediction that underlies this pregnant phrase is not borne out by a careful study of history. A close look at the history of Weimar Germany would disabuse us of empirical confidence in the market analogy. Will is especially amused that the market analogy is defended by liberals who are quite dubious of the workings of market economics. If we are willing to regulate the market in goods, why the childlike trust in the exchange of ideas (BM, 46–70)?

Second, liberal justifications for free speech and press tend to decline from dubious empirical claims to radical skepticism. The liberal theorist assumes, explicitly or tacitly, that all ideas have equal value, and insists that no one should impose one set of views. Adopting this strategy is clearly self-defeating. If no ideas are superior, liberal tolerance is no better than totalitarian repudiations of it. Liberalism that has lapsed into radical egalitarianism concerning the value of ideas loses the ability to defend itself. We are reduced to the claim that might makes right (BM, 1–70).

Liberalism need not recur to dubious predictions or self-defeating skepticism. Liberals can share with Will the view that liberty is an intrinsic good that government ought to recognize and protect. If a liberal makes this sensible move in Will's direction, there are still critical issues to be explored. Recognition that liberty does not automatically yield truth should be accompanied by an awareness that liberty is dangerous. We can use freedom to destroy freedom along with other basic goods. Liberals from John Stuart Mill onward have recognized the dangers of freedom. American jurists have addressed the dangers of liberty by developing "the clear and present danger" doctrine. This doctrine holds that a government may restrict the exercise of a basic liberty if it poses a clear and present danger of an evil that the government has the authority to prohibit. Will notes that the clear and present danger test has been used exclusively against the states rather than against the national government, but that is not his primary concern. Will's principal concern is to repudiate the toleration of "evil" views.

Will quotes Learned Hand's famous version of the clear and present danger test: "In each case [courts] must ask whether the gravity of the 'evil' discounted by its improbability, justifies such invasion of free speech as is necessary to avoid the danger" (BM, 99–100, brackets in the original). Will retorts that "the difficult question raised by Hand's formulation is this: Why should any person or any government adopt, as a matter of principle, the practice of 'discounting' great evils"? (BM, 100). The idea of discounting great evils is not as odd as Will asserts. On his television appearances, Will frequently chides those who demand too exacting standards of safety and security with a telling example. He remarks that we could radically reduce auto accidents by banning left turns. Will discounts a great evil for the sake of convenience!

A more important criticism involves Will's failure to pursue a key distinction in liberal thought from Locke onward—the distinction between thought and action. Liberals insist that evil thoughts are less odious than evil actions. Is this simply liberal prejudice, or can it survive the tests of common sense and philosophical analysis?

At the level of common sense, a friend comes to mind. My friend has an uncle who is rather unsavory. He is apt to express anti-Semitic and racist sentiments and enunciate the wildest conspiracy theories imaginable. His thoughts and words are indeed evil, but he is quite harmless. Everyone positioned to act on his lunacies ignores him. Would anyone be better off if we jailed him?

At the level of philosophical analysis, we have to begin with basic assumptions. Will is, as previously noted, usually a consequentialist. Unfortunately, he sometimes lapses into selective consequentialism, much like he rightly accuses our liberal jurists of selective skepticism (BM, 99). Will asks: "What social good can we reasonably expect to come from tolerating a known evil until it becomes a clear and present danger? What does a polity gain from the non-lethal, peaceful promotion of (say) totalitarian or racist causes" (BM, 70)? A consequentialist will indeed ask what good will come of a policy. A consequentialist will also ask what evils a policy will avert. Toleration averts the evil of depriving a person of a primary good—liberty. It also avoids the trap of giving the government too much power to intervene. When we concede the advantages of toleration, the burden of proof shifts, and the advocate of intervention must show what good will come of repression or what evil will be avoided.

Absent a showing of clear and present danger, can the burden of proof on behalf of repression be met? Will thinks so. First, he resists the claim that the danger must be "present" in the sense of immediate (BM, 79). A liberal can agree with this. The Supreme Court has on occasion adopted what is best described as a "clear and probable danger" test.[24] This test requires a genuine likelihood that the evil would triumph if left unchecked. Critics of the Court's decisions using the clear and probable danger test argue that the Court overestimated the strength of the Communist Party in America. It would be difficult to downplay the threat of totalitarian and racist threats in Germany; therefore, a liberal could consistently criticize banning totalitarian parties in America while grudgingly accepting the policy in Germany. Will wants to resist more than unnecessarily generous estimates of danger, however. He wants us "to consider arguments for suppressing political activity which is clearly innocuous in effect as it is evil in purpose" (BM, 102). What consequentialist arguments would support such suppression?

Will argues that we could get good results by outlawing racist and totalitarian parties (without outlawing racist and totalitarian speech). The effect would be "constructive repression." What does that mean? Will thinks that repression can be constructive because of its educational effects. From repression we would gain "confidence that questions about the usefulness, the goodness, of totalitarian policies are closed questions" (BM, 412). We would also learn to "affirm the nation's commitment to . . . the principle that no intelligent policy of tolerance is opposed to placing some things—those essentials to which we are most intensely and justifiably loyal—beyond the reach of majorities" (BM, 412). Finally, we would learn "that care should be taken to assure the living power of the public philosophy" (BM, 412).

We should indeed educate our citizenry in all the things Will mentions. Our citizens need to avoid moral slackness in the face of evil and to affirm those things that hold us together. Once that is conceded—nay, affirmed—there are still critical questions concerning Will's proposal. Is it not possible to teach these things affirmatively rather than invoking the example of the bludgeon? John Stuart Mill insisted that we should be taught virtue as children during the time when our liberties are most properly restricted and our capacity for learning most alive. Can we not ask our schools to teach that racism is wrong without denying racists the freedom of association?

Is repression a safe device for education even if it works? Milton opposed censorship because he thought truth requires freedom. He also opposed censorship because he feared that government would abuse its power to instill virtue by repressing those who are virtuous. Will is correct to insist that we have the power to make useful distinctions between racists and nonracists and between totalitarians and nontotalitarians. The key question is this: Do we trust our officials to observe scrupulously these distinctions when we make them masters of the dictionary?

Even if we repress the right people, is not Milton correct that we risk driving them underground and making them both more virulent and martyrs to boot? While Germany's policy of repression is rational, it has not been totally effective. Neo-Nazis have grouped and regrouped about as fast as they have been outlawed.[25] What have the German people learned from their policy of constructive repression? A study of that empirical question would be needed to resolve the disparity between Will's assertions and my doubts.

Will has retained his focus on the educational value of law and public policy in instilling virtue and building community throughout his career. The two chapters that follow offer a review of some specific policies that relate to the core aims of his legal and political thought.

Chapter Four
Making Community
and Issuing Virtue

What is common to us matters much less than what differentiates us. What makes life precious for us is difference, not identity. We do not prize our equality. We think of ourselves not as human beings first, but as sons and daughters, fathers and mothers, tribesmen and neighbors. It is this dense web of relations and the meanings which they give to life that satisfies the needs which really matter to us.

Michael Ignatieff

It is not a question of being inhumanely blind to the monstrous faults of the old order, of all old orders. It is simply a matter of learning inductively the impossibility of any new program too sweeping, any progress long sustained. Only dead chemicals can be sweepingly reorganized, sustainedly perfected; everything alive is indefensible because infinitely precarious. Humanity is wilful, wanton, unpredictable. It is not there to be organized for its own good by coercive righteous busybodies. Man is a ceaseless anti-managerial revolution.

Peter Viereck

I'm on the pavement thinking 'bout the government.

Bob Dylan

As a practicing journalist, Will is engaged in the task of thinking through our daily concerns. He diligently attempts to connect the problems of the day with the larger meditations of political philosophy. I examine a few of the issues he addresses and evaluate how well they further his project of repairing the defects in the American order while maintaining a fundamental commitment to constitutionalism. The issues are abortion, censorship, racial politics, English as an official language, the university curriculum, and political correctness. I continue the discussion of topical issues in the following chapter by reviewing Will's views on gay rights, minority rights, and the degree of unity appropriate for a free society. The issues I discuss are useful for understanding Will's thought because they reflect matters to which Will has returned repeatedly, and each represents some important aspect of Will's attempt to produce community and virtue within our culture.

Abortion

Perhaps the greatest divide in American culture is the issue of abortion. It is a wrenching moral issue that disturbs those urging moderation. It attests to the resiliency of the liberal tradition that such a potentially divisive issue has not threatened the survival of the regime in the way that slavery did.[1]

Will has urged a number of sensible points on abortion. Accepting his claims does little to defuse the issue, however. Will cites medical evidence supporting the claim that the fetus is alive (MA, 166–68). He further contends that the Supreme Court's decision in *Roe v. Wade* "rests shakily on this doubly absurd proposition: No one knows when human life begins, but the Court knows when 'meaningful life begins' " (SUD, 313). Will acknowledges that these observations do not settle the debate in favor of right-to-life advocates. "The argument, in which thoughtful people differ, is about the moral significance and hence the proper legal status of life in its early stages" (SUD, 314).

Will's main argument against the Court's abortion decision derives from his version of judicial restraint. His criticism of the Court illuminates his moral theory. Will argues that removing the abortion issue from the legislative arena diminished our opportunity for serious moral discussion. A free society must make room for serious moral debate: "Absent good moral argument, bad moral argument will have the field to itself. People should and will find political ways for venting their moral dimension, and for raising the perennial questions about how we ought to live. People who assert that values are incommensurable are people who have no place in politics, because politics is in the business of weighing values against one another and preferring some to others" (SS, 92.) From Will's perspective, removing the abortion issue from the legislative arena robs us of the opportunity to reflect seriously on our condition and our aims. Will believes that liberals err in assuming that abortion is a "private" matter. It is a decision that helps to shape our character and is, consequently, subject to scrutiny.

What is unacceptable to Will is settling the abortion debate by judicial fiat precluding democratic deliberation (SS, 84–85). Will's focus on democratic deliberation is questionable. Liberal societies need not maximize debate. Since Mill, we have grown accustomed to praising robust debate, but Hobbes, Locke, and Spinoza were eager to remove divisive issues from the public arena. The aim was not to force these issues into the underground, but to privatize them. Divisive issues were sapped of their public significance by removing the desire to debate them in public arenas. A liberal culture creates moral idiots (using Heraclitus's sense of idiocy as pertaining to private rather than common matters). By consigning large chunks of our moral lives to the private sphere, liberal culture allows us to avoid intractable issues while allowing robust debate on other matters.[2]

Will agrees that some things are not appropriate for public discussion. Indeed, as previously noted, his dissertation called for "constructive repression." Taking something off the public agenda does not require any sort of legal repression. We simply treat people who hold certain views as crackpots. As Will stated during the interview with me, "In theory everything is discussible. In fact, we do close questions. . . . Should women be chattel? We decided against that. Should there be slavery? No. We figured that one out. Should there be forcible segregation of the races? I thought we had figured that one out. It turns out we have not. We now have segregation from the left, and all the rest. So there is regression, I suppose. It's not just a straight line of progress as we close out errors" (Will, interview).

The abortion issue has followed the liberal script perfectly. A stable consensus collapsed as demands for abortion rights emerged. The issue reached a pitch of moral enthusiasm calculated to divide the republic into warring camps. As the debate heated, proponents of abortion struck upon the classic formula that this is an issue better suited for private conscience rather than public disposition. The formula is well in tune with our political tradition.

Will may want to argue that the issue should remain in the public arena, believing that good arguments would settle it. Agreement seems improbable. A pro-life enthusiast may want to keep the issue alive for the sake of righteousness, but can the issue serve as a vehicle to elevate public discourse?

Two outstanding works have attempted to refute the claim that abortion is an issue unsuited for public debate.[3] Mary Ann Glendon argues that the American debates, in contrast to those in Europe, deploy the language of rights rather than emphasizing the goods that public policy might produce. Rights talk tends to preclude compromise and encourage extreme positions.[4] Were we to ask what good our policies produce rather than what our rights are, we could have civil debates over abortion. European laws recognize the interests of both pregnant women and the fetuses they carry. While abortions are common in European countries, American-style vituperation is not. Most parties agree to respect a variety of interests, and listen to everyone.

James Hunter argues that there is a fairly broad consensus on abortion issues disguised by the extreme, acrimonious rhetoric of political activists. Because extremists dominate our rhetoric, we face bloody conflict. The conflict may diminish, Hunter thinks, if we substitute democratic deliberation for partisan rhetoric. Deliberation would be possible only if we developed forums to hear all considered opinions. That would require learning to listen to nuances missed in the ideological wrangling that passes for debate today. Hunter fears that suppressing debate, on this or other subjects tangled in our "culture wars," might lead to violence and social disruption that respectful debate might avoid.[5]

Will's position is quite close to Glendon's and Hunter's. He argues that there are "splittable differences" in the abortion debate (SUD, 311–17). We can manage our differences if we have recourse to deliberation: "This democratic nation needs vigorous argument, not judicial fiat, about abortion. Politicians will hate it. Still, they can split some differences if the argument is not about when in pregnancy life begins but when in pregnancy abortions should stop" (SUD, 315). Will thinks that legislatures can split differences because they work against a background of consensus. The consensus would allow some abortions, but many fewer than would be permitted under *Roe v. Wade*. Will believes "there is . . . a vague but broad and plausible intuition that the moral status, and hence the protection appropriate for, a fetus changes with its developmental stages (hence the power of, and fury from pro-abortion people concerning, photographs of aborted fetuses sufficiently developed to resemble infants)" (SUD, 316–17).

Survey data analyzed by Hunter in *Before the Shooting Begins* support Will's perception of the dominant view among Americans. Hunter demonstrates that Americans diverge sharply from both pro-life and pro-choice activists.[6] The important question concerns the proper use of this information. How are we to express the consensus within the public and constrain the dissensus among activists? Put somewhat differently, how do we secure the blessings of both deliberation and peace simultaneously? In his useful typology of arguments about legal privacy, Michael Sandel classifies the argument I am presenting as "the minimalist or pragmatic view [that] says that, because people inevitably disagree about morality and religion, government should bracket these controversies for the sake of political agreement and social cooperation."[7] My version of the argument only requires that we bracket some issues. I agree with Sandel and Will that eventually we must appeal to some conception of the good. Peace is a good that frequently outweighs others. At times we must even allow evils for the sake of peace.[8]

Will seems to assume that legislatures are good forums for deliberation on testy issues. On some issues, that assumption is undoubtedly true if our aim is peaceful adjudication of issues on which there is broad consensus. The key, however, is not public consensus but rather dissensus among different publics. Political scientists distinguish between attentive and inattentive publics. Legislators typically listen more carefully to those for whom an issue has high saliency and intensity. The evidence suggests that the most attentive publics on abortion are the activists. Consequently, the likely tone of legislative debates would be set by activists. I do not find this an exhilarating prospect. Surely the broader public consensus could constrain legislation. Even if it did, that would not ensure quality deliberation. Absent that gain, the main question would be: What best serves the Hobbesian interest in peace? My guess is that we have reached a stable consensus that allows peaceful living with or without *Roe*—a consensus solidified and partially created by the courts. Is Hunter right that we risk violence without democratic deliberation? We risk it, indeed experience it, anyway, but I place little trust in more talk. I am much more sanguine about the abortion debate than Hunter. My sense is that liberalism has triumphed, and the issue is more or less off the public agenda. Those, such as Paul Hill, who turn to violence will be ostracized and defeated. If *Roe* were overturned, as seems unlikely, most states would keep relatively liberal abortion policies. Some would adopt restrictive policies. Many places would maintain the current pressure of public condemnation that makes exercising the abortion right difficult. In any case, I see no scenario where good debate would occur.

On balance, we may be better off retaining the notion of abortion rights. Glendon and Will are surely correct that we overuse the language of rights. The trouble is that the tendency is so deep in the American psyche that it is difficult to imagine avoiding it.[9] Rights talk did not emerge full-grown from the head of some liberal Zeus. It grew with the American order primarily because it served a purpose. Nothing privatizes judgment better than rights talk. If I have a right, I do not owe you an explanation. The problem is how to reintroduce the language of the good without exacerbating our differences over the good. At least part of the solution: Be selective. Some things we need to talk about; others we do not. Most Americans are sporadically attentive to politics. The language of rights distances us from our leaders and filters their messages to us. What we cannot expect is for most of us to take the lead in reformulating an issue we find frustrating to discuss. Certainly Glendon and others are right in urging us to discuss ways to help children and explore our common interests in promoting strong families. Nothing in our history suggests more productive debate if abortion is a legislative issue.

None of these comments imply that discussion about abortion should not occur. Opponents of abortion can still use moral persuasion and attempt to create a moral atmosphere hostile to frequent abortions.[10] Vivid moral discussion is quite possible over matters that are not on the legislative agenda. In a society saturated with rights talk, it is still possible to distinguish between legal rights and ethical propriety. E. J. Dionne Jr. makes the case for depoliticizing moral issues quite well:

> If we are to end the cultural civil war that has so distorted our politics, we need to begin to practice a certain charity and understanding. We need politics to deal with the things it is good at dealing with—the practical matters like schools and roads, education and jobs. Paradoxically, by expecting politics to settle too many issues, we have diminished the possibilities of politics. After years of battling about culture and morality through the political system, voters are looking for a settlement that combines tolerance with a basic commitment to the values of family and work, compassion and the rule of law.[11]

Will seems to be of two minds concerning the extent to which moral issues should be politicized. On the one hand, he castigated the speakers at the 1992 Republican National Convention for their "thick soup of values blather." "Is there no public business—roads, schools, national defense, stuff like that—they could attend to" (LW, 303). On the other hand, he told me "you can have politics . . . of the sort that American contemporary liberalism is comfortable with—the politics of material distributive justice. Taxing the rich and giving it away, and building highways and infrastructure, and talking about bridges. Sorry, that doesn't happen to be what people are worried about. They're worried about their children. They're worried about the coarsening of life. They're worried about values. In this attempt to narrow the political conversation to the old, comfortable political vocabulary . . . that may have been more comfortable, but sorry, that's not our politics anymore.

And shouldn't be. And never was to tell you the truth" (Interview, 25–26). I sympathize. It is exceedingly difficult to decide what should be on the public agenda, and what our publics should concern themselves with is quite relevant. But the answer to the question "What shall we argue about?" simply cannot be: "Everything." Our "values" are not always the best subject for political debate.

Pornography and Censorship

Will decries efforts by contemporary liberals to shuffle our concerns with books, pictures, and film into the private realm. Writings and images should be subject to public scrutiny because the ways we entertain and teach ourselves have a distinctive bearing on how we live. There is no "right" to produce pornography.[12] Will does not confine his penchant for censorship to obscene materials, insisting as he does that all sorts of expression may damage our character.

Will is not willing to recognize an untrammeled right to free expression. He powerfully denounces subjectivist arguments that deny our capacity to distinguish among various forms of expression (however difficult it may be to make distinctions in practice). Civilized judgment presupposes the capacity to distinguish worthwhile expression from trash. What remains for consideration is the gravity of various assaults on our sensibilities and the ways to properly regulate them.

For Will, threats to civilized sensibilities are grave indeed. He insists that a good society must blush: "A public incapable of shame and embarrassment about public vulgarity is unsuited to self-government" (MA, 52). Are we in danger of losing our capacity for self-government? According to Will, we have seen an increasing "coarsening" (a most favored Will word) of life reflected in the precipitous decline from the high moral demands of *She Wore a Yellow Ribbon* to the moral laxity of Steven Spielberg (MA, 51). Will correctly gauges the shortening attention span of the American public and accurately connects it to the public's demand for more sensational spectacles. Forgive me, however, for failing to grasp the grand elevation of John Ford's movies or the sordid degradation of Steven Spielberg's.

Will has a variety of complaints against popular culture. He finds many of our most popular films, such as *Star Wars,* morally suspect. I do not fully understand Will's revulsion to that film. I suppose one could view it as an appeal to an easy and superficial moralism. To the contrary, one could discover archetypal themes with deep resonances.[13] I see both.

In any case, some moral superficiality is a precondition for decency. With respect to some cultural products, Will's standards for objection are clearer. He dislikes *E.T.* because the kids are foul-mouthed and the movie puts scientists in an unfavorable light (MA, 34–36). The suspicion of government scientists is a long-standing theme in science fiction movies. We may be alarmed that science fiction reflects and reinforces American anti-intellectualism, but we should be pleased that these movies reflect a healthy skepticism about people who have not always behaved responsibly. In any event, Will has worried more persistently about coarsening than about assaults on science or moral superficiality.

Will's worries largely derive from an image of decline from, if not a golden age, a better age in American popular culture. His moral balance sheet is quite problematic. People raised on westerns do not automatically qualify as people I would want to know.[14] Nor do I stand in fear and trembling when I learn that someone spent time watching *Three's Company*—a show Will describes as "execrable" (PV, 69). Why does Will attach such importance to pointless and seemingly harmless diversions? He correctly describes himself as someone so straight he "wouldn't recognize marijuana if a bale of it fell on" him (PV, 347). Fervid straightness (combined with a streak of snobbishness) allows for charming and insightful prose. Unfortunately, straightness and snobbery create a blind spot about the lives of the "vulgar"—used in the original sense of ordinary folks. Indeed, Will consistently fails to distinguish between cultural manifestations that are merely vulgar and those that are toxic for civility.

On *This Week with David Brinkley,* Will asked a guest whether she would allow her children to watch *Married With Children.* The guest (who apparently had higher standards than Will) replied that she had never seen the show. Will's question intrigued me because I love the show, and it is one of few programs I bother to watch regularly. I like the show primarily because it is funny, but I appreciate it precisely because it (like Aristophanes) captures the rhythms and pathos of vulgar (ordinary) life so well by exaggerating common features of contemporary experience. My aesthetics may be bad, but are my morals? Well, let's not get into that. My relatives, who are charismatic Christians, also love the show. It seems not to have ruined them.

Assume Will is right about the need to elevate our moral lives by elevating our aesthetic standards. How do we do it? What sort of soulcraft can we deploy? Will praises the efforts of Donald Wildmon, a Mississippi family values activist, for leading national boycotts of television and movies he considers immoral (PV, 69–71). Surely defenders of a

moral perspective may use boycotts along with persuasion to pressure us
into right thinking. If Wildmon were successful in promoting the
agenda Will endorses, would popular culture improve? Many of us
would not regret the demise of *Three's Company* reruns, but many people
I know would miss the opportunity to see a variety of films and television programs that would surely offend my fellow Mississippian's consti-
pated sensibilities.[15] In Wildmon's America, I probably would not have
had the delightful opportunity to spend a summer studying Nietzsche
under the sponsorship of the National Endowment for the Humanities.
I did have to wait longer than urban dwellers to see an excellent film,
The Last Temptation of Christ. Boycotts, like laws, are blunt instruments.
They should be allowed, but we should refrain from too willing
applause. (The same criticism applies to those on the left who would
shut down *Basic Instinct* or *The Silence of the Lambs.*)

The issue of pornography is different. Liberals who worry that prohibiting *Deep Throat* puts us on a slippery slope where we will necessarily
ban *Carnal Knowledge* or even a Robert Mapplethorpe exhibit are too
dogmatic. Will insists that a civilized society must retain its capacity to
make distinctions. The serious questions are: Why bother to regulate
pornography? How well are we likely to do in regulating it?

Unfortunately, Will does not always tie his claims concerning the
desirability of regulating pornography to evidence concerning its
effects.[16] Is pornography producing deleterious results for either individuals or the community at large? At best, the evidence is inconclusive.[17]
Not having firm evidence, we must rely on our best guesses. My best
guess is that many people who watch porno flicks quickly become bored
and develop no desire to repeat the experience. People who watch these
movies now and then probably do not experience a deep or lasting
impact. There are, of course, a few people obsessed with pornography.
These people may or may not have problems requiring attention, but
we should not simply assume that their vice unfits them for citizenship.
Similarly, liberals who worry about the effects of violence in film and
television rely on empirical studies of doubtful value.

Will has shown some sympathy for feminists who contend that
pornography is either intrinsically dehumanizing or sustains cultural
values in need of eradication (LW, 13–15).[18] Will's fulmination against
rap music relies on a combination of claims that misogynist celebrations
of violence lead to misogynist violence and that the words are themselves an assaultive affront to womanhood. The first claim is unproved.
The latter is legally problematic.

The Supreme Court has ruled that while time, place, and manner restrictions on free expression are allowable if narrowly drawn, regulating the content of speech is much less acceptable.[19] The mere offensiveness of the speech has not justified an exception to the rule against regulating content. In the case of pornography, the Court has held that its "expressive content" is so low-grade as to warrant lessened protection. Pornography seeks to build "prurient interest" rather than express ideas. Misogynist ideas, however, have a political content that requires protection. Consequently, we may ban misogyny as pornography but not as misogyny.[20] This line of argument has incensed feminists and critical race theorists who wish to promote codes and laws against hate speech. It also runs counter to the argument in Will's dissertation for repressing racist speech.

Will, along with feminists and critical race theorists, is surely correct in seeing the dead end of relativist defenses of "expression." Who's to say what opinions are better or worse? Anyone willing to govern will prefer some opinions to others. It makes no sense to ban discrimination if we have not decided between racism and antiracism.

Milton, in the *Areopagitica,* captured the (essentially Augustinian) case against censorship. Censors tend to be stupid. If you leave your liberties in the hands of people less capable of judgment than you, you will quickly lose them.[21] The argument from mistrust is far superior to the kind of argument that would assign some serious value to, say, Nazi propaganda. Moral crusades are morally suspect because moralists are often dense people. We surely need them to preach, but not to govern.[22]

There is some reason to resist even the preaching. Corruption in the arts is not always a bad thing. Rousseau argues that corrupt forms of art (particularly the theater) do not belong in a virtuous republic but are desirable in a large, corrupted, cosmopolitan community. In a virtuous regime, the arts will divert citizens from the simple moral messages that simple people need to reinforce their citizenship. In a cosmopolitan regime, the rustic arts will leave patrons bored. The more sophisticated arts will allow corrupted people to become distracted from their miseries and less of a public nuisance.[23] Put more charitably, a liberal regime encourages people to turn toward their private circles for sustenance. Living a private life requires diversions. Edifying art may not satisfy our lust for diversion. Absent the diversions there is potential for mob action in search of a meaningful life.

There is a seamier side to these observations. Pascal considered diversions the clear mark of spiritual emptiness—an emptiness filled with an unending quest for novelty.[24] On that view, the seeds of "coarse" popular arts are sown in *Ozzie and Harriet,* which is, after all, a diversion. If this is true, what can we do? Sweetness and corniness breed boredom. How long will John Wayne satisfy? Coarseness breeds excitement followed by ennui—followed by more coarseness.[25]

People easily bored need a preacher, I suppose. In my interview with Will, he stressed the important role John Wesley played in helping to address the problem of gin in England. Will hopes for a similar source of renewal in the face of our drug problems (Will, interview). The problem involves getting good preachers without surrendering the keys to a theocratic kingdom. The dynamic of mass culture engendering a quest for excitement seems endemic to a technologically advanced liberal regime. If boredom and anxiety create enough sense of crisis, there is powerful potential for authoritarian politics.

Politically, the problem of ennui may be less disturbing than Pascal thought. Our diversions do divert. They effectively substitute a satisfying vicariousness for real living. We do not have to "get a life" if we have television. As a youth in the sixties, I imbibed the revolutionary posturing of Jefferson Airplane to no apparent effect other than an ersatz but effective sense of belonging to something bigger than me. Then I grew up (though I still like the music). Most of today's kids listening to gangsta rap or heavy metal will do the same thing. They will experience a sublime sense of communally shared alienation and then get on with raising families and worrying about the coarsening of life. This does not mean that mass media cannot have sinister political uses. Aldous Huxley's description of the "feelies" in *Brave New World* rings true. The greatest problem, then, is not social disruption but quiescence. Television and popular music work more like soporifics than amphetamines.

Maybe we do need preachers, and not just as prophetic goads. Without efforts at censorship, there may be an aesthetic loss even if there is no moral crisis. We may lose the sense of the forbidden that provides spice to human experience. If those who urge full acceptance of our sexuality have their way, we may become too good for our good. Milan Kundera ends his novel *The Book of Laughter and Forgetting* with a description of life in a nudist colony:

> A group of people are discussing many things: the temperature of the water, the hypocrisy of a society that cripples body and soul, the beauties of the island. . . . A man with an extraordinary paunch began developing the theory that Western civilization was on its way out and we would

soon be freed once for all from the bonds of Judeo-Christian thought—
statements Jan had heard ten, twenty, thirty, a hundred, five hundred, a
thousand times before—and for the time being those few feet of beach
felt like a university auditorium. On and on the man talked. The others
listened with interest, their naked genitals staring dully, sadly, listlessly
at the yellow sand.[26]

Affirmative Action and the Politics of Race

The problems and perils of character formation through law and exhor-
tation are considerable. They are nowhere more taxing than when we
attempt to address the American dilemma of how to live up to our
ideals in pursuing racial justice. One of the ways we have attempted to
deal with the American dilemma is through affirmative action.

Will repudiates affirmative action because it violates the "core concept" of American justice—equal opportunity for individuals—and
replaces it with "statistical parity for government-approved groups" (PV,
129).[27] Will's point resonates in American political culture. Equal
opportunity for individuals is a comforting and familiar ideal shared by
most of us. Commitment to the ideal explains much of the political
resistance to affirmative action—resistance that we cannot dismiss as
open or disguised racism. Appeal to the ideal is somewhat odd in Will's
case. He invokes the individualism he castigates as the major defect in
our regime. Does he really think that the language of individualism is
adequate to describe race relations in America? Furthermore, Will usually makes a Burkean appeal to prudent management of consequences
rather than asserting abstract rights. Here he offers more of a critique of
pure injustice.

Fortunately, Will does more than appeal to core principle. He argues
that affirmative action has undesirable consequences. Will avers that
affirmative action in professional schools would be ruinous because "the
pool of qualified minority applicants is shallow" (PV, 129). If this is true,
a policy that even resembled quotas would indeed be ruinous. Nevertheless, the notion of being "qualified" is not clear-cut. Amy Gutmann has
cogently argued that a sane idea of affirmative action must include a
threshold conception of being qualified.[28] Every applicant seriously considered for a benefit (school admission, jobs, contracts) ought be qualified. Once we assemble a pool of qualified applicants, we then have the
unenviable task of devising a method of ranking them. The issues are
these: Do we have clear, reliable, objective criteria for merit that do not

simply mask prejudice? Can race or gender be used as a factor in ranking qualifications?

Will does not address the first question in any depth. He does address the second, and in one unusual case he surprisingly answers: Yes. Will gives an excellent example of race counting as a qualification. In an evocative essay on drug stings in Miami, he pauses to reflect on the racial composition of the Street Narcotics Detail: "The Detail is composed of black and white officers, but when the task is a sting, and the place is the ghetto, the black officers must do the dealing. A black officer watching his colleagues scoop up drug buyers says matter of factly, but also pointedly and unanswerably, that what we are watching is made possible only by affirmative action. If Miami's police force had remained what it, like so many other police forces, was recently—too white—this kind of law enforcement would be impossible" (SD, 186). Including racial balance in qualifications is not simply confined to jobs such as police work and newspaper reporting where having racial minorities in the labor force is essential to particular tasks. Any labor force is too white (or too male) if members of groups are systematically excluded from participation. The public interest suffers when large segments of our population become convinced that they cannot attain the American dream.

A critic can raise legitimate concerns about the propriety of affirmative action as practiced. We may question the use of quotas, especially where we have not taken affirmative action to improve the level of the applicant pool; e.g., by seriously confronting the failure of inner-city schools. Affirmative action may disproportionately benefit women and minorities who were on the fast track to begin with, leaving untouched the problems most in need of attention. The benefits of affirmative action could disappear in the backlash from a society saturated with an individualist ethos. Whatever our doubts about affirmative action, it addresses problems that are sorely in need of attention. Recall that Will bemoans the absence of qualified minorities. (Note, however, that in the famous *Bakke* case, none of the parties claimed that the university accepted unqualified candidates.)[29] Does Will think the absence of qualified minorities is an accident? If not, three explanations are available: genetic factors, social and cultural variables, and discrimination.[30] Will generally opts for the second explanation, arguing that the inner-city black population suffers from "pathologies" stemming from a disintegrating family structure (MA, 160–64).[31] Three observations are in order.

First, even if family structure explains the bulk of the problems of inner-city African Americans, it cannot explain them all. Some problems, in both hiring and promotion, stem from discrimination. Will knows this, but he consistently argues that we should not use statistics to unearth patterns of discrimination, but rather should prove specific intent (SD, 324–25). This approach ignores the insidious character of discrimination. Discrimination is not simply individuals acting against individuals. People endure discrimination *as* members of the groups to which they belong.[32] Our rhetoric is individualist; the reality certainly is not.

Second, discrimination follows subtle patterns. Minorities were not excluded from the Miami police force because a few people made overt decisions to exclude them. There was a pattern of exclusion supported by an unstated understanding that whites were preferable, as well as by institutionalized biases that appear "objective" but ensure disparate impacts. At any interview for any job, an interviewer could always find a reason for preferring a white candidate that has nothing to do with race. The result was a "too white" police force. To remedy the pattern of subtle, tacit discrimination, race-conscious remedies may be necessary. How to prove a pattern of discrimination is a difficult and contentious matter. One thing is abundantly clear: you cannot prove a pattern on a case-by-case basis. Statistics must be applicable in some way. In a case where there is a pattern of discrimination, it will not do to say: "We will be color blind; there will be no preferences." The status quo would entail preferences, and inaction would sanction them.[33]

Third, if the root problem is cultural patterns and family structure, what can we do? Will believes that most of the problems of the inner city stem from behavior that government is powerless to correct (NS, 151–52).[34] If Will is right, there are severe limits to the basic theme of statecraft as soulcraft. If statecraft is about shaping souls and we confess ourselves powerless to do the shaping we need, what does that say about the virtues of the "big government conservatism" Will has espoused? He could reply that we cannot expect to reach everyone, but that answer is disheartening considering his stress on unity—a problem that runs through the remaining issues I discuss.

Legislated Language

Will is ardent in supporting English as the official language of the United States. He connects his opposition to bilingualism to the demand for good citizenship. He asserts that providing bilingual ballots "denies the link between citizenship and shared culture" (MA, 137). He thinks that a shared language is essential to a shared culture, and that shared culture is necessary for good citizenship. He even believes that the connection between citizenship and language is rooted in human nature: "When government nurtures a shared language it is nurturing a natural right—the ability to live in the manner that is right for human nature" (MA, 138).

Why does nature require all people living in a community to speak the same language? Will's claim rests primarily on the need for unity. For Will, unity is a precondition for the good life, and it is not compatible with linguistic diversity.

Will's call to unity is not objectionable. Neither is asking Spanish-speaking people or Vietnamese immigrants to learn English. What seems questionable is the disproportion between the demands that we place on one group of citizens and those we place on another. Why not learn better ways to live with people who are different? Asking the people who are different to merely become like us makes living together harder.

We find no sure path to unity in denying obvious differences. Why not ask Anglos and Hispanics to learn each other's language and culture? Will's answer is disturbing: "The promise of America is bound up with the virtues and achievements of 'Anglo culture,' which is bound up with English" (MA, 138). This claim seems odd considering the argument, discussed in chapter 2, that places American culture within a broader, deeper tradition. Spanish culture would seem a vital part of the broader stream from which we wish to drink. Does the notion of "western civilization" make sense without reference to Cervantes? Can we understand the glories of the English language without understanding the abiding presence of Latin?[35] In any event, if the pragmatic aim is unity, it is not clear that making English our official language achieves it. How do we avoid the harsh and unappealing invitation that proclaims: "Come join me. I am better than you"? It also portrays our dominant culture as either too lazy or too stupid to learn and appreciate even a closely cognate language. (Americans are particularly bad about picking up second and third languages.) Insularity is not a particularly inviting characteristic to celebrate in ourselves.

Canon Fodder

The call to unity also dominates Will's discussion of the university curriculum. He believes that every university ought to have a core curriculum, centering on the "classics" of western civilization. The criteria for classics are not clear, and Will admits that canon formation is open to debate. The issue for him, though, is not so much which books are classics. Rather, he wants to make sure that western classics dominate the canon. He is unabashed in his defense of "eurocentrism": "'Eurocentricity' is right, in American curricula and consciousness, because it accords with the facts of our history, and we—and Europe—are fortunate for that. The political and moral legacy of Europe has made the most happy and admirable nations. Saying that may be indelicate, but it has the merit of being true, and the truth should be the core of any curriculum" (SD, 17). At least four political consequences attach to this view, none of which are reassuring for a champion of unity.

First, Will believes that European works are aesthetically superior to those of nonwestern peoples (SD, 210–12.) The consequence of this belief is telling people—whom we want to join us in a national celebration—that they should enjoy the beautiful things that we alone appear capable of creating. Second, Will asks us to affirm the uniquely civilizing quality of our texts. The problem lies in squaring this story with the fact that Germany, the most philosophically cultured nation in western Europe, produced some of the greatest barbarities in history.[36] Third, we have to pretend that there is a sublime harmony beneath the surface of our intracultural debates. We disagree wildly about the proper content and meaning of the canon, and canonical texts promote bitter arguments about the nature of the good life. Where is the harmony beneath the discord?[37] Fourth, an assumption that a political assessment of a canon must center on "truth" is subject to radical questions posed within the canon itself. Plato, Machiavelli, and Nietzsche (merely to produce the short list) all affirm the value of lies and salutary myths for political harmony and good living.[38]

We cannot assume that we should select works for our students on the single criterion of "greatness." We may serve our moral purposes better by choosing less than great works. Susan Wolf explains this point well in her commentary on a piece by Charles Taylor. She asks whether discovering great works by Africans, Asians, and Native Americans is necessary for wanting to include them in our curriculum. She answers that refusal to do so constitutes a failure of respect. "This failure of respect, however, does not depend on any beliefs about the relative merit of one culture compared to another. Nor does the need to remedy it rest on the claim, presumed or confirmed, that African or Asian or Native American culture has anything particularly important to teach the world. It rests on the claim that African and Asian and Native American cultures are a part of our culture, or rather, of the cultures of some of the groups that together constitute our community."[39] Most of our students will never be connoisseurs of high culture. The point of a curriculum is to make them welcome and well-functioning citizens. Were appreciating the finest things (Arnold's "best that has been thought and known") a precondition for citizenship, most of our people would have to be disenfranchised.[40] Will shares a quaint, popular notion that there was a golden age when people were highly literate and that our current generation has suffered from miseducation, depriving them of the common culture we once shared (SUD, 216–18). Survey research on Americans' knowledge of politics has consistently shown, from the '40s onward, a dearth of knowledge about government. I have no reason to believe that, outside a circle of Princeton graduates, the picture is any better concerning history or literature. We have always had educated elites and everybody else. Absent high literacy, we must expect something less than greatness in our curricula. That leaves room for many serviceable books.

Even if the canon possesses undeniable nobility and moral instructiveness, there is a deeper problem that Will does not touch. He exhibits the peculiar American faith in the saving power of curricula. We assume that students become inspired by being exposed to great books. Many of them become sleepy. Will almost wholly neglects the problems of pedagogy, choosing instead to bank exclusively on depositing our intellectual capital without assurance of a receipt. This is especially unfortunate in a plural culture where the teaching must effectively cross cultural divides. We cannot think of our culture as a museum to display a few pretty baubles. Reaching students is difficult. In a television age, preserving mere literacy, much less high culture, is a challenge. Frequently a good teacher will ask: Will this book entice students toward further reading? Often good books serve better than great ones. Indeed, C. Wright Mills notes that bad books are sometimes more intellectually stimulating than good ones.[41]

The great canon debates clearly absorb more of those people who spend time thinking about prescribing reading lists to others than those people who are interested in sharing the joys and frustrations of reading with students. That is hardly surprising since our prestige universities hire people who spend more time researching and preaching than teaching (irrespective of which end of the political spectrum they inhabit). The debates on the canon, as with the battles over "political correctness," are distorted by the intense focus on prestige universities. Christopher Lasch, in his last book, observed that: "The noisy battles over the 'canon' which have convulsed faculties at a handful of leading universities, are completely irrelevant to the plight of higher education as a whole. Four-year state colleges and two-year community colleges enroll far more students than renowned universities like Harvard or Stanford, which receive a disproportionate share of attention."[42]

Russell Jacoby captures the distortions that result when we focus on reading lists at prestigious universities rather than on teaching. He notes the notorious gap in prestige between teaching literature and composition. As a result, regular faculty stay away from composition courses, leaving them to underpaid and overworked graduate students. Jacoby insists that complaints about "politicizing" English courses ignore these realities. Jacoby observes that

> George Will . . . denounced as "political indoctrination" proposed course revisions of a University of Texas English course. "Politicized professors" from the sixties, he wrote, were attempting "to give a uniform topic and text" to the English course. Yet critics crying politics avoid the nonpolitical problems English composition courses face.[43]

Jacoby relates the background for attempting to create a set of required readings on race and gender. The readings were requested, not by tenured radicals, but by graduate students in literature forbidden to use the novels, poems, and short stories held as a monopoly by the literature faculty. The students were looking for something to structure courses for which they were not trained and to arouse the interest of their students. From Jacoby's perspective, those who do not understand the problems of ill-prepared instructors struggling to cope with a difficult situation will inevitably reduce difficult problems of pedagogy to flat ideological disputes over book lists. Until the debates focus more on pedagogy than curriculum, the prospects for a satisfying conclusion to the debates about the future of our universities are not good.

Virtuous Correctness

George Will has joined a large chorus of conservatives in complaining about "political correctness." The term was coined by leftists protesting ideological rigidity among those with whom they shared a number of convictions, but it was hijacked by those on the right seeking an effec-

tive epithet to use against opponents. Like any phrase in common
coinage, the appellation is imprecise. Increasingly the term has assumed
an odd political correctness in that it is used to describe any conviction
that defies conservatism. Thus, a letter to the editor in the *Clarion Ledger*
of Jackson, Mississippi, claimed that the paper had succumbed to political correctness by refusing to drop a popular comic strip ("For Better or
Worse") that had depicted a gay teenager.

Whatever the imprecision and abuse of the term, Will correctly
insists that we should not abandon it or accept the assertion that political correctness is simply the invention of right-wing ideologues (LW,
119–21). Political correctness, broadly, is the attempt to enforce orthodox modes of expression to protect groups of people from injury or
insult. Using this definition, political correctness can come from any
portion of the political spectrum; however, the most publicized examples have been leftists attempting to enforce orthodox expression, especially in universities.

In assessing political correctness, we need to distinguish among the
various ways we can enforce orthodox expression. We have at least three
ways of ensuring good behavior. We enforce correct speech and behavior
through manners, morals, and law.

We enforce manners indirectly through irony and exclusion. Ill-man-
nered people are either subtly shamed into conformity or denied association with those who insist on standards of civility.[44] We enforce morals
through persuasion, public opinion, and social condemnation.[45] We
enforce laws with the coercive power of government. Each mode of
enforcement raises different questions concerning the propriety of its
use. Unfortunately, the discussions often fail to make the appropriate
distinctions.

One thing is clear. Almost no one is willing to abandon all standards
of decent comportment. Who among us will grant an unrestricted
license to insult whomever we wish, however we wish, whenever we
wish, with utter impunity? My students, being good Americans, pay lip
service to openness and candor. When I ask them to think through the
implications of an encounter group ethic, they invariably balk. I ask
them: Who would like to live in a world where everyone speaks his or
her mind at will? I find very few takers. Consequently, the issue is not
whether we will have standards of correctness, but whether we will have
correct standards.

How far will Will go in enforcing correct comportment? He is surely
suspicious of those who would enforce uprightness. He complains that

many political ideologues are (to use Joseph Epstein's term) "virtucrats," people who enter all political arguments with a firm conviction of their righteousness. For virtucrats, opponents are not mistaken but wicked (NS, 162–63). Virtucrats are the people who are most likely to insist on sweeping enforcement of political correctness. Self-righteousness combines well with another source of political correctness—excessive sensitivity. Will decries the growth of victim status in America, especially when combined with delicate sensibilities.[46] For Will, the combination of victimhood and sensitivity is disastrous: "Many of today's Balkanizing policies are products of a desire to show sensitivity to the feelings of particular groups. Sensitivity is a good thing. But remember: The four most important words in political discourse are 'up to a point.' Armies, police, taxation, even freedom and equality are good only 'up to a point' " (LW, 130). Will is sure that we are past the point at which sensitivity is the reigning concern. Candor is in order.

What have we become too sensitive about? The most common examples of political correctness concern the way we use language. Will does not oppose prohibiting abusive language. He took the American Civil Liberties Union to task for supporting the legal right of Nazis to march in the heavily Jewish town of Skokie (PV, 84–86). His objection was not to the danger created by the march. Although Will would allow restrictions on the content of speech, that was not his primary concern about the Skokie march. Rather, his objection to allowing the march boils down to this: In this setting, this speech is grossly offensive to an audience that ought not to suffer the offense. He would protect Jews from "the pain" the march would cause (PV, 86). Will is surely correct to find the march insulting and painful for victims of the Holocaust and their descendants. Moral condemnation is in order. Is legal restriction appropriate?

Here is the problem. Protecting one group of victims against insult rather than injury opens the floodgate for protecting all who have been or have been thought to be victims. Will, who supports legislation against pornography, recognizes how far the fight against pornography as an insult to women can carry us. He castigates Catharine MacKinnon for swallowing freedom of speech in her crusade against pornography. Here he expresses the liberalism of mistrust quite well. Speech codes are wrong because the wrong people will invariably capture them. Indeed, he provides a valuable warning to radicals like MacKinnon who assume the hegemony of patriarchy in our society. "She simply ignores the familiar contradiction in radical programs for therapeutic government: If society is so sick that it needs radical therapy, what reason is there to trust the government produced by that society to be therapeutic?" (LW, 30). The question of mistrust runs deeper from an Augustinian viewpoint. When can we trust government to protect our sensibilities? Conservatives like Will and William F. Buckley who once dreamed of political institutions that would enforce a correct correctness now balk when the wrong people are in charge.[47]

Advocates for teaching virtuous attitudes need to consider Chappell's theorem on the circulation of elites: Sooner or later (usually sooner), the wrong people will be in charge. Will seems to have realized the significance of this. In my interview with him, I asked if he would still enforce the Supreme Court's old "fighting words" doctrine, which allowed government to punish words calculated to incite a breach of peace.[48] He replied:

> When I wrote my dissertation, I would have said a university is a special place. It exists to have its own atmosphere and purposes that are not the same as those of the larger society, and it can take measures to condition the atmosphere on campus. I no longer believe that because I look at who has captured the campuses. People have captured the campuses as part of the long march through the institutions. Now it turns out to be a very short march. These virtucrats have gone to earth in the English Departments, and that's it! They are not getting to the capitol. (Will, interview)

The only quarrel I have with these remarks concerns their narrow target. Political correctness runs across the political spectrum.

Will assumes that political correctness is principally a product of the left. According to him, "the right wing has its share of virtucrats of the 'when Jesus returns he will register Republican' sort. But Epstein says virtucrats are found more frequently on the left. People on the left, he says, need to feel they are good-hearted, whereas conservatives are content to feel they are obviously correct. Disagree with a conservative and he will call you dense. Disagree with a liberal and he will call you selfish, insensitive and uncompassionate" (NS, 162–63). There is much truth to this, but not as much as Will thinks. Has he listened to enough Pat Buchanan speeches? Or Rush Limbaugh broadcasts? Or Jesse Helms? Will's comments on the (disastrous) 1992 Republican National Convention are apt: "Republicans have caught a particularly virulent version of the Democrats' quite-virulent tendency . . . to turn political disagreement into moral assault" (LW, 303).

The left and the right both have passions that drive them toward political correctness. Both groups threaten liberal tolerance. People on the right have passions for hierarchy and order and consider these passions rooted in "nature." Both passions are threatened by lapses in moral rectitude.[49] People on the left are animated by the (frequently contradictory) desires for progress and equality. Devotion to progress encourages a puritanical denial of the present for the sake of the new world to come. The passion for equality requires that differences be ignored (or homogenized) so that we can live together as virtuous equals, resisting all "elitist" demands to excel.[50]

Classical liberals possess a passion for liberty. They do not share the passions of leftists. Equality is a secondary concern, so they do not expect the all-for-one solidarity of Rousseauian citizens. Just regimes secure only as much of the good as a free society will allow; therefore, genuine liberals are not chiliastic.

Classical liberals do not share the passions of rightists either. Order and hierarchy are necessary, but not good in themselves. They are desirable insofar as they conduce to the blessings of liberty. Liberty is compatible with freely circulating elites and radical (if slow) shifts in the principles governing hierarchy and order. Some sort of order is necessary, but conservatives frequently delude themselves about their indispensability to an ordered society.

The case for locating political correctness on the left is most convincing when the focus turns to campuses, if for no other reason than the fact that campuses house the largest aggregation of leftists in America. The problem with observations about university campuses is that they tend to be unsystematic and selective. For instance, Dinesh D'Souza's highly influential book on political correctness draws from a few (often poorly analyzed) anecdotes and uses them to support sweeping generalizations.[51]

I spend much time at conferences, institutes, seminars, and workshops. The academics I meet tend to be a diverse lot. Like me, they probably spend more time than they should—with less circumspection than they need—saying exactly what is on their minds. If their speech has chilled, I have not noticed the freeze. My observations do not confirm the anecdotes. The anecdotes also tend to skew toward elite campuses with leftist offenders. Furthermore, conservative critics of political correctness do not tend to report examples of political correctness on the right; e.g., the efforts of the Alabama legislature to defund a gay rights group at Auburn University by prohibiting funding for college organizations that oppose Alabama's sodomy law.

Will has good reasons to denounce speech codes. They violate our legal traditions irrespective of their prevalence or place on the political spectrum. But what of the complaints against political correctness that focus on manners and morals? When Will and other conservatives report horror stories about P.C., we learn that tenured professors were "driven" from teaching their favorite classes by student criticisms.[52] Most lists of vital virtues include courage. How much sympathy do we owe people with protected jobs who simply refuse a fight? They should follow the example of Eric Voegelin, who sharpened his considerable polemical skills by arguing with coteries of Marxists at Bennington.[53]

By focusing on speech codes, critics of political correctness underplay the serious moral issues surrounding the use of language. Like ideas, words have consequences. Do not confuse rigidity in applying an idea with the worthlessness of the idea. Surely it is foolish to insist that everyone use "Native American" when many Indians prefer "Indian," but the recommendation for reforming the language reflects serious concerns about how we understand and have understood a group of people. Do critics of political correctness want to deny women the opportunity to criticize men who feel compelled to dismiss serious points with the casual use of "honey"?

Both sides in the political correctness debates share the same problem. They want to prescribe without justifying. At some point this is inevitable. Rules of usage work best when we do not think about them. During a period when our notions of acceptability are in transition and disputed, we need to be more willing to calmly ask and answer the question: Why? What we ask this question about will vary over time. Most people no longer ask why we do not call people "cripples" or "retards." That these terms are demeaning is (now) relatively transparent. Why "handicapped" (from the phrase "hand-in-cap") might offend is less transparent and requires patient discussion. When Representative Dick Armey (inadvertently?) referred to Representative Barney Frank as "Barney Fag," almost everyone, including Armey, admitted that it transgressed the bounds of decency. The debates over the use of "sexual perversion," "sexual preference," and "sexual orientation" are less clear and decisive to most Americans. In cases where the etiquette is transparent, social approbation will take care of transgressions. In debatable or poorly understood cases, we owe one another explanations, not reeducation seminars or sensitivity training. Indeed, without clearly understood rationales taught noncoercively, teaching sensitivity is likely to be counterproductive.[54]

In a strong column, Miss Manners stated the issue correctly. She denounced those who would use her criticisms of P.C. as an excuse for bigotry. She averred that there are two kinds of political correctness—a good and a bad version. The bad version is "ridiculous, touchy, hostile, humorless responses to ordinary, previously acceptable, harmless, even pleasant, human discourse."[55] The good form of P.C. involves the polite rebuke of people rude enough to express their bigotry. We should not allow people to use complaints against political correctness to excuse bigotry. Miss Manners observes that "it has become common now to preface offensive statements with, 'I suppose I'm not being politically correct, but . . .' This does not work on Miss Manners who never lets people off from the charge of being rude because they acknowledged that they are being rude—sort of the opposite of the temporary insanity plea" ("Good P.C.," 7E). All too often criticisms of P.C. wear the mask Miss Manners removes. Excusing bigotry is no way to practice the necessary virtue of politeness.

Reissuing Virtue

So far, I have considered issues that are more matters of empirical than philosophical dispute. The issues can be decided by assessing the evidence concerning the probable effects of proposed policies. Do boycotts engender good character? Does affirmative action contribute to national unity? Questions of this sort are crucial in evaluating Will's work, but deeper issues need to be explored. Among the deepest and most contentious issues in contemporary political philosophy are the status of "nature" and the meaning of political identity. Will's contribution to these disputes can be assayed by looking at his writings on gay rights, minority rights, and the imperative of national unity. Those are the topics of the next chapter.

Chapter Five
Natural Unions

According as his divine power hath given unto us all things that pertain unto life and godliness, through the knowledge of him that hath called us to glory and virtue; whereby are given to us exceeding great and precious promises: that by these ye might be partakers of the divine nature, having escaped the corruption that is in the world through lust.

2 Peter 1:3–4

And the tongue is a fire, a world of iniquity: so is the tongue among our members that it defileth the whole body, and setteth on fire the course of nature.

James 3:6

A man needs a maid.

Neil Young

Understanding how Will's commitments to virtue and community translate into debates about concrete issues requires us to probe his philosophical understandings a bit deeper. Efforts to build a virtuous community frequently build on theories of nature and political identity. The theorist will tell us what is right by nature and who "we" are or ought to be. Will does not offer elaborate philosophical theories on these matters; rather, he builds on the work of others and expresses his ideas concerning particular issues.

I explore his views on nature via an examination of his views on the politics of homosexuality. I then turn to the issue of political identity by reviewing Will's positions on national unity and minority rights. Many of the points about political identity build on points discussed in the previous chapter.

Virtuous Sexuality

Will has written about homosexuality throughout his career as a journalist. His essays on the subject reveal the problematic connections among the notions of nature, community, and virtue in his thought.

In an early essay, Will defended the campaign in Miami to repeal a gay rights ordinance. He maintained that, as a result of the ordinance, "people must be coerced into disregarding homosexuality when, say, hiring teachers" (PH, 56). This is an odd way to describe an antidiscrimination law. I will return to the issue of discrimination shortly. For now, the key question is: Why does Will regard the coercion as wrong? He repudiates claims that gay people pose a clear danger to others. "The idea that homosexuals are bent on recruiting children is a canard" (PH, 56). Rather, gay people threaten to disrupt the social order.

The role of choice is at the center of Will's arguments. Will observes that "the causes of homosexuality are a mystery. There is no evidence that it is congenital. . . . Surely homosexuality is an injury to healthy functioning, a distortion of personality. And the grounds for believing that it is a socially acquired inclination are reasons for prudence. To the extent that homosexuality is, in some sense, a 'choice' of character, as many homosexuals insist, then that choice may be influenced by various things including a social atmosphere of indifference, or sustained exposure to homosexual role models, such as teachers" (PH, 56). Will has retreated somewhat from his confident claim that no evidence of genetic influences on sexual orientation exists (he does not seem to use medicalizing terms such as "congenital" so much either) but still insists on caution because "postnatal events, including choices, influence sexuality" (LW, 118).[1] The notion of choice is confusing in this context. Most people do not choose a sexual orientation, although some people can choose to engage in acts that do not conform to their basic orientation. Will's worry seems to be that people whose basic orientation is not gay will choose enough homosexual acts to alter their orientation. Surely some (though I doubt very many) will make this choice. The key question is: So what?

Will's answer to the question typically takes two forms. First, the community has a right to enforce its moral judgments. Second, the community needs to enforce standards of naturalness.

Will believes that those who insist on a right to engage in homosexual acts undermine the right of the community to express its moral standards. He applauded an appeals court decision upholding a school district's decision to dismiss a bisexual woman as a guidance counselor. Will insisted that "the community has a right to act as it did in expression of its convictions" (MA, 96). He chided Justices Brennan and Marshall for wanting to grant certiorari in the case because they would "stigmatize as immoral the community's expression of its values" (MA,

97). Will's attempt to frame this as a community rights issue seems incongruent with his stance about affirmative action and other issues of personal rights where he consistently repudiates notions of group rights. Elsewhere he insists that we not "retreat from the Constitution's core principle, that rights inhere in individuals not groups" (LW, 217). This apparent incongruence is easily remedied. Will wants to maintain, along with a bare majority of Supreme Court justices, that the community has the authority, under the police power, to enforce its moral code.[2] As a constitutional principle, that may be correct, but Will himself notes that the constitutional issue is severable from questions concerning the wisdom of legislation (MA, 96). We need to recall Burke's constant reminders in his speeches on conciliation with the colonies and not succumb to the temptation to confuse what we have the authority do with what we ought to do. Leaving aside the constitutional issue, we can ask: Is there a communitarian argument for legislating against gay people?

Invoking community leads straight away the question: Which community? In a pluralist society, claims on behalf of one community frequently conflict with those of others. The majority of voters in Colorado voted to deny local communities the authority to enforce gay rights ordinances. What is the community to whom a communitarian may appeal in this dispute? Does community mean the current expression of the will of a majority? Even were we to accept such a shallow conception of community, why would "our" community be the state rather than the locality?[3] Furthermore, Will's endorsement of community expression borders on an expressionism, subjectivism, and relativism that he commonly abhors. Regarding any particular community, we may ask: Is it a good community? Within a good community, we may ask of any of its actions or beliefs: Are they good actions or beliefs? Of course the standard for a good action could be its contribution to preserving a good community. Thus we could ask, along with Lord Devlin, if liberalizing laws against homosexuality threatens our character as a people. To say that it does would require more evidence than Devlin and Will have produced.[4] If community survival is not at stake, we need a standard for action independent of mere community will.

Will appeals to an independent standard: nature. He believes that the call for gay rights reflects a serious flaw in our political culture. "The notion that no form of sexuality is more natural, more right than any other is part of something larger. It is a facet of the repudiation of the doctrine of natural right on which western society rests. According to that doctrine, we can know and should encourage some ways of living that are right because of the nature of man" (PH, 57).[5] Will believes that a liberal society can allow for a wide range of freedoms but must enforce limits based on nature: "True freedom is impossible without comprehension of, and submission to, the natural order" (PV, 27). If nature is the standard to which a good community must aspire, what is nature?

Will does not operate within the ambit of Christian natural law, which builds on the idea that God has established a set of rules for right living for all to obey. Our God-given ability to reason allows us to discern (imperfectly, given our fallen state) what God intends and how we may conform ourselves to His plans.[6] Will rejects natural law because "natural law usually comes freighted with a religious premise—that there is a lawgiver. Now I believe there is a great blank universe there. That is why what I am saying is not natural law. I believe in natural right in the sense that there are ways of living that are right for creatures of our nature" (Will, interview). Will's view is close to Aristotle, who believed in human nature as a standard without believing in anything like natural law.[7]

There are problems with applying an Aristotelian naturalism to the issue of homosexuality. First, we must ask whether we can sustain an Aristotelian view of nature without recurring to Aristotle's standards of scientific knowledge and the cosmology they supported. Second, we must consider whether a conclusion that homosexuality is unnatural yields a condemnation of it.

Aristotelian science relies on the notion of teleology—the idea that things have ends or purposes toward which they naturally incline. Christian philosophers such as Augustine and Aquinas accept the notion of teleology and apply it to sexuality. The argument against homosexuality relies on the notion that sexuality has one and only one knowable purpose: procreation. All nonproductive sex (oral sex, anal sex, masturbation, or sex undertaken in "unnatural" positions) is wrong. Sex undertaken for the sake of pleasure is condemned as well on the theory that pleasure is a by-product rather than an aim of sex.[8]

Christian sexual teleology is not in vogue (to say the least). Much modern science has abandoned the idea of teleology altogether.[9] Even if we retain a place for purpose in nature, it is not clear that the ascetic reading of sexuality is the best. Why must something have one and only one purpose? What precludes us from seeing pleasure as a natural aim for sex?

Appealing to Aristotle to condemn homosexual acts is odd in any case because he makes no clear condemnation of either natural or unnat-

ural desire for same-sex unions. He divides males who desire sex with
males into those who have a natural desire and those who acquire the
desire through habituation (roughly the line Will draws).[10] All Aristotle
concludes from his discussion is that same-sex desire is not in the same
class as incontinent behavior (*akrasia*). He does not single it out as
deserving ethical condemnation. Nor does he conclude that homosexuality is a perversion of nature worthy of serious condemnation.[11] Why
does Aristotle not write against same-sex unions? For Aristotle, the final
purpose for human action is the highest good, *eudaimonia*—the happiness, flourishing, or well-being appropriate to human beings. The issue
concerning any particular act or occurrence is: Does it destroy our
capacity for happiness? Will has asserted that same-sex unions are
destructive of happiness. On what does he base this conclusion? The
empirical research has not supported his claim. In situations in which
gay people appear to do worse than the rest of the society (e.g., higher
rates of alcoholism), no explanations for these differences are evident,
and from these rates we cannot infer anything about individuals.

Even if Will had evidence, we would still need to consider the merits
of the standard he wishes to apply to community decisions. Can we use
nature as a norm for moral and political judgments? John Stuart Mill
has raised some serious questions about the propriety of doing so—especially for people like Will who accept the authority of modern science.[12]

Mill seeks to discredit nature as a standard of right. He observes that
"nature" is a term burdened by deep imprecision and ambiguity. The
most serious ambiguity, from his point of view, involves the failure to
distinguish nature as the order of things from nature as a norm. For
Mill, nature properly refers to what is, not to moral rules. Mill defines
nature as "the aggregate of the powers and properties of all things"
("Nature," 368). Thinking that there are distinctly human purposes,
Mill wants to confine ethics to the human sphere. He insists that nature
cannot provide a standard for emulation independent of human ends.
Many things happen "in nature" that are inimical to human purposes.
Being eaten by a lion is quite "natural." We cannot conceive of nature as
a providential voice guiding our conduct. To appeal to nature in this
sense is morally obtuse: "To bid people conform to the laws of nature
when they have no power but what the laws of nature give them, when
it is a physical impossibility for them to do the smallest thing other than
through some law of nature, is an absurdity." ("Nature," 374).

The only standards appropriate for us are those we set ourselves; "the
sentiment of justice is entirely of artificial origin" ("Nature," 394). This

does not leave us rudderless. Not all ends we choose are suitable to guide our actions. Our artifice stems from the principle of utility and our inevitable desire for happiness. Whether this standard is "natural" or "artificial" is unclear.

Mill's criticisms apply to a variety of recent attempts to generate naturalist ethics while adhering to the canons of mainstream philosophy of science. The critique strikes home even more when we accept (as Will presumably does) the principle of evolution in which what is "natural" alters over the course of time. Some writers, such as Julian Huxley, have met the challenge of evolution head on, attempting to construct an evolutionary, naturalist ethics. These writers typically fall prey to Mill's criticisms. Huxley proclaims that we are in nature and are its product. Yet, somehow, we stand over and against nature as its master. Huxley relieves the paradox, momentarily, by viewing humanity's "consciousness" as an "emergent" property. This solution is suspect because Huxley wants to invest ethical significance in the property.[13] Huxley and others are still caught in the trap common to naturalistic ethics. The naturalist takes "Nature" as norm while elevating an aspect of nature above the rest. Why is our ability to manipulate genetic codes more valuable than a rat's ability to become immune to our poisons? Even if we interpret the good as "good for us," we have no guidance concerning which of our actions and desires are truly human and which are defective. How do we escape the charge that we have arbitrarily elevated those aspects of nature we happen to like?[14]

Mill's assertions are not applicable to all appeals to nature. His criticisms derive from a metaphysical vision that bifurcates the world into natural facts and human values. Mill's arguments are quite effective against fellow positivists and naturalists such as Herbert Spencer. They simply talk past Aquinas and others who affirm classical doctrines of a transcendent "natural law." Mill replaces a theocentric vision of reality, in which the moral law is an integral part, with an anthropocentric naturalism. Once this step is taken, his critique of naturalism is rather effective. Will needs to show how he can accept Mill's initial move toward naturalism without absorbing Mill's powerful criticisms.

Must we fight the battle over homosexuality with high-level abstractions like "nature" and "community"? Are there not common principles to which at least some of us can appeal without recourse to nearly intractable metaphysical disputes? Perhaps. Will suggests that a civil society needs to develop the virtue of social sympathy. He is not entirely clear about what this means in relation to gay issues.

Perhaps social sympathy requires refusing to look at people as mere abstractions. When we meet people, we have a tendency to size them up and reduce them to a few qualities. We habitually commit what Alfred North Whitehead calls the fallacy of misplaced concreteness—treating an abstraction as if it were a real thing.[15] We can reduce a person to a bad quality they happen to have. This is a failure of tolerance—refusing the good a person has to offer because of a bad quality. Will has not failed in this respect. In an interview, he was asked how "conservatism with a kindly face" would deal with the AIDS epidemic as it affects homosexuals. Will replied: "I have written that practicing homosexuality is an injury to normal functioning, that it's not just another preference. That doesn't mean that homosexuals are pariahs of any sort. They are citizens, human beings. Their homosexuality shouldn't complicate your normal duty to love them as neighbors."[16] "Love" apparently does not extend far toward acceptance, however. In a more recent essay, Will claimed that there is a "dilemma of social policy: We should combat irrational prejudice about and injustice toward homosexuals, and affirm their human dignity. But we should not communicate societal indifference, thereby weakening social promptings toward heterosexuality" (LW, 118). The message seems to be: tolerance, yes; acceptance, no. As a legal matter (more of which shortly), that formula may be right, but is it a good moral message? On one level, Will focuses on a threat I find hard to take seriously. Most of the young people I observe do not need much "prompting" to become interested in members of the opposite sex. If the future of procreation is not in doubt, what do we have to worry about?

People who balk at accepting an alternative sexual orientation appear to be caught in another aspect of the fallacy of misplaced concreteness— substituting an abstraction for concrete experience; seeing a who as a what. Whitehead explains why it is important to look past our abstractions.

> The disadvantage of exclusive attention to a group of abstractions, however well founded, is that, by the nature of the case, you have abstracted from the remainder of things. In so far as the excluded things are important in your experience, your modes of thought are not fitted to deal with them. You cannot think without abstractions; accordingly, it is of the utmost importance to be vigilant in critically revising your *modes* of abstraction. It is here that philosophy finds its niche as essential to the healthy progress of society. It is the critic of abstractions. A civilization which cannot burst through its current abstractions is doomed to sterility after a very limited period of progress.[17]

In short, reducing things to the current abstractions surrounding them deprives us of the full understanding needed for a rounded judgment. The noun "homosexual" is an abstraction of recent coinage. Many societies in the past would have found the noun incomprehensible while surely understanding the adjectival references to same-sex acts. Homosexuality is the invention of 19th- and 20th-century psychologists.[18] The primary effect was to create invidious and celebratory categories to define people.[19] What do we gain by treating homosexuality as an identity?

In criticizing this abstraction, we should ask: To what extent are someone's sexual attractions and their private sexual behavior relevant? Will has suggested that homosexuality is relevant (not a matter of indifference) to employing teachers. Why? Alan Bloom's homosexuality did not seem particularly relevant to the conservatives, including Will, who showered *The Closing of the American Mind* with praise (SUD, 212–14).[20] David Brock's homosexuality seems not to have affected his standing among conservatives, including Will, when he denounced Anita Hill or Bill Clinton (LW, 149–51). Will has also showered praise on the writings of Jonathan Rauch. Should the sexuality of these writers matter for their jobs as a teacher and journalists respectively?

Some conservatives (and some liberals sniffing out hypocrisy) have criticized Will's credentials as a defender of the sanctity of the family because he is divorced.[21] The divorce is probably more relevant than Bloom's or Brock's sexual orientation, but none of these criticisms get to the point. Neither authors nor persons should be reduced to one abstract aspect of their work or character. There is more to most people than a simple predicate can convey. Edwin J. Delattre, in a book Will admires, has expressed quite well the fundamental irrelevance of sexual orientation to most things.

Neither homosexuality nor heterosexuality . . . is a lifestyle. The lives of homosexuals differ as much from one another in substance as do the lives of heterosexuals. Some of each group are honorable persons, some are not. Some are courageous, fair minded, and trustworthy; others are not. Some are promiscuous; others are not. Some of each group indulge in sexual tastes that involve predation on children and commit acts of domestic violence against their partners. Homosexuals no more think alike on every issue than heterosexuals do; and many homosexuals and heterosexuals agree on some issues. . . . Failure to take individuals into account is bigoted, no matter where it occurs: in exempting black people from racial prejudice, in indicting all religious people as prejudiced, or in claiming that all homosexuals are bad or all homosexuals are good.[22]

Intellectually and morally, we should demand of ourselves an effort to dig past our superficial categories.

Will has done a great service in criticizing the abstractions surrounding persons with Down's syndrome. He has written eloquently asking us to recognize our common humanity with his son (MA, 194–97; LW, 445–47). Such pleas are necessary in the face of prejudice and a cruel history of warehousing these children.[23] Even today, when we can see how well these children flourish outside an institutional setting, doctors regularly recommend against life-saving surgery by citing a poor prognosis for "quality of life." Regarding children, we see in full bloom the pathos of the western discourse on nature. Aristotle identified intelligence as the specific difference that makes us human. Using this abstract criterion, we have denied some of us ("retards") our full humanity. Will has performed a real service by substituting a concrete appreciation of human life for stultifying prejudice. He needs to continue his work regarding prejudice surrounding all irrelevant differences.

Even if we accept the moral task of teaching acceptance, the legal and political waters will still be muddy. Liberalism distinguishes between the moral and legal spheres. One of the ways it preserves the distinction is to promote privacy and freedom of association. Will has correctly observed that demanding acceptance of homosexuality (as opposed to tolerance) threatens these liberal principles.

Will recounts the case of Georgetown University, which was charged with violating an ordinance prohibiting discrimination on the basis of sexual orientation by refusing to grant university recognition to two gay groups (MA, 172–74). He observes that enforcing this law threatens basic constitutional liberties including freedom of religion, association, and privacy. The problem is not confined to the issue of antigay discrimination. Will complains about a suit under Massachusetts law compelling two brothers to rent, against their religious scruples, to an unmarried couple (LW, 151–53). Will has directed us to a real tension in the constitutional and political theory of liberalism. The right to be free from discrimination conflicts with religious freedom and the freedom of association.

Will seems at times to want to resolve the tension strictly in favor of association, privacy, and religious freedom, but the tension defies easy resolution. We cannot frame the issue the way Will does—as a simple choice between genuine liberty and doctrinaire liberalism (MA, 174; LW, 153). On the one hand, losing the right to choose with whom we shall associate is really sacrificing freedom. On the other hand, not being able to find a job or to move about freely also restricts liberty.[24] The civil rights movement was about serious and debilitating restrictions on freedom—not simply violations of the Equal Protection Clause of the Fourteenth Amendment. A liberal society requires that the free movement and economic choices of individuals not be unduly restricted by either government or private groups. People who cannot work, live, and shop where they choose are denied the full benefits of liberal living.

The tension between liberal opposition to discrimination and commitment to the freedom of association derives from a reality that communitarians have usually understood better than liberals. We are not simply individuals who need liberty, but members of communities who need to form bonds and associations. Indeed, some of us do not adapt well to liberal ways of living. This creates problems for liberal theory and practice that I explore more fully in the next section. For now I want to dwell a bit on the legal implications of Will's defense of the freedom of association.

Neither the right to associate nor the right to privacy is mentioned in the Constitution. Consequently, Will's defense of these rights is somewhat out of tune with his originalism discussed in chapter 3. In any case, the Supreme Court has recognized both rights. The Court has been sharply divided in its interpretation of the privacy right. In a 5-4 decision in *Bowers v. Hardwick,* it ruled that the right to privacy does not extend to "homosexual sodomy." The Georgia statute that the Court upheld in this case forbade all forms of sodomy, not just homosexual sodomy, but the plurality in the case went out of its way to emphasize the hostility of "our traditions" to homosexuality. What has gone unnoticed by most observers is the departure from communitarian theory by both the majority and the dissenters in this case.

Michael Sandel argues that both sides in the cases dealing with homosexuality have relied on procedural arguments while importing substantive arguments surreptitiously. A procedural argument brackets questions about the good and resolves legal questions with a legal principle that is neutral concerning the good. Defenders of the right to privacy argue that the law should remain neutral about questions of the good and leave moral decisions to the individual.[25] This is the sort of neutralism that Will consistently criticizes. Will is less mindful of the proceduralism of opponents to abortion and homosexuality. "Let the legislatures decide" is no less a proceduralist principle than is liberal neutralism. According to Sandel, a court engaged in constitutional review eventually will import judgments about the good envisioned in the Constitution and say no to a legislature that transgresses its rightful authority. Sandel urges a return to the privacy claims of the Court in *Griswold v. Connecticut,*[26] where the Court defended the right to use contraceptives because government regulation would threaten the goods achieved within the intimate bonds of marriage ("Moral Argument," 525–28). The power of the government was restricted for the sake of the good, not for the sake of a rule.

Had the Court turned its thoughts toward the good rather than toward legal procedures, Sandel believes a different sort of dissent could have occurred in *Bowers v. Hardwick.* The four dissenters maintained that the Georgia statute unduly restricted the right of individuals to choose. Sandel believes that this line of argument will eventually founder on the necessity to decide that some choices simply are not acceptable. He would have preferred the dissenters to state their intention to protect genuine goods of the sort mentioned in *Griswold.* Sandel suggests, following a lower court rationale, that the privacy (and one would assume the freedom of association) of gay people is defensible because these associations allow for "mutual support and self-expression" ("Moral Argument," 535). Obviously this argument would require development to function as a legal standard, and it risks merely reinforcing stereotypes about the good and promoting selective toleration.[27] In any case, the line of thinking Sandel asks us to undertake is more consistent with Will's basic commitments than the proceduralism to which Will frequently appeals. Sandel's argument should at least mark the need for redirecting the inquiry on the political and moral (if not the legal) dimensions of the quest for community.

One Nation?

The issues I have discussed so far point to the general problem that needs assaying. How far can we move toward resolving the tension between liberty and community in a liberal society? Another way of asking is: How much togetherness can we stand?

Will is a champion of national unity. He is susceptible to the criticism Aristotle (wrongly) makes of Plato—that he expects too much cohesion. Will's positions on the issues I have discussed bring us to the heart of an effort to evaluate his work. Does a call for virtue require a strong emphasis on unity? Are we to adhere rigidly to one set of rules with no exceptions? Answering these questions requires specification of the standards by which we judge. Are those standards communitarian, liberal, or a combination of both?

If our primary focus is the community, we could ask citizens to put the community first and forego diverse actions and differential claims to group rights. If our focus is the community, we must address the question I have already raised: Which community? Most Americans do not confine their loyalties to the nation. We find comfort and support in other associations. These group loyalties are quite diverse and even incompatible. Belonging to some groups precludes belonging to others. I cannot be an active contributor to the civic life of a working class neighborhood and a member in good standing of an exclusive country club. When I am called on by a nationalist to belong, I may reply: "I'll give you my allegiance, but not all of it." Such diversity seems to be the American way. The American way is quite compatible with deep cultural differences. People should not be denied citizenship in the national community because their dress, manners, and folkways do not fit a fictitious common pattern. We should avoid efforts to homogenize, even at the cost of some disunity. Our differences are not about to bring us to the state of the Balkans. Cultural nationalism is resurgent and its dangers should not be minimized, but American divisions seem shallow indeed compared to those we encounter abroad.[28]

My guess is that a too vigorous effort to educate our citizens in a common ethos would exacerbate rather than smooth our differences. Indeed, one of the main failings of multiculturalism is that it homogenizes cultural differences rather than promoting genuine cross-cultural communication. Both traditionalists and multiculturalists need lessons in the central art of a liberal society—the art of leaving others alone.

Unfortunately, we tend to think of leaving others alone as merely leaving individuals to their own devices. We also need to learn how to leave communities alone to find their resources for solving problems. That strategy involves thinning ties to the national community to allow thickening of local ties. (By "local," I mean informal associations, not local governments.)

Our courts frequently face the demand by communities to be left alone. Sometimes the demand is to exempt a communal practice from ordinary scrutiny, as in the case of Christian Scientists who want to allow faith healing for their children. In other cases, the community demands protection from intrusions that threaten its collective identity. The Supreme Court recognized the need to protect the communal integrity of the Amish by exempting their children from the obligation to attend school past the eighth grade.[29] In an appeals court case, the judges refused to extend to Christian fundamentalists the option of having their children read alternative textbooks more consonant with their world view.[30] I do not want to argue the merits of either case. Rather, I call attention to Judge Boggs's concurring opinion rejecting the claims of discrimination against fundamentalists.

While agreeing that the fundamentalists should not be allowed alternative texts, Judge Boggs chided the other judges in the case for failing to realize that they were grappling with a hard issue that could have had a different result with only marginally different facts. He noted that the other judges relied heavily on the trial record's rather inarticulate and unsophisticated testimony by the fundamentalists. This highlights a crucial point about legal and moral contests. Much depends on who masters the words. Welcoming an inarticulate participant to a contest is like using loaded dice in a crapshoot.

Attention to language as a medium of contest allows us a better grasp of the tension between inclusion and exclusion—a tension central to Will's appeal to unity. Consider the issue of Black English. To "succeed" in America, an African American usually must master Standard English. To remain comfortable in the segregated communities, the "successful" African American must be bidialectal—moving freely from one mode of speech to another.[31] To demand a uniform manner of speaking is to either exclude or include on terms that seem unjust.

Somehow a just strategy of inclusion must clear a space for difference. In the cases of fundamentalists and African Americans, securing a space of aloneness would not require a radical exodus from American society. Other cases require more forbearance for different communities by respecting their aloneness. Was it inevitable that we would encircle the Branch Davidians with an army? In any case, we need to think about leaving communities alone without invoking an easy rhetoric of inclusion on the left or unity on the right. We need to ask when it is possible and desirable to exempt others from our ordinary expectations and even from our prevailing rules. Gauging possibility and desirability requires an awareness that some people do not occupy liberal space well: they need thicker communities than liberal unity can comfortably accommodate. What we need to learn is the difference between convenience and necessity.

Raising the prospect of exemption is consistent with at least some brands of communitarian thought. Is it consistent with liberalism? One way of asking that question brings us back to Will's complaints against affirmative action: Can liberal regimes recognize group rights? The distinguished Canadian political philosopher Will Kymlicka argues that they can.[32]

Kymlicka firmly maintains that liberal regimes seek to justly distribute the good things of life to individuals. Communities have no rights other than those derived from individuals. Thus, Kymlicka shares Will's belief that equal justice is our core value even if meritocracy is not.[33] Individuals may decide how to live, but, following John Rawls, Kymlicka contends that liberal societies should provide access to the primary goods that make meaningful choice possible. Central to Kymlicka's argument is the claim that cultural membership is a primary good. Having a community that supports and orients us provides an indispensable context for choice. Consequently, destroying a minority culture and forcing assimilation into a dominant culture makes it difficult, if not impossible, for some people to effectively participate in liberal opportunities. Under circumstances where an empowering cultural identity is threatened with extinction, the cultural group may be assigned rights (even to the detriment of some individual rights) to protect itself from extinction.

Kymlicka does not wish to assign minority rights promiscuously. He believes that the end to segregation in America and the demand for integration for African Americans was an appropriate response to the American dilemma. That approach does not work as well for other groups that are more culturally distinct, such as American Indians. Kymlicka argues that Canada made a serious mistake when it concluded that American-style civil rights could apply to the problems of Canada's aboriginal peoples. In the name of justice, Canada embarked on an unjust policy of forced assimilation that made it difficult for native peoples to engage in meaningful choice (*Liberalism, Community and Culture*, 135–61). According to Kymlicka, Canada should have retained community rights to restrict land sales and marriages (even though these limit individual liberty) for the sake of preserving a communal identity (*Liberalism, Community and Culture*, 162–219).

Kymlicka realizes that "community preservation" often functions as a general defense for illiberal policies, pointing to the various movements for Islamic fundamentalism that restrict personal liberties to maintain cultural integrity. Within our own culture, we find Lord Devlin arguing that changing laws such as those against homosexuality might threaten the integrity of the culture that sustains us. Kymlicka responds by distinguishing between protecting a culture's existence and protecting its character. Reforming aspects of a dominant culture do not pose the clear threat to its existence in the way that forced assimilation of a vulnerable minority does (*Liberalism, Community and Culture*, 166–71).

Kymlicka may be right that the primary aim of liberal exceptions for community rights should be to protect culturally distinct minorities, but the principle is necessarily vague. How distinct must communities be? Must we focus on a group or can we make exceptions for subgroups? Assimilated American Indians are clearly different from those on the reservations. Middle-class African Americans are different from less-assimilated African Americans. Should these groups be treated differently? If so, does the treatment add to or restrict choices? How we answer these questions depends in part on empirical issues that are far from settled, but the questions also point to other issues we seldom discuss. Must all people in a liberal society live a life of striving for opportunity? Can we cultivate different standards of success? Can we find a space for nonliberal living for people who do not fit the liberal pattern of striving?

For Will, rendering justice for those who are persistently different is subordinate to the question of unity. He does not wish to render justice even though the heavens might fall.[34] But will the heavens fall? Must a respect for cultural difference lead to balkanization? Can we cultivate a real respect for others that allows for genuinely different ways of living? I do not know. I think the current debates advance in a way that does not allow us to discuss the issues seriously.

We tend to divide ourselves into three warring camps. Traditionalists such as Will think we are one people with a set of common standards threatened by the assaults of those who would demean our common heritage. Multiculturalists believe we are a rainbow of cultures needing most to understand and accept our differences. Particularists (e.g., Afrocentrists) think we are so diverse that understanding is impossible. We should cultivate our own gardens and not attempt to learn alien ways of thought and expression. My problem with all three camps is their dogmatism. They are all right about something, but they insist on applying their insight to everything, whether it fits a case or not.

Traditionalists frequently commit the sin of pride. They think the world was created in their image. "I have high standards. Why can't everybody be like me?" Even if the standards are indubitable, it is sheer pride to expect everyone to live up to them. The pride grows when we confuse aesthetic standards with moral standards. We should not damn our fellow citizens simply because they do not share our sense of beauty.[35] Traditionalists also err, as previously noted, in assuming that high learning is the only purpose of education, even higher education. Teaching students to become good citizens means teaching them salutary myths. Not just any story will do. The stories must begin with an awareness of and respect for who the students are. That requires some understanding of and appreciation for diverse cultural identities. People whose cultural identities have been unjustly devalued need to learn self-respect. That does not mean teaching a degraded form of "self-esteem," where one learns to love oneself regardless of one's efforts or accomplishments.[36] Rather, devalued people need to learn that people like them have done good things to which they can aspire. Excluding these stories is an affront to good citizenship.

As previously noted, multiculturalists suffer from the temptation to homogenize difference. Asking students to learn about other cultures frequently reduces learning to a passion play where everything fits a simple narrative of multicultural triumphalism. Another weakness in multicultural education is its tendency to reduce learning to perusing encyclopedias. We ask students to learn a large body of facts about diverse cultures without establishing where these facts fit and why they are important. Multiculturalism often encourages what St. Augustine derided as "curiosity," learning for the mere sake of knowing.[37] Why is it that we need to know everything we can learn about one another? Forget the impossibility of learning everything. What do we gain from the attempt? Teachers need to be able to convey some sense of the importance of learning about people who are different. Failing that, students will (rightly) view all this learning as busy work. Will correctly understands that this cafeteria style of education leads to boredom, frustration, and confusion (SUD, 210–20; LW, 137–39). Furthermore, multiculturalism overestimates the transparency of difference. Most people are fairly opaque. It defies proper humility to pretend that whole cultures can become accessible in a semester or two. Indeed, genuine learning should teach us how difficult understanding others is, rather than reducing it to formulas.[38]

Particularism overrates our differences. When I ask my students (who are mostly African Americans) to tell me what is different about whites and blacks, they discover and admit that most of the differences are remarkably superficial. When presumably big differences are mentioned, they invariably turn out to be stereotypes. The core of prejudice is treating superficial differences as if they were important. Asking students to center their studies on themselves not only creates self-centered students, it reinforces prejudices. Particularism, when it is not functioning as a shield against prejudice, does encourage the sort of balkanization Will fears.

What we need most in our debates on difference is to abandon these rigid ideologies. They obscure where our differences lie and make it more difficult to negotiate them. We also need to learn the fine art of letting be. In a liberal culture where a basic value is tolerance, we need to be able to ignore many of our differences. If we learn that, we may have slimmer textbooks, but we will have better lives.

A Conclusion?

What then can we say about the connections among community, nature, and political identity in Will's thought? There may be good reasons to strengthen communal ties, but the discourse on nature does not necessarily fortify the case for conservative communitarianism. As I have argued, the intellectual case for natural unions is weakened when a theorist abandons the ancient and medieval cosmologies in favor of modern science, as Will does. To develop a cosmology that would allow judgments about what is right by nature would require considerably more attention to philosophical issues than Will has provided.

To be sure, the rhetoric of nature continues to exhibit considerable political appeal. Unfortunately for a champion of unity, the appeal is quite diverse. In a pluralist culture, there are too many natures to lend much aid and comfort to conservative advocates of unity.

The politics of identity provides little, if any, more comfort. When conceptions like "nature" and "identity" cease to function as background assumptions and become contested, they cease to serve as philosophical or religious anchors and become politicized.[39] Will admits that many of our most cherished notions about our identity as a people are embroiled in political controversy. In my interview with him, Will referred me to Michael Barone's *Our Country*. According to Will, the book demonstrates that "the great organizing question of American politics is: Who are we? The implicit question being: What ought we to be? The assumption being: That question is in play. We can be not entirely what we want to be, but we can make ourselves into different things" (Will, interview).

In admitting that ostensibly philosophical issues are keenly political, Will positions himself rather close to the postmodernist thinkers he regularly excoriates. Will need not accept postmodern claims that nature and identity are inherently unstable notions to advance at least partway toward recognition that these notions are more likely to be contested in political rather than disinterested philosophical arenas. Once we concede that nature and identity are political conceptions, the direction of our inquiry shifts. We are free to ask: What sort of politics do we practice? What sort should we practice? These are the central concerns of the following chapter.

Chapter Six

Representing a Virtuous People

Public speaking is far, very far, from the meanest or least important utility of a Legislature. The debates of the House of Commons have educated the people of England in the science of politics more widely and fundamentally than all the works of all our writers.

Samuel Taylor Coleridge

In the past Gingrich has made powerful arguments for term limits. Now he has become a powerful argument for limits.

George Will

Republican Theory: Civic Virtue and Representation

As I previously noted, George Will hopes to draw inspiration from the republican tradition in political thought. He wants to infuse the American regime with enough civic virtue to correct the defects that our founders left us. One major problem, however, with drawing sustenance from the republican tradition involves the doubts that some scholars have expressed concerning its existence.[1] Pocock's magisterial study, *The Machiavellian Moment,* sought to identify a republican tradition stretching from Aristotle through Machiavelli, James Harrington, and a variety of British and American thinkers. A major problem with Pocock's erudite catalog of republicans is the stunning diversity of positions it reflects. Indeed, since the term "republican" was long an honorific in political discourse, very different people contested for title to it. Indeed, one of the great coups in political history was the successful wresting of the terms "federalist" and "republican" from the antifederalists who were more clearly heirs to both appellations.[2]

At best we can discern a "family resemblance" among those grouped as republicans rather than a paradigm persisting through the ages.[3] Perhaps we can discover more unity if we focus on some problems that republican theory attempts to address rather than on common positions. My focus is on unity and citizenship.

It will be profitable to begin, as Pocock does, with the Greeks, especially Aristotle. The ancient Greeks, being a fractional society, faced the problem of unity. Of particular concern was the problem of faction, as Greeks were prone to divide into groups seeking dominion over other groups. One way of dealing with the problem was to attempt to extinguish differences by creating a strong sense of civic duty. Indeed, the strongest attempt to create civic virtue would entail cultivating civic virtue to the virtual exclusion of private flourishing. The most robust attempt to exalt civic virtue was in ancient Sparta, which Paul Rahe regards as the paradigmatic example of an Ancient Republic: "Of all the Hellenic communities, she came closest to giving absolute primacy to the common good. She did this by turning the city into a camp, the polis into an army, and the citizen into a soldier."[4]

Sparta was a garrison regime dedicated to cultivating martial virtues. The education of Spartan boys and men centered on hardness and unity. Achieving these qualities required excluding aspects of living that we take for granted. There was, for instance, no conception of rights or personal freedom here or anywhere else in ancient Greece.[5] For the Spartans, the great enemies of hardness and unity were commerce and moneymaking. Consequently there was little commerce, and land was not a commodity.

Inculcating civic virtue required more than sheltering citizens from adverse influences. The Spartans embarked on a rigorous course of instruction to extinguish all but communal feelings. An ambitious plan of civic education required educating every aspect of existence. Nothing was so "private" (in Greek terms, idiotic) as to escape regulation. For instance, the Spartans encouraged homosexual courtship between boys and men to develop a martial character. In other Greek cities, boys were coy with male suitors, but not in Sparta. As Paul Rahe explains:

> When a boy reached the age of twelve, he aggressively sought out and took an older lover (*erastes*) who would be his patron, his protector, his friend. This was not just a practice sanctioned by custom; as among the tribesmen of Australia or Melanasia, it was a political institution. It was not only the case that a boy lacking lovers was an object of disdain: a young man of distinguished background could, in fact, be severely punished by the magistrates for refusing to select a *paidika* or for preferring a wealthy boy to one of virtuous character; and as a surrogate father, the *erastes* would be held personally responsible for the behavior of the boy that he chose. (*Republics Ancient and Modern*, 154)

Pederasty was a political institution because it cultivated loyalty, unity, and military ardor among men. Because it was a public ritual, it served to turn the sexual impulse away from private concerns. As Rahe notes, the social and economic arrangements at Sparta "seem to have been aimed almost entirely at suppressing the private element in human life, at making the Spartan an almost entirely public being by eliminating to the greatest degree possible the last refuge of privacy—the family" (*Republics Ancient and Modern*, 155).

Not all Greek regimes, and surely not all republican theorists, took the quest for unity so far as the Spartans, but the struggle against factions was a common concern. After surveying the causes for rebellion, Aristotle proposes remedies. After discussing a variety of institutional and economic techniques, he turns to the most important remedy—education:

> Of all the things which I have mentioned that which most contributes to the permanence of constitutions is the adaptation of education to the form of government, and yet in our own day this principle is universally neglected. The best laws, though sanctioned by every citizen of the state, will be of no avail unless the young are trained by habit and education in the spirit of the constitution, if the laws are democratic, democratically, or oligarchically, if the laws are oligarchical. For there may be a want of self-discipline in states as well as in individuals. Now to have been educated in the spirit of the constitution is not to perform the actions in which oligarchs or democrats delight, but those by which the existence of an oligarchy or a democracy is made possible.[6]

While sharing the Spartan concern with education in civic virtue, Aristotle takes a less extreme approach. He realizes that the kind of civic virtue taught must fit the kind of regime it supports. Furthermore, civic education need not extend to every aspect of existence. Aristotle severely criticizes Socrates' proposals for communism in property, women, and children on the ground that they foster too much unity (*Politics*, bk. 2, ch. 1–5, 1261a–1264a). We can conclude that republican theorists want to use education to foster unity, but how much unity and what methods of education to use are open issues. As I argued in chapter 2, there is no decisive break between republicans and liberals on the matter of civic education. Liberal civic education leaves much in the private sphere, but many republican theorists do so as well.

Some have thought that republicanism diverges from liberalism regarding citizenship. Republicans stress attention to public matters and the dignity of the public life. Liberals assign priority to private satisfaction. Though there is some reason to stress this divide, the ways we can enact and categorize citizenship are far more complicated than any simple division can entail.[7]

At least two dimensions of citizenship need to be distinguished: participation and voice.[8] Participation concerns the active role that citizens assume in managing public affairs. Both republicans and liberals have assumed a limited role for the populace in governing themselves. Liberal democracies allow for near universal suffrage, but most of the actual decisions belong to small bodies of formal and informal representatives. Ancient republics and Italian city-states during the Renaissance allowed a wider scope for citizen assemblies to govern, but participation was possible for only a minority of the population. In any case, these small republics bear little resemblance to the large "extended republics" Madison envisioned ("Federalist No. 10"). Even the most radical modern republican, Rousseau, limited the populace to lawmaking while assigning governance to the few (*Social Contract,* bk. 3). Liberals, republicans, and most conservatives unite in opposition to populism, which assumes a large mass of people can assemble and govern themselves. Will's comments on "conservative populism" are pungent: "Populism historically involves impatience with complexity, suspicion of big institutions and big people, and reverence for whatever 'the people' are thought to believe this week. So 'populist conservatism' is an oxymoron" (NS, 84).[9]

By creating a political system where people play a minimal role in governance, we have virtually lost the distinction between subjects (for whom decisions are made) and citizens (who decide for themselves). We have developed a passive conception of citizenship. Aristotle recognized a valuable role for participation. He contended that governance is an art with two parts—learning to govern and be governed. For Aristotle, a citizen is someone who assumes some share in the offices of governance and the administration of justice. Someone who shares in rule can learn the job fully only by being ruled as well as by ruling (*Politics,* bk. 3, ch. 1–5, 1252a–1254b). Aristotle's analysis comports well with his general claim that virtues flourish through habituation. Why should civic virtue be any different?

In our time, citizenship is more anemic. The Fourteenth Amendment defines citizenship this way: "All persons born or naturalized in the United States, and subject to the jurisdiction thereof, are citizens of the United States and the State wherein they reside." All that most of us need for citizenship is to be born. Will seems to endorse the weak conception of citizenship when he emphasizes the role of voice to the neglect of participation. He asserts that the Constitution designs the

92GEORGE F. WILL

American Republic to temper pure democracy. The constitution incorporates "the republican principle, which is the principle of representation: In a republic, the people do not decide issues, the people decide who shall decide."[10] Will's identification of republicanism with representation contrasts with Rousseau's claim that representation is incompatible with republican virtue (*Social Contract,* bk. 3, ch. 15). But Rousseau's view is not universally accepted, and, since the time of James Madison, we have come to associate representation in a large society with republican government. Two aspects of Will's claim require remark, however.

First, saying that republicanism can incorporate a principle of representation in an extended regime is not the same as identifying republicanism with representation. If a republican government requires only a system of representation that restrains pure democracy, there is no basis for distinguishing the republican tradition from the liberal tradition. Second, Will's acceptance of Schumpeter's dictum that the people do not govern, but rather choose who shall govern seems to abandon the role of participation in civic education.[11] J. S. Mill argued that extensive and regular participation in public affairs serves as civic education in a community. By deliberating on public affairs, citizens turn their concerns from the small circle of private affection toward their common interests. Furthermore, only citizens who learn through active involvement can acquire the skills of deliberation necessary for a people worthy of self-rule.[12] Mill may be too optimistic about the benefits of participation, but he marks a problem to which Will has given insufficient attention: How do we train our people in civic virtue when most of our lives revolve around private affairs? I will return to the connection between representation and participation shortly.

As his identification of republicanism with representation would suggest, Will has devoted considerably more attention to the issues concerning voice—the best ways for the populace to have its concerns expressed. The remainder of the chapter focuses on the issue of representation. Before turning to Will's writings on the subject, I provide the reader with an outline of the major theories of representation that compete for our allegiance in America.[13]

Theories of Representation

In saying that the people only decide who will decide, Will rejects what is superficially the most appealing theory of representation—the delegate theory. This theory holds that a representative should follow instructions from his or her constituency. In a government based on consent, a representative should reflect the wishes of the people. Despite its surface plausibility, the delegate theory suffers serious difficulties.

First, who are "the people"? Do we mean the people now? If so, how does the representative deal with the fickle character of public opinion? The people change their opinions rapidly. How can we best reflect these changes? By abrogating treaties that have become unpopular or eliminating programs that have had little time to prove themselves? The identity of the people is not simply in doubt diachronically. Who are "we" at any particular moment? Are we the majority? Have we consented to policies simply because they benefit a majority? If the common good means no more than what is good for a temporary majority, someone in a consistently disadvantaged minority has no reason to exhibit the loyalty that a stable republic demands.

Even if we are a fairly homogenous lot, there is still doubt that we can instruct a representative. Can an election send fine-tuned messages on every issue that a representative will face? Most of us give issues only superficial attention (though polling research shows that many of us are willing to offer opinions on issues about which we are poorly informed or even on nonexistent issues). What is the representative to do when faced with issues about which only vague opinions or no opinions at all have been offered? When we elect representatives, they frequently face unforeseen issues demanding quick and decisive action. How are we to instruct our representatives on these unforeseen topics?

Some people argue that we cannot instruct representatives on how to vote, but we can hold them accountable after they vote. There is some truth to this, though less than meets the eye. Only a few of us who vote regularly base our decision on issues. We are more likely to vote based on party affiliation, the appeal of the candidate independent of issues, or a vague perception of the nature of the times. Even when issues are decisive, we base our votes on a few salient ones, blissfully ignoring most of the votes that a representative has taken for us.

Even if we could supervise our representatives, would it be a good idea? The main criticism of the delegate theory concerns what delegates represent. A delegate represents our wishes, but is it wishes that we want represented? The remaining theories answer "no," claiming instead that a representative should, in some sense, represent our interests. What we most immediately desire is not always what is good for us. Our representatives should vote our interests rather than the transitory will of a majority.

Will swears his allegiance to the trustee, or Burkean, theory of representation. As the second name for the theory suggests, it was enunciated by the great conservative writer Edmund Burke.[14] Burke attacked the notion that a representative should serve as a delegate. What a representative owes constituents is "mature judgments" and "enlightened conscience," not slavish obedience. What does a representative represent? For Burke, the representative must reflect the common good. Burke did not regard the principle of "one person, one vote" as necessary for fair representation. Since each representative must reflect on the good of the whole, we attain "virtual representation" even without representation in proportion to our numbers. Burke's theory of virtual representation requires that a representative deliberate properly on the common good. It also requires some idea of how to hold accountable a representative who deliberates poorly.

Among the most popular theories of representation in America is pluralism.[15] Pluralists argue that we cannot expect representatives to be fully accountable to individuals. Individuals do not have the time, knowledge, or resources to secure accountability. If people are to hold politicians accountable, they must do it through the groups to which we belong. Our interests aggregate through pressure groups who give voice to our concerns. We secure our good through competition among interest groups. Government is obligated to create an impartial arena where the groups can compete. The common good lies largely in maintaining the process of competition.

Criticisms of pluralism are sharp, as one might expect of a theory that has maintained dominance for so long.[16] One concern is the representativeness of the groups themselves. It is fine to say that groups represent us, but do the groups really hear us? How much voice do we have in the groups?[17] Furthermore, saying that the groups represent "us" assumes that the groups are relatively equal in influence—a quite dubious assumption. What of the many people who never join groups? Who represents them? Even if the groups represent us, we can still ask: Do they represent us well? In chapter 2, I discussed Jonathan Rauch's claim that interest group politics has created an inability to deliberate. Are we well-represented if all the groups do is maintain an unsatisfactory status quo? I also discussed in chapter 2 Will's argument that pluralism relies on a "cuisinart" notion of the common good. Will's argument is quite effective against pluralist theory.[18]

Another theory of representation that has become popular recently is a variation on pluralism and older theories of proportional representation and is known as categorical representation. This theory builds on the idea that we belong not only to associations we have freely chosen, but also to unorganized groups into which we are born. We form part of our identities and interests through membership in these groups. Consequently, the groups deserve a voice, perhaps a proportional voice, in government. This is the theory Will likes least, believing as he does that it sustains the notion of "group entitlement" that we saw him excoriating in his discussion of affirmative action. One could conceivably oppose affirmative action and favor categorical representation, since they raise different issues and require different justifications. I will defer further discussion of the theory until I present Will's thoughts on representation, merely pausing to observe that the theory provides the sharpest contrast and deepest challenge to his approach.

Will's most sustained treatment of representation occurs in his book on term limits, *Restoration*. Before I review that work, I examine his comments on the American party system and presidential politics in *The New Season*. Discussing parties in relation to republican theory is somewhat odd since the very existence of a party system runs counter to most republican theory, stressing as it does unity and the common good. Regardless of republican theory, parties have become an indelible part of our political life. Thinking about the quality of our representation requires thinking about political parties and presidential politics.

Thinking about these matters is important because they are integral to our political life and because Will has given much thought to them. More important, they highlight a dimension of representation that is frequently given insufficient attention—rhetoric. "The people" are not just "there" waiting to be represented. Having a people is, in part, a political act. We create ourselves through our political activities. Part of this creative activity involves our leaders talking us into being. A good portion of who we are results from the rhetorical skills of our leaders. Would America be what it is without the soaring rhetoric of Jefferson's Declaration of Independence or Lincoln's Gettysburg Address or Martin Luther King's "I have a dream" speech?

Will is quite cognizant of the power of rhetoric to represent us as who we are. Rhetoric is crucial to a successful president. In criticizing Gerald Ford's abilities as chief of state, Will observes that "rhetorical skills are not peripheral to the political enterprise, and they are among the most important skills a person can bring to the presidency. . . . An inarticulate President is like a motorcycle motor installed in a Mack truck. Only a President can persuade this impatient nation to accept short-term pains for long-term gains, which is the essence of government. Without a persuasive, articulate President many important government decisions do not get made, and those that do are in the subjunctive mood" (PH, 165). With the end of the cold war, Will has welcomed a diminished role for the presidency, and he has denounced the excesses of "the rhetorical presidency" (LW, 306–8; RES, 129–36).[19] Nevertheless, Will recognizes that our system could not function effectively unless our political parties and presidents represented us by attempting to give us words to live by.

The Rhetoric of Representation

Will has written one book-length study of campaigns and elections in America—*The New Season.* In his other books, electoral politics is a constant preoccupation. In his regular appearances on *This Week with David Brinkley,* Will frequently appraises the prospective fortunes of parties and candidates.

Will argues that the American electoral process is, over time, rational.[20] He contends that the American voters respond to ideas and evaluate them in a deliberate and responsible way. That a party succeeds or fails is, then, dependent largely on its ability to produce a satisfying message matched by successful policies. The rhetoric builds support for the policies, and the success of the policies allows us to gauge the resonance or hollowness of the rhetoric. Will does not make extravagant claims for voter rationality: "The voters are, on balance, sensible. That is not to say the electorate invariably makes the wisest choice. Rather it is to say only—although this is actually quite a lot—that elections are about substantial things, and most voters know that" (NS, 16–17). Voters give voice to their concerns over substantial matters when they vote, but they do not articulate solutions to problems. Voters respond to large themes and broad choices. These themes and choices filter through well-known leaders (especially presidents) and political parties.

Will is aware that America does not have a disciplined and centralized party system like Great Britain's. Nonetheless, the parties do offer differing visions and real alternatives that voters can understand.

According to Will, the direction of party activity and political rhetoric shifted under the weighty influence of Ronald Reagan. Reagan became a towering presence in part because of his leadership and the resonance of his rhetoric, but that is not the whole story. According to Will, Reagan's influence will extend well into the 21st century. Reagan "will control the future debate and agenda more than any post-war President has done. The reason for this, paradoxically, is his biggest failure, the deficit. The government, which is energized by money, is out of money" (NS, 34). Competition between Democrats and Republicans must address continuing deficits and the resulting mammoth debt. From the vantage point of 1988, it also appeared to Will that Reagan had forestalled serious disagreement on the future of the welfare state: "To the recurring surprise of some of his most ardent and least observant supporters, Reagan is a 'New Deal Conservative' quite reconciled to modern government's steady impulse to build a 'social insurance state' " (NS, 83). Neither Will's recent reconsideration of the role of government (discussed in chapter 2) nor the stunning 1994 midterm congressional elections that gave control of the House and Senate to the Republicans fundamentally alter Will's assessment that Americans are committed to a "mild social democracy" (NS, 83; Will, interview). The will to cope with the problem of deficits became apparent following the Republican triumph in 1994, but that does not belie our commitment to extensive subsidies, especially for the middle class.

For Will, Reagan's most important legacy, as a strong president preaching against an overreaching government, is to remind us of the limits of the presidency: "The presidency is an inherently, meaning constitutionally, weak office. There is little a President can do on his own except sway the country and by doing so move the Congress. Thus, the power of the presidency—unlike the office of the British Prime Minister armed with party discipline—varies substantially with the qualities of the occupant. And the power of a particular President can vary radically with swings in the public's perceptions of him" (NS, 37). Will applauds the weakening of the presidency since he, good Lockean that he is, believes in the primacy of Congress. In 1988, he deplored the continuing dominance of the presidency: "The political geography of Washington is now sixteen blocks askew" (NS, 178). Now with the end of the cold war and the consequent diminution of the presidency, he encourages "the miniaturized presidency," hailing the "restoration" of congressional supremacy (LW, 311–13; RES, 132–38).

Wherever leadership resides, Will is convinced that to represent us properly each party must accept the challenge of articulating a coherent vision for America. Quality representation requires articulating ideas that will move people. Each party has peculiar problems, but Will believes that "there is nothing wrong with parties that unifying, animating ideas won't cure" (NS, 39).

To lead, the Republicans must overcome their long-standing status as the minority party. Since Kevin Phillips wrote his famous study predicting realignment, Republicans have eagerly awaited the day when a majority of Americans would identify with them.[21] It has not happened. The Democrats have lost party identifiers, but that loss has not always resulted in Republican gains. The trend has been toward more independent voters. Will observes that trends in party identification may reflect dealignment rather than realignment (NS, 44).

Republicans face special problems in conveying their message. One problem is the stridency of their core activists. Americans have never accepted the laissez-faire nostrums to which many activists adhere. Beyond the American penchant for "mild social democracy," Will thinks laissez-faire policies are unrealistic because modern political economies require rather heavy doses of planning, intervention, and management (NS, 64–65). Reagan did not defeat Jimmy Carter because his conservative message was pure. Rather, he moderated his image, allowing him to beat an unpopular president. "Reagan won because he kept the election from being a referendum on conservative ideology" (NS, 48).

Reagan's legacy was not an unpalatable ideological consistency. Rather, the uncertainties he bequeathed resulted from inconsistencies in his policies. "Reaganomics" succumbed to the theory that tax cuts would be self-financing. Will recognizes that reducing marginal rates of taxation can indeed improve overall revenues—up to a point. When tax cuts are not accompanied by spending restraint, however, massive deficits result.

The new breed of Republicans dismissed those who urged either higher taxes or lower rates of spending as "traditional Republicans." Will acidly comments that "times are truly out of joint when the adjective 'traditional' becomes, in the name of conservatism, an epithet" (NS, 62). By not exerting the will to raise taxes or cut spending, Republicans lost some of the high ground in criticizing Democrats. Will laments: "In 1980 the conservative critique of liberalism boiled down to its essence: Liberalism has lost the capacity to establish rational priorities and make hard choices. Less than six years later that has a hollow ring" (NS, 69).

Expecting an abrupt and radical change in our spending patterns defies conservative prudence, according to Will. He marvels at Reagan's fondness for "that stupendously dumb statement by Tom Paine: 'We have it in our power to begin the world over again.' " Will retorts that "Paine's statement is the most unconservative statement that ever issued from human lips. Conservatism is grounded in an appreciation of the immense constraining givenness of life. Conservatism is the politics of prudence, which begins with acceptance of the fact that, more often than not, and to a degree that is humbling to human beings, the inertia of society and history severely limits the pace and degree of change that human willfulness can bring about. Or, as a wise man once said: In the battle between you and the world, bet on the world" (NS, 81). "The world" is the American penchant to sacrifice some degree of economic dynamism for the security that government can provide through common provision.

Will's estimate of the temper of the American public did not change radically in the face of the stunning Republican congressional election victory in 1994. The Republicans offered proposals to slow the rate of growth in government and proposals for balancing the budget. The 1994 midterm elections produced serious discussion of devolving responsibility to the states. None of this appeared particularly revolutionary to Will. Although the balance between risk and security may shift somewhat, Will has shown no serious proclivity to revise his judgment that Republicans are bound to conserve much of the legacy of Franklin Roosevelt: "FDR is the only President to have altered, fundamentally and irrevocably, the relationship between the citizen and the central government. That government assumed responsibility for the nation's economic health—the aggregate economic output—and for a minimum material well-being of the individual. If Reagan really wants to repeal those federal responsibilities (a repeal that would constitute a real revolution), he has never said so" (NS, 88).

Democrats, as one would expect, face a different set of challenges if they are to resume their status as majority party. Will traces the decline of Democratic affiliation to the disastrous 1968 national convention in Chicago (NS, 99–100). One thing that that convention revealed was the sheer divisiveness of the Democratic coalition. From Will's perspective, a successful party, at least in presidential elections, must enunciate unifying themes. Increasingly the Democratic party appears as the voice of a series of special interests. That appearance is ruinous in a presidential race: "To be elected President in the 1980s you must get 55 million voters to vote for you. Now consider: What do 55 million Americans agree about? Precious little. Or to be more precise, precious little other than propositions couched in a high level of generality. Mondale tried to cobble together the 55 million from lots of groups. Against Mondale, as against Carter, Reagan took a different approach. Reaganism is politics as evangelism, calling forth a majority with a hymn to general values.

Mondaleism is politics as masonry, building a majority brick-by-brick"
(NS, 100–101).

The major thematic problem for the Democrats is America's deeply
ingrained antigovernment rhetoric. Democrats, being the champions of
vigorous government, are obvious targets for the rhetoric. Many Americans have prospered as the result of government actions while continuing to think of government as doling out benefits to the (undeserving)
other guys. What is worse from the standpoint of Democratic electoral
prospects, the success of many government programs has undermined
the party of government:

> The great event at the Democratic convention of 1984 was Walter Mon-
> dale's pledge to raise taxes to continue financing the protective state. The
> problem with the proposal was illustrated when a young Democratic
> professional called from the convention to get his father's assessment of
> things. The father, a blue-collar worker in the Northeast, said: "The
> Democratic Party has been good to me—Social Security, G. I. Bill, stu-
> dent loans. The Democratic Party made me middle class. But Reagan
> will keep me middle class."
>
> There, neatly put, is the paradox at the heart of the Democratic
> Party's problems. Many federal programs, most of them pioneered by
> Democrats, have produced a prosperous and socially competent middle-
> class nation that feels less need for the modern state and hence is less tol-
> erant of the taxes needed for that state. (NS, 123)

According to Will, the problems occasioned by success are exacerbated
by wounds the Democrats have inflicted on themselves.

One incision results from the Democrats' failure to attune themselves
to the symbolic realities of American politics. The brick-by-brick
approach to attracting a majority is especially difficult if the candidates
not only fail to enunciate themes that resonate, but also make noises
that grate. According to Will, Americans respond as much to symbolic
commitments as to concrete policies.[22] What Americans want are politicians who signal that they are on their side. The Democrats, by viewing
"law and order" as code words for racism, ceded a deeply resonating
issue to the Republicans (NS, 128–29).

Will thinks the Democrats are handicapped in seeking resonance
with the American public because of their addiction to "fairness." The
pursuit of fairness leads the Democrats to attempt fine tunings of tax
and fiscal policies. These labyrinthine efforts tend to be both ineffective
and open to abuse: "The justice of the market is not perfect. However, it

is, more often than not, preferable to a politicized system in which the allocation of wealth and opportunity is heavily influenced by government tax code decisions that are themselves heavily influenced by the 'influence industry'—the expensive, sophisticated, Washington-based lawyer-lobbyist complex that works to make government a servant of the strong" (NS, 135).[23]

In Will's view, the ideology of fairness leads to the self-righteousness of virtucrats. It also leads to an obsession with equality that can be debilitating for a party seeking a majority of votes. The search for fairness led the Democrats to adopt categorical representation in its national conventions. This leads, in Will's estimation, to a balkanized party that has difficulty appealing to poor, ethnic white voters that Democrats need to form a majority (NS, 154–56). Will concludes that, by weakening their electoral base, the Democrats have become resigned to using the courts to achieve results that the electorate will not support (NS, 156–60).

Another area where Will sees decline in Democratic support is foreign policy. Will lauds the Democratic Party for its role in resisting communism. The Democrats were instrumental in resisting Republican isolationism and turning American foreign policy toward a vigorous pursuit of the cold war. During the late '60s and beyond, a substantial portion of the party, repelled by the Vietnam War, turned to a more dovish stand in international relations. Many in the party became so disenchanted with American foreign policy that they became (or became easily perceived as) anti-American. In 1988, Will thought that the Democrats needed to return to "the flinty realism and longheadedness of the Truman-Acheson Cold War tradition" (NS, 139).

The focus that the cold war gave to foreign policy disputes is lost. The direction of Democratic and Republican thought in this area is opaque. In any event, the Republicans may have lost a real edge in public perception with the decline of communism.

Will has provided a valuable outline of some broad divisions within our party system. Anyone who seriously wishes to represent us must consider the challenge of developing a rhetoric suitable to govern. Once in power, the problem of representation assumes different forms. How does a representative maintain the power that the electorate has granted? More important, how can the representative do a good job of serving the people? Will is most concerned with the second question, and he addresses it in developing his ideas on deliberative democracy.

Term Limits, Deliberative Democracy, and the Republican Tradition

On the surface, Will's book *Restoration* is simply advocacy of a controversial policy—term limits. The book is unusual and more exciting than most books on the subject, however.[24] It transcends the narrow terms that typically frame debates on institutional reforms because Will connects his thoughts to key issues in democratic theory. The book is a timely and provocative interpretation of the idea of representation and a troubling meditation on the role of Congress in contemporary America.

Will centers his thoughts on two themes: classical deliberative democracy and republicanism. I examine how he connects his advocacy of term limits to each.

Deliberative Democracy and Term Limits

Many advocates of republican virtue envision an active citizenry devoted to the public weal. Will tempers his devotion to civic virtue and his case for term limits with a largely Burkean notion of representation, which he labels deliberative democracy. Will rebukes those who would reform Congress to make it more "responsive" if responsiveness involves representing citizen desires rather than their common interests. What Americans desire are low taxes along with lots of services. To these desires Congress has been excessively responsive. The cost has been budgets that mortgage the future of our children. What we need is a Congress capable of reflecting our interests rather than the "cognitive dissonance" of our wishes (RES, 107–8).

Will attributes the pathological responsiveness of Congress to professionalism; the cure is to make professionalism impossible. Will differs from other advocates of term limits who want to bring representatives closer to the people. Proponents of term limits frequently argue that rotation in office would bring representatives closer by forcing them to live among their constituents under the laws they make. Conversely, Will favors term limits because they would create more distance between representatives and constituents.

By serving limited terms, representatives could avoid the constant pressures for reelection. Under the current system, representatives need to campaign constantly and raise funds for reelection. The campaigns require them to be highly attentive to the demands from the public and interest groups. That makes it difficult to do their job, which is to deliberate on the common good rather than reflect particular interests. Will sounds almost like Rousseau in stressing the common good in deliberation: "By 'public opinion' we should mean something other than, something richer and more political than, the mere tabulation of private judgments arrived at in private" (RES, 125).

Representing the common good requires "constitutional distance from the people" (RES, 110). Attaining that distance requires a free people to create, or in our case restore, deliberative institutions: "Today the sensible reason for enacting term limits is not to forestall oppression but to nurture deliberation, meaning a disposition to reason about policies on their merits rather than their utility in serving the careerism of legislators. A deliberative institution is one in which members reason together about the problems confronting the community and strive to promote the general interest of the community. The deliberative process involves identification and investigation of social needs, the evaluation of programs currently attempting to meet those needs, and the formulation of new legislative remedies for recalcitrant problems" (RES, 110–11). Will believes that term limits would free legislators from particularizing pressures, thereby creating institutional space to deliberate.

Will takes great pains to distinguish deliberation from leadership. He derides the popular notion that we need to improve our estate by improving leadership. Leadership calls forth emotions and brings people to act. At its core is the art of rhetoric, which has increasingly dominated the presidency. Effective representation in legislatures demands deliberation rather than leadership. There is some overlap, but deliberation and leadership require different qualities:

> A deliberative legislature, composed of people exercising judgment, can do what leaders are supposed to do. It can inspirit people by the dignity of its deliberations. It can persuade by the gravity of its procedures as well as the plausibility of its conclusions. This is the noble power possessed by ordinary people who take up the republican task of deliberating for the community, in public. Let us call these deliberating people "leaders." Let us call what they do "leadership." But let us not lose sight of the fact that what they are doing is deliberating. What they are exercising is judgment. (RES, 115)

For Will, the aim of legislation is to represent what Madison calls the "cool and deliberate sense of the community" (RES, 117; "Federalist No. 63"). A legislator must note the opinions and desires of the constituency, but the opinions must be divorced from the turbulent whims of passion and the wants separated from what we really want.

Will knows that even cool deliberation will not lead to unanimity.
We ought not expect too much unity in the deliberative process:

> The first ten words of the Constitution are "We the people of the United
> States, in order to . . ." Those words are the beginning of the Preamble,
> which is a Statement of intentionality by a unity, the American people.
> But when are we "a people"? Are we always one? Always to some extent?
> It is a premise of our pluralism, and a glory of our open society, that we
> are not always, and for all purposes, united, or even aspiring to unity.
> Indeed, we are rarely in serried ranks about anything short of war, and,
> come to think of it, rarely even about war.
>
> However, it is not just nice, it is often necessary for even a pluralistic,
> open society to think and act as a community. Now, the word "commu-
> nity" implies unity, but a unity short of unanimity. It is unity compatible
> with an easy, friendly, neighborly acceptance of differences within a
> framework of consensus on essentials. But a community needs institu-
> tions that reconnect its actual diversity with its need for some unity. One
> of these institutions is government. (RES, 118–19)

This eloquent passage reflects Will's acceptance of the basic outlines of
our liberal tradition. It also reflects the difficulty in developing a theory
of deliberation for a liberal regime.

In his classic analysis of deliberation (*bouleusis*), Aristotle insisted that
we can deliberate only about ends, not about means (*Nicomachean Ethics,*
bk. 3, 1112b).[25] In ethical and political discourse we reason about the
ways to attain the natural ends we discover. The key word is discovery.
In both personal and communal deliberations, Aristotle emphasizes
what we find on our way to happiness. His conception of public deliberation has little of our modern idea of "lawmaking."[26] Deliberation is a
process of understanding rather than making.

Aristotle's theory of deliberation runs counter to modern sensibilities
in two respects. First, by tying deliberation to teleology and the cosmology that supports it, he upholds a view, as I noted in the previous chapter, rejected in much modern thought. Second, the idea of deliberation
as discovery violates our modern faith in legislative supremacy—the
idea that we can "make" the laws to which we consent.

Will does not suggest a vigorous reintroduction of "nature" into our
legal deliberations, as strong advocates of natural law do. In any case,
there is no clear way to move from nature-driven deliberation to the legislative supremacy he defends, even if we add a theory of balancing to
preserve against legislative abuses. The question still remains: What are
we deliberating about?

Will seems to follow the treacherous path most of us travel eventually by invoking consensus to produce the ends of deliberation. "We" (there's that devilish figure again) agree on fundamentals that entail ends. Will finds the ends in the Preamble to the Constitution, fully aware that these ends are quite vague: "The Constitution has been compared to a loose-fitting suit of clothes. The most apposite comparison would be to work clothes—or play clothes. The Constitution does not bind during strenuous exertions" (RES, 105). The problem is not so much the vagueness or adaptability of the ends (something endemic to political reality). Instead, we may wonder what sort of legislative process encourages fidelity to them.

Will's focus is definitely on process. The key is a well-organized structure of opinion formation. The ideal procedure would be circular:

> The sentiments of individuals, and of individual factions, should indeed flow to a representative government. But there, in bodies that are both representative and judicious, these sentiments should become the stuff of deliberation. And by the action of such a political body on the raw material of public sentiment, those sentiments can acquire the shape and weight of truly political principles and arguments and judgments.
>
> This process should be observed by attentive constituents of the deliberating politicians. The observation is assisted by journalism and by such political communications as party publications and legislators' newsletters. Such communications complete the circle. And the members of the public, being attentive to and hence participants in the process, become *a public*. (RES, 125)

I confess some puzzlement at how public awareness improves the quality of deliberation in this process, even if keeping the public informed does promote unity and a sense of (always?) belonging. My deeper concern is the faith in the process of communication that this quotation exhibits.

In centering his discussion on communication, Will echoes Aristotle in connecting human nature to the capacity for reasonable speech: "Man is a political animal because he is a language-using animal. . . . Language is intrinsically connected with reasoning, and hence with two indispensable facets of popular government, persuasion and deliberation" (RES, 122). Term limits would, Will thinks, allow our nature to flourish.

In connecting language to persuasion and deliberation, Will captures a substantial part of the liberal ethos that stresses persuasion over power. Will thinks liberals are especially prone to blunders in foreign affairs because they carry the will to discussion into the international arena where it does not work. Does it work that well in the domestic arena?

Jürgen Habermas has struggled to develop a theory of democracy grounded in a theory of communication.[27] He maintains that democratic life depends on creating unconstrained discourse where people are free to say what their reason dictates rather than what external forces dictate. Habermas seems to believe we would flourish were constraints on discourse to disappear. Two questions are in order. Would we? Could we? There is no clear reason to think that simply speaking our minds will lead to harmony even when (especially when?) we speak freely. There is no clear reason to believe that we can lift all constraints on discourse.

Asking about the constraints on discourse is useful because we can occasionally identify barriers to the best practicable discussion. If our deliberations have gone awry, why? I know of no legislator who does not want "to form a more perfect union, establish justice, insure domestic tranquillity, provide for the common defense, promote the general welfare, and secure the blessings of liberty to ourselves and our posterity." If legislators fail to deliberate properly on these ends, why are they failing? We could locate the failing in the available candidates, in the way we select them, or in the process by which they deliberate. Will opts to focus on the second explanation. The process of deliberation has been corrupted by the professionalism sustained by our method of election. In his view, term limits would mitigate the corruption.

I will discuss the adequacy of term limits to secure good deliberation momentarily. I conclude this section by posing some large questions, the significance of which should be clearer after the concluding sections of the chapter.

If we dispense with the discourse of nature and rely on consensus, how do "we" maintain the sense that we are a unity in the face of division? Can a facially fair process bridge deep disagreements? Can we ensure that the people we chose to deliberate for us will indeed seek the common good? Will's proposals for a civilization of discussion presuppose a "we" about whose common good we are deliberating. Does the fact that we have a few hundred people relatively isolated from public pressure and voted for by a majority of a relatively small electorate guarantee virtual representation?

The Republican Ideal and Term Limits

George Will seeks a revival of "classical republicanism." I have already examined some of what he has written on the subject and connected it to the themes of citizenship and civic unity. What remains is to examine some additional comments by Will on classical republicanism and to see how he connects term limits to republican theory.

The title of Will's book on term limits recurs to the concerns of many modern thinkers concerned with restoration. Will singles out Machiavelli in particular. Machiavelli and other moderns have sought to restore a lost glory from a republican past that was thought submerged. The idea of restoration connects well with a major theme in republican thought: decay. Will thinks that the theme connects Machiavelli to the ancients: "Machiavelli, so unlike the ancients in so many ways, shared with them an intense interest in the problem of preventing decay, and the possibility of regenerating a society when decay has not been kept at bay. These are the themes—degeneration and regeneration—that connect today's two controversies about the condition of Congress and the meaning of representation with the largest and most enduring argument in the Western political tradition" (RES, 150–51).

What has decayed? Will summarizes the key features of the tradition he wishes to restore. Classical republicanism includes "the ideas of social man, the central importance of public participation in civic life and the struggle of the virtuous people out in the country to contain the corruption associated with those who cluster around the central power, like the court around the king" (RES, 152–54). How these ideas connect to term limits is not entirely clear.

Will wants to maintain, against what he takes to be an excessive individualism in Locke's thought, the image of human sociability: "The crucial difference with Lockean liberalism is the emphasis classical republicanism gives to man's natural sociability. That sociability entails both a need and a disposition to participate in civic life and to develop and display public virtue" (RES, 155). Will, relying on Pocock, affirms an unbroken chain of republican thought built on this premise. Like Pocock, Will wants to make Aristotle the founding father of the republican tradition.

> Classical republicanism is rooted in Aristotle's notion that man is a political animal. Man, to Aristotle, is not political in the tentative, limited and diffident manner of the Lockean man who enters into political society only negatively, as a necessary concession to inconveniences. Rather, said classical republicans, man is political in the sense that his nature can not be realized, and his natural inclinations can not be fulfilled, without active involvement in a particular kind of political order. It is a kind that makes possible political participation, which Aristotle considered a defin-

ing attribute of citizenship. Such a political order is right for man's nature. Which is to say, it is a natural right. (RES, 155–56)

I think that the chain running from Aristotle to Pocock is quite broken, but this is not the occasion to redeem that claim. Rather, I want to suggest that this reading of Aristotle and the contrast with Locke need qualification. I want to focus on "nature" again to blur some differences drawn too sharply.

What does Aristotle mean by claiming that we are "political animals"? Any answer I give is disputable, so let me begin with what he does not mean. He does not mean that anyone born human will act sociably. That expectation is so contrary to the facts that Aristotle never seriously entertained it. Our sociability is "natural" insofar as we realize our telos when we associate. Outside some sort of association we would be either beasts or gods (*Politics*, bk. 1, ch. 2, 1253a). Unlike bees, however, we do not associate instinctively. We must educate our children to achieve their natural potential by living well in association with others. It is not at all clear that Aristotle thinks we need to participate in public affairs to fulfill our nature. The main virtues he discusses are personal, but political science provides the necessary frame for living the good life. The community is as much an instrument for the good life in Aristotle as in Hobbes or Locke. His arguments against Plato preclude the idea that the community can have a goodness independent of the good it produces for its members (*Politics*, bk. 2, 1261–65).

Furthermore, the particular order Aristotle defends is more particular than Will allows. Aristotle does not defend a principle of widespread participation. Participation was severely limited in all the ancient Greek polities because women, slaves, and alien workers (*metics*) could not participate. What Aristotle defends is the compact city-state against sprawling empires like Persia. Our commercial republic would seem quite unnatural and barbarian (meaning non-Greek) to him.

What is the difference between Aristotle and Locke? Will is correct that Locke does not believe in natural sociability, but that does not mean Locke denies the need for sociability. How do we secure the sociability we need? We educate our citizens and provide incentives for right action.[28] How does that differ from Aristotle? The aim is to educate in the appropriate virtues. If we succeed, what difference does it make if the impulses are natural or artificial? If we dispense with the prop of nature, the issues become: How much civic participation do we need and how can we effectively attain the right level? When the issue is formulated this way, Lockeans and Aristotelians have something to talk about.

Still lurking in the wings is the crucial question: What does our need for civic fulfillment have to do with term limits? The notion of civic virtue is thinly connected, in *Restoration,* to term limits. How would the reform promote civic virtue? More crucially, whose civic virtue would be promoted? Removing the pressure for reelection would create a space of freedom for a member of Congress to promote the public good, but would it create an environment in which we foster zeal for the public interest in the general populace?

Will admits that a large commercial republic restricts the opportunity for participation, but he thinks term limits would open new opportunities for those citizens who are "effectively excluded from the pool of talent from which lawmakers are drawn" (RES, 164). That may be true, but even the most radical proposals for a citizen legislature would open opportunities for only a few of us to participate.

Will falls back on the educative value of a reformed Congress. Somehow observing the dignity and sustainability (gravity and piety?) of a reformed process would teach civic virtue by example. The problem with this is that it defies Aristotle's central claim that we learn virtue through habituation.

The other aspect of Will's connecting term limits to classical republicanism is more plausible. He argues that our current system of interest group politics and categorical representation encourages factionalism and undermines the unity we need for action. Resisting factions depends on deliberating for the common good rather than on particular interests. The time has come to ask: Will term limits improve the quality of deliberation?

Will Term Limits Work?

Will does not believe that term limits are a panacea. Nevertheless, he does think that the reform would improve the quality of our representatives' deliberations and of our civic life (RES, 144–45). Would it?

If we assume that professionalism is the central motivating force tending toward promotion of private interests, the reform might transform attitudes among members of Congress. But is professionalism the root of all evil? No complex problem reduces to a single variable. The sources of congressional irresponsibility are numerous. Along with professionalism, Will lists three reasons for congressional irresponsibility that would not necessarily respond to his proposed remedy: a culture of spending, congressional delegation, and presidential ascendancy.

Will produces compelling evidence of a culture of spending in Congress that tends to eliminate resistance to budget deficits (RES, 59–61). Representatives do not challenge requests for spending by other members, thereby protecting their requests from challenge. Some of this culture feeds on the need to produce pork for the reelection platter, but not all of it. Legislators disagree about what is in the public interest. Frequently, they have to swallow their reservations and relent on dubious projects to promote a vital interest. Will says that term limits would not "purge from politics the traditional arts and crafts and skills of negotiating, conciliating, logrolling and the rest. However, term limitation is an attempt to enlarge the domain of deliberation, to improve government's 'aptitude and tendency' to behave reasonably" (RES, 145). How much enlargement do we get? There is a comfortable tendency to avoid conflict when possible. Why wouldn't our legislators continue with the get along, go along strategies that have served them so well? The temptation toward logrolling will always be present in an undisciplined and decentralized legislative process, and term limits would not touch the highly decentralized committee structure of Congress.

Will also mentions the problem of delegation (RES, 172–73). Congress tends to write laws that are more statements of purpose than detailed plans for addressing problems or needs and providing the appropriate level of funding. Congress abdicates too much of the legislative process to executive agencies. Term limits would not touch this problem—indeed they could exacerbate it by minimizing the possibility of expert legislation and oversight.[29]

Will also notes the ascendancy of the presidency during the latter half of the 20th century. We have come to expect our leadership—our policy and budget initiatives—to come from the president. Will may be right that a citizen legislature would enjoy more respect from the American public, but it hardly follows that the legislature would assume a more active role in policy making. As with the problem of delegation, the disparity could worsen. In any case, Will observes that the end of the cold war should lead to a weaker presidency with or without term limits.

Even if Will is right in that the source of our troubles is professionalism, term limits, as he conceives them, may not remedy our condition. Will favors a version of term limits where both Senators and members of the House serve up to 12 years (RES, 220). Would this eliminate profes-

sionalism? I can envision an enterprising professional who would stay in
the state legislature for, say, 20 years and then move on to the House
and Senate for another 24 years. If the career track breaks, our professional could move into the governor's mansion for a few years. For a
dynamic careerist, the presidency is not out of reach. If the office seeker
cannot assume an elective position for a few years, strong incentives
would entice our professional to enter the revolving door into a high-
paying political appointment in the bureaucracy or in lobbying. In
short, to eliminate professionalism, term limits will have to be more radical than Will desires.

Perhaps a more fundamental proposal to create a citizen legislature
would yield a better balance between public and private interests. We
could limit members of Congress to one term and forbid them to hold
executive appointments or lobby. I doubt that we could insulate even a
genuine citizen legislature (or the executive agencies to which it would
delegate much of its business) from well-organized, heavily-funded, and
articulate interest groups. Somehow we must arouse civic virtue among
the citizens themselves so that they will demand a responsible rather
than a responsive legislature. We cannot accomplish such a difficult (and
dangerous) shift in our political culture with simple institutional reform.

Will does an excellent job of criticizing the arguments against term
limits. He asks devastating questions for opponents. Could a citizen legislature do worse with the deficit? If government is so complex that citizens cannot learn its workings in a few years, sholdn't we simplify government for the sake of democracy? In any event, showing that the
opponents of term limits are wrong about the disasters that would ensue
is not the same as showing the merits of term limits.

One of the most interesting sections of *Restoration* pertains to the
motives of term limits' opponents. Will notes that political scientists
tend to be vigorous opponents of term limits and attributes the opposition to a variety of ideological and institutional factors (RES, 213–15).
His observations are challenging and deserve investigation. I want to
note Will's venture into "the sociology of knowledge," which explores
the causes of our beliefs and judgments.[30] The venture is perfectly legitimate, but the sociology of knowledge has an unnoticed bearing on
Will's theory of representation. If we admit that who we are and the
context from which we judge has bearing on our judgments, can we
simply assume that we can divorce deliberation from group membership? That brings me back to the issue I have left in abeyance: Categorical representation.

Categorical Representation and Deliberation

Will considers categorical representation to be as much a threat to deliberative democracy as the interest group politics that has dominated congressional politics. He finds it perniciously manifested in the drawing of election districts to increase minority representation (RES, 47). Will views this as an unwarranted entitlement for "a particular government favored ethnic group" (RES, 42).

Will has some important criticisms of the redistricting plans. The new districts encourage the "ghettoization of representation, and this ghettoization diminishes the incentive of minority and white voters to build inclusive coalitions" (RES, 48). He further observes that the new districts have violated the traditional desire for compactness to protect the interests of incumbents. Republicans in the South have been particularly compliant in creating majority black districts because draining black voters from districts strengthens Republican voting (RES, 48–50). These concerns are fair, but Will shares them with writers whose perspectives sharply differ from his. For instance, Lani Guinier advances essentially the same objections as Will, but she has sought alternatives to both redistricting and traditional schemes of representation by exploring cumulative voting alternatives that would keep blacks and whites in the same districts.[31] Will does not rest content with denouncing the particular versions of categorical representation we have tried. He objects to categorical representation on principle. Why? Will thinks that any scheme of representation that recognizes group membership defies our core principles of justice and comity.

The case against categorical representation is weaker than the case against affirmative action. We cannot pretend that the only thing that counts in voting is the individual. Will's commitment to the tradition of compactness means that where you live will count along with who you are and how you think. Were we acting on a pure theory of Burkean representation, we could assign each person randomly to a district. What difference would it make?[32]

Notwithstanding his faith in virtual representation, Burke thought group membership counted. Hannah Pitkin has shown that Burke believed in a theory of "unattached interests" rather than fidelity to an undifferentiated "common good."[33] He thought that interests deserve representation, but that someone other than a member of the interested party could voice them. There are distributive goods that assume political importance along with the common good. For example, a nation has agricultural interests that are not equivalent to the prosperity of farmers but surely include it. The nation as a whole should promote these interests even if not everyone benefits or benefits equally from their promotion. If a vital interest receives no voice, we cannot simply assume that it is being represented by right-thinking legislators. If vital interests or the interests of justice (for, say, the Irish) are not being voiced, we need to find a way to voice them.

That leads to the obvious question: Has anyone voiced the interests of groups who have suffered the most exclusion in our society? For most of our history the answer would have been no. There was a clear need to grant actual representation to African Americans in the South and women throughout the nation. Most of us now concede the justice of the Fifteenth Amendment, the Nineteenth Amendment, and the Voting Rights Act of 1965. These measures secured actual representation where virtual representation was no reality.

The Supreme Court laid out in *Thornburg v. Gingles* a rationale for redistricting to increase the chances for electing a member of a minority group.[34] In showing "purposeful discrimination" in violation of the Voting Rights Act, a plaintiff must prove that (1) a minority is large enough and compact enough to form the majority in a single-member district, (2) the minority is politically cohesive, and (3) the majority votes together enough to deny minority candidates the effective opportunity to win elections.

In *Thornburg v. Gingles,* we have a valid criterion for categorical representation. A group cannot receive virtual representation if the majority has shown hostility to the group. You cannot represent my interests if you are hostile to me, and bloc voting is a sign of hostility. In his analysis of a redistricting case involving Native Americans, Will has shown that bloc voting can be seriously misread to the disadvantage of a minority group.[35] Nevertheless, showing that a principle has been abused does not invalidate the principle. There are districts in the South with a manifest history of racial intolerance where the chances of electing African Americans are slim indeed. That may be changing, but caution is in order.

Assume that a history of hostile patterns of voting regulation justifies limited use of categorical representation. That assumption would not yield a positive reason for categorical representation in selecting delegates to the national convention of the Democratic Party or in those cases where boards and commissions encourage or require inclusion of minorities and women. Any case for these practices must be advanced cautiously and tentatively.

Some advocates of categorical representation advance dubious arguments for it. The most extreme version posits a granite block conception of consciousness. Each ethnic group has a distinct way of thinking that members of another group cannot represent. The least plausible versions of the granite argument ground it in biology by postulating a racial basis for consciousness.[36] The more plausible version of the argument asserts diverse cultural identities that preclude easy understanding by members of out-groups.

The cultural argument suffers two major defects. First, members of cultural and racial minorities (and surely women) do not think alike over a large range of issues. Second, the beliefs and desires of groups significantly overlap with the dominant groups (however defined). In the face of these difficulties, theorists of granite consciousness will typically retreat to a distinction between those who are authentically members of the group and those who are inauthentic representatives. Gnostic elites frequently claim that only they can measure authenticity while seeking to protect the vulnerable masses from the brainwashed pawns of privilege. Sometimes solidarity justifies the posture of special insight into membership, but abuse of the privilege of separating sheep from goats is all but inevitable. The notion of block consciousness wrecks the possibility for communication with out-groups—a serious cost in most cases.

If advocates avoid appeals to granite consciousness, is there a positive, as opposed to protective, case for categorical representation? The best arguments appeal to common experience. One argument appeals to the common experiences of degradation and pride. People who are taught that they are less valuable than a dominant group need to see members of their subordinate group in key positions in public life, especially in governance. It makes a difference to say that people like me count. Will expresses the value of some degree of ethnic consciousness persuasively.

> Behind the vague and often mindlessly used slogan of 'Black Power' lies a plausible insight which casts doubt on the old humanitarian axiom: that 'racial consciousness' is a hindrance to the good life and is a thing to be cured rather than cultivated. But powerful new evidence from the social sciences points to the conclusion that the task of aiding the self-development of America's mal-treated Negro population is made tragically more difficult by the absence of racial pride that would generate coherence in the community, and through that stability, and through that a social life that stimulates confidence and initiative and other signs of wholesome, hopeful self-respect. (BM, 9–10)[37]

Even if encouraging ethnic unity secures a sense of self-respect, we have still not discovered a clear connection to the problem of representation. Can the experiences that one has as a group member improve the deliberative process? There are plausible reasons for answering yes, but the differences among group experiences are probably not as great as strong advocates of categorical representation think. Those who thought that Clarence Thomas's experiences would color his decisions on the Supreme Court were largely mistaken. Ideology has outweighed other factors.

If group membership is to be relevant, it will show itself in ways that are not particularly dramatic. ABC aired a segment on *20/20* about the shortage of women's bathrooms in public buildings. At one point, a female architect who was designing a new building noted the obvious: Most buildings were designed by men. Experience counts! Men have not had to stand in those insufferable lines. Furthermore, the difference in experience is relevant to deliberation.

We should not decide the relevance of group membership a priori. Proponents of categorical representation should carefully expound the differences that make a difference. Critics such as Will should be more inquisitive about differences as well. Will cited as "social insanity" a New York "affirmative action program to recruit homosexuals because (according to the notice posted in gay bars) police officers must be representative of the community they work to serve" (NS, 132). Will delights in recounting a seemingly pertinent query by Daniel Seligman: "How will the community know the sexual orientation of the person on the beat?" (NS, 132). The cute answer to this cute question is: "Once the guy calls you a faggot and hits you with his nightstick, you'll know." Instead of being cute, we might ask: Is there any experience behind the request for gay police officers? Asked that way, sensible answers can emerge.

Will was right to venture into the sociology of knowledge when asking about my tribe—political scientists. Who we are affects the quality of our judgments. Once we take the first step, the field is open for further inquiry about how our situation affects our deliberation.

Chapter Seven

The Virtues
of a Conservative Writer

To be conservative . . . is to prefer the familiar to the unknown, to prefer the tried to the untried, fact to mystery, the actual to the possible, the limited to the unbounded, the near to the distant, the sufficient to the superabundant, the convenient to the perfect, present laughter to utopian bliss.

Michael Oakeshott

Philosophy may not neglect the multifariousness of the world—the fairies dance, and Christ is nailed to the cross.

Alfred North Whitehead

Fourier had promised that Socialism would turn the seas into lemonade, and so the Party members had swallowed sea water as if it were lemonade. But eventually their stomachs turned, and from time to time they had to retire and vomit.

Michael Polanyi

In Search of Conservatism

George Will is a conservative. What does that mean? One way to write about someone being something is to define the something that that someone is. Asking people to define terms is reasonable. Unfortunately, conservatism is a word that has defied previous attempts at definition, and I have little hope of breaking the impasse. The impasse may lie in the very nature of the tendency for which a definition is being sought.

Nietzsche maintains that only those things that have no history can be defined.[1] Conservatism certainly has a history. Indeed, conservatives appeal to the wisdom of tradition, which entails that we cannot divorce politics from the history of a people. Furthermore, conservatism is a term of honor or derision, which means that its meaning is regularly contested, perhaps essentially contested.

Not defining conservatism is a controversial option. William Buckley is fond of quoting Richard Weaver's definition of conservatism as "a paradigm of essences towards which the phenomenology of the world is in continuing approximation."[2] Despite thinking that this is "as noble effort" as any he has encountered, Buckley, unsurprisingly, finds his audiences unsatisfied by the definition.[3]

Buckley is in search of an empirical definition of conservatism. This is strange enough, but invoking Richard Weaver in an empirical search for a definition is even stranger. Weaver donated to conservatism its most durable cliché, "ideas have consequences," in a book by that title.[4] Weaver thought modern man had fallen from grace under the baleful influence of William of Ockham. Ockham defended nominalism—the doctrine that general qualities or essences are no more than names we assign to individuals arbitrarily grouped together. For Weaver, one of the greatest imaginable evils—modernity itself—has flowed from the bowels of this doctrine.[5] Consequently, refusing to define conservatism may be a case of treasonous clerks refusing to do their duties. Of course, the clerks could plead that discovering the essence is beyond their capacity, but Weaver would surely condemn those who give up on the paradigmatic concern.

Leaving the field to sworn essentialists carries costs, since it would probably exclude one of contemporary conservatism's most influential voices—Michael Oakeshott. In any event, there is something to be said for an empirical approach to definition. I will at least begin my search for conservatism with self-identification—treating people who call themselves conservatives as conservatives. That allows mapping different positions within the self-identification, including disputes about the meaning of "true conservatism." Knowing how conservatives dispute among themselves will allow us to see where George Will stands.

Conservatism has its beginnings in Europe as a response to the French Revolution. Most genealogies trace conservatism to Edmund Burke. Burke's heritage is a serious part of American history, but it has never attained the dominance that many conservatives desire.[6] American soil has not been especially receptive to the seeds planted by Burke. As I have maintained throughout this book, the dominant tradition in America has been liberal and forward looking. Americans are prone to historical amnesia and smitten with novelty. Intellectually, the conservative tradition has been muted at best, submerged at worst. This is not to say that there have been no important American conservative thinkers. Neither would it be appropriate to forget the major role that temperamental conservatism and conservative institutions (especially the Constitution) have played in our history. Nevertheless, conservatism has usually taken the back seat in American intellectual life.

In the 1950s, a conscious effort was begun to create an intellectual edifice to support a conservative movement in America. Will has been a part of both the political movement and the attempt to provide it with intellectual foundations. Whether his efforts can advance us toward an agreeable definition is uncertain.

The confusion of terminology is greater in America than in Europe or Britain. In America, conservatism has (in some circles) come to describe a variety of liberalism that tends toward laissez faire economics. We normally reserve "liberalism," in the current usage, for welfare state liberalism. The opposition between liberals and conservatives is, then, an argument between two branches of liberal thought. Why, other than historical accident, call one branch conservative?

If conservatism is a defense of society's fundamental traditions, there is no reason to suppose that conservatives will take one or another ideological stand on property rights. The view would depend on the traditions of the society. For instance, conservatism in England originally grew in opposition to classical liberalism, and many conservatives opposed the political and economic doctrines of classical liberals. Coleridge, a leading British conservative, thought that liberalism was a "gospel" destined to corrode and destroy British society. It was a movement of "shopkeepers" and shopkeepers were "the least patriotic and the least conservative of any" class.[7] Today the opportunity to resist (as opposed to repel) liberalism has passed. Coleridge would probably be more accepting.

Framing conservatism as opposition to the welfare state would leave George Will out. Will not only believes that the basic American consensus is liberal, he also accepts that the dominant consensus now supports welfare state liberalism (NS, 161). Will wants to retard the growth of the welfare state and even eliminate some of its programs, but he thinks an abrupt departure is unwise (Will, interview). To war against the welfare state for ideological purity would constitute a departure from our basic traditions.

Many observers of American political life have noted the absence of intense ideological debate on "principles."[8] This contrasts sharply with the deep divisions found in Europe throughout much of the 19th and 20th centuries. One argument concerning the absence of ideological dispute centers on ideological consensus. We do not engage in intense ideological disputes because we share a common ideology—liberalism.

Americans generally agree in supporting negative freedom, limited government, private property, and have a deep, if fuzzy, attachment to some conception of progress (e.g., manifest destiny). Of course, we have disagreements. We disagree, for instance, over how much negative freedom we should have and in what areas (property rights, sexual freedom, freedom of political association, etc.). But the range of acceptable political ideas is quite limited (although some unacceptable ideas become accepted over time). We may disagree over the extent of government interference in the lives of individuals, but we agree that there are major limits. We may disagree over the degree of regulation rightly applied to private property, but we tend to ignore people proposing the abolition of private property. In short, we think that anyone who strays too far from the basic liberal consensus is a crackpot.

Now, if this characterization of American political life has any merit, we have a paradox. The only viable tradition in American politics is liberalism. Therefore, in order to be a conservative (defender of tradition) in America, you must be a liberal. Note, however, that the liberal tradition is an elite tradition.[9] When political leaders manage to activate the most disaffected strata of the population, we get some very illiberal politics. The movement surrounding George Wallace is a good example.[10]

Some writers have argued that conservatism needs to appeal to the public against the elite. Willmoore Kendall thought that a recovery of congressional supremacy combined with a less civil-libertarian reading of the Bill of Rights could restore "the deliberate sense of the community" that the liberal "enemy" had distorted.[11] In Kendall's vision, America was beset by liberal crusaders intent on destroying its character as a "Christian society with a secular constitution" (*Conservative Affirmation,* xxviii). The challenge of liberalism required, in his view, championing Congress against the presidency and the courts, and restricting civil liberties to respect majority rule. More recently, some conservatives, such as Pat Buchanan, have urged a Gaullist strategy that would bypass our political institutions and press an appeal directly to "the people."[12]

So far I have already surveyed three tendencies within (self-described) conservative thought. Will is the sort of conservative who would moderate liberalism and renew it with infusions from other traditions. He stands in opposition to "populist conservatives" who would radically reshape our political loyalties in the name of the people and laissez faire liberals who would sacrifice our concrete traditions for ideological principle.

Will thinks that populism speaks to serious concerns, but, on balance, it threatens the conservation of our basic political tradition. His

comments on the subject are compelling and deserve quotation at
length.

> There is a sense in which conservatism, as a criticism of the concentration
> of power in a large central government, is the natural inheritor of the
> American impulse called "populism." This is so because the modern state
> is inherently unfair. It is so because it is susceptible to manipulation by
> well-heeled and well-connected interests. But caution is in order when
> identifying conservatism with populism.
>
> 'Populism' is by now another word pounded to mush by careless
> usage. The most successful populist of this half-century was a Democrat:
> George Wallace. He shaped the vocabulary, and hence the agenda of
> national politics. He could give today's Democratic populists a lesson in
> Washington bashing. Remember his 1968 promise to toss the pointy-
> headed bureaucrats' briefcases into the Potomac? But today's Democrats
> are implausible Washington-bashers. Their party is primarily responsible
> for Washington's swollenness and hubris.
>
> Populists are people who adore 'the people,' so populists must be
> swell people, right? Not necessarily. Populism has a chip on its shoulder
> and self-pity in its heart. Its fuel is resentment, usually of some conspir-
> acy directed from afar by an alien elite. Populism often has been xeno-
> phobic, racist, nativist, anti-Semitic and paranoid. Still, real populism,
> that of the late 19th century, did have the dignity of moral seriousness
> about the country's core values in an era of wrenching social change.
> (LW, 281)

Whatever the affinity between the populist and conservative critiques of
the American political order, Will is not willing to invite populists into
the ranks of true conservatives. He questions Buchanan's credentials,
describing his primary contest with George Bush as a choice between
"Pat Buchanan's bad ideas (nativism, protectionism, isolationism) or
Bush's lack of ideas" (LW, 287).

Will's quarrels with libertarians have been more frequent than his
battles with populists, if for no other reason than the greater presence of
libertarians in American conservatism. The main reason for Will's concerns should be clear from reading chapter 2. The dynamism of capitalism makes it difficult to sustain a traditional order. Will argues that

> true conservatives distrust and try to modulate social forces that work
> against the conservation of traditional values. But for a century the dom-
> inant conservatism has uncritically worshipped the most transforming
> force, the dynamism of the American economy. No coherent conser-
> vatism can be based solely on commercialism, but this conservatism has

been consistently ardent only about economic growth, and hence about economies of scale, and social mobility. These take a severe toll against small towns, small enterprises, family farms, local governments, crafts-manship, environmental values, a sense of community, and other aspects of humane living.

Conservatism often has been inarticulate about what to conserve other than "free enterprise," which is institutionalized restlessness, an engine of perpetual change. But to govern is to choose one social outcome over oth-ers; to impose a collective will on processes of change. Conservatism that does not extend beyond reverence for enterprise is unphilosophic, has little to do with government and conserves little. (PH, 191–92)

Will, then, distinguishes true and false conservatisms, excluding both libertarians and populists from the fold. Will pitches a big tent under which conservatives might rest, but that does not mitigate the need to say who belongs in or out (Will, interview). In any event, we are some-where near where we began. We have a better idea of what Will thinks conservatism is not, but we have yet to learn what it is.

The last quotation offers a major clue. Will writes about conserving "traditional values." Whatever conservatism is, then, it is about tradi-tion. I do not think Will would quarrel with Willmoore Kendall's gen-eral definition, though he would surely have doubts about how Kendall applies it. Kendall writes that "in any given time and place Conserva-tives are those who are defending an established order against those who seek to undermine or transform it" (*Conservative Affirmation*, xxv).

Kendall's definition ties conservatism to a variety of concrete orders. He insists on defending "American Conservatism" rather than "Conser-vatism in America" (*Conservative Affirmation*, xxv). This puts him at odds with Weaver's "paradigm of essences." Kendall also specifically rejects Russell Kirk's notion of a "conservative mind," and probably would have rejected Kirk's war on behalf of the "permanent things."[13]

The key appeal for Kendall and for Will is to the working consensus of society and the fear of radically adjusting that consensus. But what if the consensus we adopt is evil? Is there an appeal beyond tradition? Asking these questions brings us to the most interesting and thorny dis-putes within conservatism. The disputes also point up the difficulties in resting a definition on the authority of tradition.

In chapter 1, I argued that a conservative journalist could make a valuable contribution to our moral and political discussions precisely because conservatives must take seriously the need to link the citizenry with its traditions. That contribution assumes that our tradition has moral authority. Does it? If so, how far does the authority extend?

Tradition as Moral Knowledge

Using tradition to guide moral and political thought is a venerable but problematic tradition. Will, like many other American conservatives, traces his ancestry to Edmund Burke. Notoriously, Burke challenged the apostles of the age of reason by defending the sanctity of prejudice and prescription in political judgment. Nonetheless, Burke's affirmation of tradition is not straightforward. As Burleigh Taylor Wilkins has argued, Burke struggle mightily with the problem of distinguishing good prejudice from bad prejudice. Burke was a powerful critic of many British policies sanctioned by deep and long-standing prejudice. How then to distinguish between those traditions that deserve and those that do not deserve censure?[14] Will is well aware of the problem of sorting good and bad prejudices. He writes: "The development of the ability to distinguish between the good and the traditional was an important accomplishment in the history of the human race. But that invention posed a problem which is perennial: assessing the traditional and deciding which portions of it to relinquish, and which to transmit" (SS, 154).

At least two approaches are available, both of which Burke seems to adopt at one time or another. First, one can claim that tradition is the bearer of a higher authority—a sanctioning wisdom that stands above it.[15] There may be deviation within a tradition from the wisdom it carries. Normally, we can trust prescription, but in a few instances tradition must be brought to judgment in terms of a higher law.

Second, one can assume that a tradition embodies a hierarchy of principles. We may then criticize long-sanctioned prejudices that violate core principles of our tradition without seeking extratraditional authority. This approach serves well those people who hope to circumnavigate the natural law tradition while avoiding ethical nihilism.[16] Will reads Burke's conception of political reason in largely traditionalist terms, downplaying its transcendent dimension (SS, 154–55). As previously noted, Will accepts the notion of nature as a standard, but rejects the idea of natural law.

How well a traditionalist can avoid appeal to extratraditional standards is a difficult, but pertinent, issue. Will does appeal to both nature and human nature as standards to judge tradition, but his arguments along these lines are infrequent and, as I argued in chapter 4, in need of development and defense (PV, 27; SD, 28). Nevertheless, Will appears to need an extratraditional standard because his major theoretical treatise, *Statecraft as Soulcraft,* alleges that the American tradition is fundamentally flawed (SS, 25–46). He can appeal to a hierarchy to criticize

America, since he places us within the broader stream of western civilization, but he merely postpones the day of reckoning. What constitutes the proper hierarchy within a tradition does not appear to be a question for which there is a satisfactory, traditional standard.

As Michael Walzer has stressed, many of our traditional categories carry enough consensus at least to allow civil disagreement and may even allow us to arrive at agreement.[17] There is reason, however, to doubt that "we" can have, much less sustain, a common tradition. Alasdair MacIntyre argues that our ethical language is a series of incoherent fragments from a forgotten past.[18] On issues such as abortion, we deploy different moral languages and talk past, rather than to, one another. MacIntyre's search for a whole and rational version of ethical life may be chimerical. Was there ever wholeness or coherence in the theories of great philosophers such as Aristotle or Aquinas, much less in the public affairs of concrete communities? MacIntyre has explored the possibility of comparing traditions and finding a reason to prefer one over another.[19] Making the kinds of comparisons he calls for requires a level of sophistication and historical knowledge that most of us lack. Lacking MacIntyre's erudition, citizens must trust or mistrust his reading of the rationality of tradition. Is that trust any more rational than simply trusting our traditions?

Perhaps there is no supremely rational way of life. Let us entertain the Augustinian thought that all forms of (earthly) community are fragments—that thought and life do not come in satisfying wholes. All ways of life express incompatible aims requiring trade-offs that involve costs.

Will believes that "pessimism about politics is built into American history" (RES, 14–15). Pessimism can easily extend to understanding and implementing the standards of justice. Leo Strauss famously remarked that the great modern thinkers build on low but firm ground. Liberalism, in seeking to satisfy our "lower" concerns, sacrifices glory. It also sacrifices some degree of justice for the sake of peace.

From an Augustinian viewpoint, the sacrifice is necessary. Perfect justice is unattainable; therefore, we must settle for the peace of Babylon. An Augustinian would conserve a liberal order for the same reason he or she would conserve most orders that are not grotesquely unjust. We cannot expect much better. But I may have given the game away. Almost no one, Augustinian liberals included, will agree to accept peace at any price. "No justice, no peace" is a good slogan to aim at both those who love peace and those who love justice. In the worst cases, the order under which we live requires destruction.

There is a way to preserve conservative credentials and favor an occasional rebellion or revolution. The conservative can appeal to willful departures from the tradition by those who happen to be in power. Thus, many conservatives, to explain Burke's sympathy with the American cause, have contended that the American revolution, unlike the French and Russian revolutions, was a conservative event sustaining traditional rights against assaults on the British constitution.[20]

There may indeed be cases when we need to destroy the government to conserve the constitution, but that does not solve the problem of affirming tradition against power. At least three problems remain. Hannah Arendt has skillfully exposed the first. She argues that traditions sometimes face rupture.[21] The traditions that sustain us collapse. In the face of rupture, we must engage in the act of founding. The founding generation styled their stab at a new beginning as a "new order for the ages." Unfortunately, the very act of founding reminds us that we can begin again without appeal to tradition. Arendt argues that foundation legends aim to solve "the problem of beginning—a problem because beginning's very nature is to carry in itself an element of complete arbitrariness. . . . They confronted the abyss of freedom, knowing that whatever would be done now could just as well have been left undone."[22] All politics carries within it what Arendt calls "natality," the capacity to begin things anew. In a tradition that constantly refers us back to the founding, a rupture with tradition is not only possible but can become, as in some of Jefferson's phrases, exalted.

Another problem with traditionalism relates to Will's appeal to republicanism. Republican thought stresses resistance to corruption. One way of viewing corruption is as a failure to live up to tradition. We have lost our past glory precisely because the voice of tradition is no longer heard, but if a corrupted people is a people out of touch with tradition, how can we cure their corruption by appealing to tradition? Those wishing restoration are in no better shape than those seeking a new order for the ages when making an appeal to tradition. When corruption passes a certain point, we need what Rousseau calls a "legislator"—someone who stands outside the political arena but who can inspire us to adopt new basic laws (*The Social Contract,* bk. 2, ch. 7). When a people becomes corrupted, we need prophetic, not traditional, authority.

A final problem with traditionalism concerns cross-cultural discourse. Ancient Roman legal theory stressed a natural law, understood by all humans, and a law of the peoples (jus gentium)—a set of rules agreed to by the common consent of all humanity. There is a third level of law that is peculiar to particular peoples, but the natural law and the law of the peoples provide a basis for common legal discourse across territorial boundaries.

Traditionalists like Willmoore Kendall and Michael Oakeshott stress the idiosyncrasy of tradition. What happens when the peculiar understandings of diverse peoples clash? Eric Voegelin illustrates the problem when discussing the encounter between representatives of the Mongol court and Christians in the 13th century. The Christians insisted that the Mongols receive baptism and submit to the authority of the pope. Kuyuk Kahn declined the invitation and wrote Innocent IV explaining his reasons. Kuyuk Kahn claimed that Genghis Kahn was the true representative of the order of God, and that victory in battle would vindicate the claim.[23] Voegelin does not suggest—nor shall I—that Kuyuk Kahn's (or Pope Innocent's) claims are beyond criticism. My point is this: The claims are not adjudicable merely through an appeal to tradition. When traditions clash at the most basic level, we must seek grounds for criticism other than the authority of tradition. Of course, we may discover common ground not previously discovered, but the authority of tradition is irrelevant to the common ground.[24]

The three problems I have discussed seem intractable if the clash of traditions is deep. Societies that lack agreement on a common tradition look like the former Yugoslavia at the end of the cold war. An appeal to tradition requires consensus on the authority of the tradition. Traditions yield authority; traditionalism does not.

If I am right that the liberal tradition is both dominant and relatively intact, there is room for the kind of conservatism that Will urges. He is more in the lineage of Peter Viereck, Walter Lippmann, and Clinton Rossiter than Russell Kirk. Both Rossiter and Viereck criticize Kirk for seeking to conserve traditions that have lost their vitality. Viereck describes Kirk as someone who confuses "concrete living roots with abstract yearning for roots."[25] Clinton Rossiter says Kirk sounds "like a man born one hundred and fifty years too late and in the wrong country."[26] These criticisms may or may not be fair, but they are the kind of criticism Will makes of certain strands of conservative thought. Is the "new conservative" appeal to concrete traditions the final word on defining conservatism in a society whose traditions are basically stable?

Many self-described conservatives, especially those associated with *National Review* in its early years, were eager to read Lippmann, Rossiter, and Viereck out of the conservative movement. They were unable to find sufficient distance between the new conservatives and the liberals that the *National Review* circle wanted to banish. They, like Will, wanted to criticize the direction of American politics. We still have a crucial issue: Even if we affirm the rationality or acceptability of the tradition as a whole, how do we criticize tendencies in it?

We need not find a hierarchy that all can agree on. Let me put that more bluntly. We cannot find an irrefragable hierarchy. What we can do is appeal to a series of "trumps" that allow us to play one principle against another in particular contexts.[27] For instance, our courts have consistently argued that national security can trump free speech in time of war.[28] We may claim that allowing pornographic theaters in a neighborhood is unacceptable because they would destroy its character. Maintaining a livable neighborhood may trump the desire to have entertainment nearby or to protect the fringes of free expression.

Playing trumps is not like using a deductive scheme. We just play our cards, call trumps, and see what happens. What we cannot do is dispense with the claim that one value outweighs another. Even though liberty is our central value, it is not our only value, and it is not always a trump. Will effectively expresses the need to negotiate rankings among our values:

> Conservatism, properly understood, rejects the idea of a single overriding aim. Real conservatism is about balancing many competing values. Striking the proper balance often requires limits on liberty, and always requires resistance to libertarianism (the doctrine of maximizing freedom for private appetites) because libertarianism is a recipe for the dissolution of public authority, social and religious traditions, and other restraints needed to prevent license from replacing durable, disciplined liberty. (PV, 45)

Because of the emphasis on liberty at the expense of other values, Will once remarked that there are "almost no conservatives, properly understood" (SS, 23).

Can there be a conservatism that weighs competing principles without affirming a great chain of being that finds a place for everything within a single hierarchy? Can we play trumps without knowing the rules? Will has asked the right question: What are we conserving? Answering western civilization yields two serious problems. First, the answer is vague. Second, we still need to explain what is so good about western civilization without simply begging the question. We need a conservatism that finds some middle ground between dogmatic metaphysics and mere acceptance of what is.

A conservatism of the middling sort can begin with a sense of transcendence. The good is beyond any formal principles I can announce. An in-between conservatism would end in a sense of tension cultivating both the desire to preserve the good embodied in our traditions while excoriating the evils they transmit. The tension between a desire to do good and the realization of our imperfection is what ought to be conserved.[29] Conserving tension may not sound as high minded as maintaining principles or values, but it is consonant with an Augustinian understanding of the human condition.

An Augustinian ethic does not succumb to a flabby relativism. Not all societies are equally just; some societies are peculiarly unjust. A well-ordered society ought to maintain an abiding respect for the competing traditions that compose it. Traditions are the filters through which peoples express their longing for the good life. One of the main jobs of ethical theory is to maintain rather than resolve the tensions between general authority and the vitality of competing traditions.

The need for tension is a theme Will stresses. The main tension that concerns him is between the rights of individuals and those of communities. He complains that "the rights of communities are by now so attenuated that there is not nearly enough tension" (SD, 206). Will also writes: "America's story is about the tension between the celebration of energy, expressed in restless individualism, and the desire for community, which must be inclusive and exclusive" (MA, 94–95). These are basic expressions of the conservatism of in-betweenness.

Affirming our way of life requires reflection on how we express or suppress voices in our conversation. Will wants to argue that some parts of our tradition need more voice to create more tension and better balance. His contribution to political thought and political journalism can be evaluated for its contribution to maintaining essential tensions— which is what I do in the concluding chapter.

Chapter Eight

Between Impotence and Destruction: The Politics of Tension

Suppose ye that I am come to give peace on earth? I tell you, nay, but rather division.

Luke 13:51

"No reason to get excited," the thief he kindly spoke.

Bob Dylan

George Will makes a significant attempt to incorporate communitarian and republican themes into American political discourse, but he also illustrates the difficulty in adapting the languages of community and civic virtue to a nation as large and diverse as the United States. There is reason to doubt that the classical languages of community and republican virtue bear any relation to our real possibilities. As Michael Ignatieff writes:

> Words like fraternity, belonging and community are so soaked with nostalgia and utopianism that they are nearly useless as guides to the real possibilities of solidarity in modern society. Modern life has changed the possibilities of civic solidarity, and our language stumbles behind like an overburdened porter with a mountain of old cases. . . . Our task is to find a language for our need for belonging which is not just a way of expressing nostalgia, fear and estrangement from modernity. Our political images of civic belonging remain haunted by the classical *polis,* by Athens, Rome and Florence. Is there a language of belonging adequate to Los Angeles? Put like that the answer can only seem to be no.[1]

Notwithstanding Ignatieff's observations, there may be room for retaining some of the language of classical republican thought. What we need are fresh forms of expressing our desire for belonging. Ignatieff reminds us of "the nineteenth-century city and the richness of its new forms and possibilities of belonging. Those great cities—Manchester, New York, Paris—were as strange to those who had to live in them for the first time as ours may seem to us. Yet we look back on them now as a time of civic invention—the boulevard, the public park, the museum, the cafe, the trolley car, street lighting, the subway, the railway, the apartment house. Each of these humble institutions created a new possibility for fraternity among strangers in public places."[2] If we are serious about strengthening the bonds among us, we may need newer forms of living together rather than simply recurring to old ideas.

Will, at one point, claimed to discern "a small republican renaissance" in some of Ronald Reagan's policies (MA, 247). Will was far too sanguine about the changes Reagan would bring, but he has the right idea about the republican tradition. Before Madison, republican thought centered on the desirability of decisions made in small face-to-face communities. There is little of that in America today. If we are to take classical republicanism seriously, we must find ways to decentralize decision making, allowing new modes of togetherness to emerge. Unfortunately for Will's nationalist impulses, decentralization would surely require more diversity and more experimentation than he desires.

When we think of decentralization, we tend to think of states and cities. Both are sprawling, complex creatures that dwarf the republican communities for which our nostalgia longs. When politicians talk about devolving power, they mean giving to entities that Will's republican mentor Jefferson would have observed with abject horror.

How would a genuine infusion of republican virtue appear today? Will, as do many conservative thinkers, stresses the role of "intermediary institutions."[3] Will believes that Robert Nisbet rightly identifies "the major theme of Western conservatism: the defense of society against the political state; the preservation, to the extent feasible, of the autonomy of social groups against politicized control" (PV, 202). Although Will once considered himself a big government conservative, he never placed exclusive trust in the efficacy, or even good will, of the central government. For Will, "to say that statecraft is soulcraft is not to say that the state should be the primary, direct instrument for soulcraft. An aim of prudent statecraft is to limit the state by delegating many of its chores to intermediary institutions. Government can become, to a dangerous degree, an interest group, as self-interested as any other, and more abusive than most" (SS, 145). Stressing the role of associational groups is venerable and quite in tune with American conservatism, which traces many of its insights to Tocqueville. Venerable or not, we still may wonder in the face of this familiar prescription: Is the call for "delegating" power to intermediary institutions more than nostalgia? Or, put differently, where in a place like Los Angeles does someone go to develop thick community ties?

To develop thick community ties in a place like Los Angeles would require more letting go—more recognition of community rights. The acceptance of community rights would need to extend beyond even the limited role they assume for a liberal like Will Kymlicka. Developing a strong sense of community along with the vigorous virtues needed to sustain community rights requires more than panegyrics to virtue and community by conservative intellectuals; we need to clear spaces where robust communities can flourish. A rebirth of communal liberty where people instilled with republican virtue fend for themselves requires the national, state, and local governments to give them the freedom to cultivate their own gardens.[4] We must be willing to let go of people who do not occupy liberal space well.

Letting go is not something we do graciously. We are more likely to grasp than release. Walker Percy captures our grasping propensities quite well in his novel *Love in the Ruins*. Percy's main character, Thomas Moore, chastises "death-dealing" America—possessor of great power and a magnificent cultural heritage: "All you had to do was pass one little test, which was surely child's play for you. . . . One little test: Here's a helpless man in Africa, all you have to do is not violate him. That's all. One little test: You flunk!"[5] Failing the test is not merely a matter of greed and lust for power. We grasp out of benevolence as well.

When we see a group of people acting in ways we think destructive, we call for intervention. We then assume the power required to set things right. This is not the place to argue at length the case against paternalism. Indeed, I have no unshakable objections to forceful intervention. By intervention, I mean that care can be exercised, even with some degree of compulsion, if the party with power really has a reasonable expectation of nurturing the subject. What constitutes a reasonable expectation is a contentious matter, but many paternalists simply assert to the subject: "Do what I say! Father knows best." That attitude can be disastrous.

Intervention is not always the best policy. Some people cannot or will not live up to our standards, and our dogged efforts to lead them to virtue come to nothing or even become counterproductive. What makes us think that we can guide everyone along the path of righteousness? We sometimes find people who simply resist our best ministrations. Perhaps prevention of a great wrong would justify intervention with people who will not accept our guidance; a stifling will to do good would not.

When we hope to intervene, we need to reflect more on the otherness of others. What makes others fail to meet our standards, excluding themselves from our midst? Without pretending to have a complete answer, I can suggest an aspect of an answer that speaks against ready intervention in the affairs of the excluded. To be excluded is to fail to travel in the world inhabited by others. A world is not a physical space; rather, it is a series of interpretations, beliefs, attitudes, and actions that allow people who share the world to comport themselves in predictable and more or less acceptable ways toward one another. I cannot be a part of the world of high society, to choose a small example, unless I learn how to select, at the proper moment, from among all those damned knives, forks, and spoons on the table.

The interpretations that constitute a world are both unstable and controversial. Having power, as Hobbes understood better than anyone, involves mastering interpretations (*Leviathan*, pt. 2, ch. 18). If I can determine what is or is not a reasonable way to believe, and behave and enforce my interpretation with sanctions, I have power over you. If you do not share my understandings, the threat of sanctions can only appear arbitrary. If our understandings are sufficiently distant, my rule and my world will seem incomprehensible and cruel.

I assume that many of those who are not a part of our "we" are other, not because of some indelible character flaw, but because of our failure to allow them to find a world in which they can live. If we pretend to let them go but continue to watch them like jailers, they will continue to experience domination by aliens from a world in which they do not belong.[6]

Really letting go would mean allowing groups of people to step outside our world and decide for themselves how to live. Much of the rhetoric of conservatism since the 1980s has borrowed from the radicalism of the 1960s. Conservatives speak the language of "empowerment." Indeed the term has become a staple of political discourse across the political spectrum. There are cogent uses for the word. For instance, Jack Kemp, while he was secretary of Housing and Urban Development, deployed the language of empowerment to promote home ownership and tenant management for people in housing projects. This was laudable. Nevertheless, caution is desirable concerning the language of empowerment. Empowerment is a gift from someone with power to someone with less power, but it is a dangerous gift. People who empower frequently retain their own power over those empowered. Letting go is different. When we let go, we leave others free to decide for themselves.

The notion of letting go carries radical implications. For instance, we normally assume that law enforcement is a state and local responsibility. We reserve the function of policing to subnational governments because we assume they are close to the problem of crime. In many cases, the bureaucracy downtown is as distant from neighborhood concerns as any agency in Washington. Were we to take localism more seriously, each neighborhood (not city) could pursue its own approach to safety and happiness.

Stuart Scheingold concludes his critique of "the myth of crime control" with a vision of "neighborhood justice."[7] He wants policing centered in the neighborhoods where the crimes occur rather than relying on centrally dispatched units and auto patrols. Despite his professed radicalism, Scheingold exhibits a commitment to experiments managed from a political center. A strong commitment to devolving power would be indicated by a willingness to trust neighborhoods to police themselves without interference.

Trusting neighborhoods to police themselves is risky business, but a uniform policy carries high costs as well. This is particularly true in minority communities. James Baldwin's image of the police officer in Harlem as "an occupying soldier in a bitterly hostile country" captures some of the realities of criminal justice quite well.[8] The provision of resources and freedom to these neighborhoods would carry on the tradition of republican localism in an energetic way.

Securing this energy and the unity to sustain it would require us to depart from the tradition of simply relying on voluntary associations freely (and often transiently) created to secure stronger bonds among the people in our localities. Most of us need instrumental associations to secure the conditions for the good life. Some of us need the permanent bonds of affection that constitute a community in the stronger sense. We may need to let go of those people who need strong communities and to give them the opportunity to form or sustain them, although a liberal community can never completely abandon the principle that those who wish to escape the constraints of a tightly knit community should be able to form less permanent alliances.

Will agrees, up to a point, that letting go is the precondition for reviving republican virtue. He accepts David Frum's argument that lessening government activity will enhance virtue in two ways. First, reducing government activity would allow tighter controls by localities, especially if we take a less expansive approach to enforcing antidiscrimination laws. Second, leaving people to fend for themselves would encourage what Margaret Thatcher calls the "vigorous virtues" needed for self-reliance (Will, interview).[9] Both of these claims are doubtful unless there is a more radical devolution of power than Will anticipates.

Merely pruning the welfare state and devolving power would not touch some of the main causes of rootlessness in modern society. Perhaps foremost among the sources of our freedom from traditional restraints are urbanization and job mobility. Enforcing morals through public approbation requires a public capable of watching those who might stray from the fold. It is most difficult to maintain surveillance by citizens in large cities. Frum is surely correct that the modern welfare state, with its independent source of income and its laws against discrimination, prevents the sort of economic restraints that fostered visions of virtue in the 19th century, but mobile capital has done as much. Will is right in believing that success in a commercial regime depends on cultivating virtues of self-reliance, but, again, mobile capital makes it difficult to sustain those virtues. When General Motors closed its plant in Flint, Michigan, a predictable decline followed in both the standard of living and the quality of behavior in the city. The virtues that lead to an industrious citizenry prevail only when people tie their actions to a reasonable expectation of success. Perhaps advocates of an unfettered economy are right in believing that the mere growth in opportunity would call forth the proper virtues, but Will has doubted the wisdom of mechanist economics throughout his career, and there is no clear reason to dispatch with his doubts now. For those people who claim that loosening the restraints on capital will call forth the vigorous virtues from the vast depths of human nature, we may respond with Hotspur's question: Will they come when you do call for them?

When we see industries freed from restraint, do we see solid character in the making? Economic power does not always translate to nurturing virtue. Stories of slavery and sweatshops in successful enterprises such as agriculture and the garment industry appear with revolting frequency. Will understands the problem of sacrificing virtue for profit well, which is why he still refuses the libertarian sirens on the farther shores.

Whatever the benefits of trimming the welfare state and devolving power to states and cities, these measures do not touch serious problems with promoting virtue. Will, along with conservatives like Robert Nisbet and James Q. Wilson, understands that we cannot separate character building from neighborhood building. The chances for developing good character are intimately related to the sorts of neighborhoods in which we live. How we do in this society depends heavily on where we come from. Decaying neighborhoods secrete failed lives. Many (like me) leave poor neighborhoods. Many (like me) would have remained in these neighborhoods without government assistance. If we leave government out of the equation, the only way of improving the life chances of many people is to change the communities from which they came.

If we leave enough room for local communities to develop republican virtue, a dilemma emerges. Devolving power enough to build character threatens to ruin unity. We really are a diverse people, and allowing "experiments in living" (to recur to Mill's phrase) permits a thousand Jim Joneses and David Koreshes to bloom. On the other hand, taking measures to secure conformity is not really devolving power. A forced overlay of conformity of the sort championed by the apostles of political correctness is likely to be ineffective and to produce resistance. The probable fruits of a planned devolution of power (apart from a contradiction in terms) would be a more oppressive order.

The tension between local initiative and public unity is an enduring tension within American political life. Will insists that tensions of this sort not be labeled "problems." To describe enduring conditions as problems is to wish them otherwise, but our tensions are integral to our political identity. Will writes: "America's story is about the tension between the celebration of energy, expressed in restless individualism, and the desire for community, which must be inclusive and exclusive" (MA, 94–95). Removing the tension would likely have the same effect as removing the tension from a suspension bridge—the entire thing would collapse.

We can view tensions differently, as sources of destruction tearing us apart. Viewed this way, the tensions that have endured should be eliminated by excising one pole of the tension. Demanding excision is appropriate only in a political culture that has lost its ability to harmonize diverse traditions. The call for excision is radical rather than conservative.

American culture may bear tensions that threaten to upset the balances we have sustained these past 200 years. If so, we may need radical reform of the sort Will refuses to sanction. If not, what is the role of a conservative critique? A viable political culture offers roles that a conservative critic can assume. The critic may claim that the delicate compromises we have maintained over the years are out of balance and need redressing. There is surely much of that sort of criticism in Will's writing, and it lends value to his work. The idea of restoration is central to his writing. Nevertheless, the values he champions—community and civic virtue—are secondary values in the American order. To put them center stage would be radical indeed. How then to champion these themes without securing, perhaps without wishing, their triumph?

One way to champion them is to urge nuances in public policy that do not radically alter our course but rather encourage adjustments in our attitude toward rights and duties. For example, Amitai Etzioni enunciates a high-sounding commitment to community, but one of his most serious policy recommendations involves establishing sobriety

checkpoints to discourage drunken driving.[10] There are serious constitutional and policy arguments for and against this measure, but no one
can seriously suggest that a decision about the program will fundamentally alter the character of the republic. Most of Will's proposals are like
Etzioni's. Will proposes measures that are well within the mainstream of
American political discourse. We usually get a nudge rather than a push
from him. Nevertheless, a conservative critique has more to recommend
it than a few mainstream policy recommendations.

One way to practice the politics of tension is to maintain remembrance of ideas that have become submerged. Remembrance is different
from nostalgia. Nostalgia longs for a past that is lost—often well lost.
Remembrance asks us to honor persons, places, things, and ideas that
are not in the forefront of our consciousness. Eric Voegelin captures the
theme of remembrance beautifully in choosing the epigraph to *The New
Science of Politics*. He quotes Richard Hooker: "Posterity may know we
have not loosely through silence permitted things to pass away as in a
dream." Even if community (better yet, the great community) and
republican virtue cannot be realized in their fullness without disrupting
a vital regime, they deserve the remembrance with which Will has
graced them. Even if they have limited applicability in our society, they
still serve as paradigms to which we can aspire in some aspects of our
lives. They are indeed central to a satisfying private life even though a
liberal regime cannot mandate the ideals.

Another service of a conservative critique is to actually maintain the
tension that our society needs. John Stuart Mill realized that a liberal
society must incorporate conservative elements to survive. A liberal
society does indeed run the risk of ruining itself through excessive individualism. To save liberalism, liberals need conservative voices to
restrain them.[11] Liberals, left to their own devices, are tempted to
march us toward illiberalism. Taken to extremes, political virtues
rapidly become vices. The energy, innovation, and freedom that liberalism loosens are dangerous, and liberals need sober people to remind
them of the dangers.

The most important contribution Will makes is to our intellectual life.
Michael Oakeshott conceives our intellectual life as a conversation.[12] A
conversation requires diverse voices. Remove conservatives from the discussion and it becomes markedly duller. The great sin of political correctness is
intellectual rather than moral or political. We need intelligent voices from
all quarters to sustain the life of the mind. Will stands out as a major voice
among 20th-century journalists in sustaining our conversation.

Notes and References

Chapter 1

1. Upon reading this sentence, Bernard Bray observed quite correctly that the notion of "mediation" is problematic. A mediator would transmit ideas and information two ways—to and from experts. Most journalism transmits one way, conveying authoritative thoughts to a lay public. Some of Will's best essays put those in power in touch with ordinary life. Most of the writings I survey transmit highbrow thought to a wider public. The thoughts of ordinary citizens are more difficult to systematize and summarize than those of elite writers.

2. See Benjamin Barber, *Strong Democracy: Participatory Politics for a New Age* (Berkeley: University of California Press, 1984) and Kai Nielsen, *Equality and Liberty: A Defense of Radical Egalitarianism* (Totowa, NJ: Rowman and Allanheld, 1985).

3. For good introductions to the debates about foundationalism and antifoundationalism, consult Kenneth Baynes et al., eds., *After Philosophy: End or Transformation?* (Cambridge: MIT Press, 1987) and John Rajchman and Cornell West, eds., *Post-analytic Philosophy* (New York: Columbia University Press, 1985).

4. Note that I describe moral judgments as correct rather than true; however, I do not want dogmatically to rule out the possibility of moral truths. What I want to affirm is a weaker notion of moral correctness involving judgment in congruence with a standard. I want to resist the foundational claim that there are well-demonstrated moral principles. This resistance is quite consistent with a serious search for moral truths. We cannot equate a search for transcendent truth with an acceptance of dogmatic metaphysics. For powerful affirmations that we can search for truth without claiming to possess it, see Michael Polanyi, *Knowing and Being* (Chicago: University Press, 1969); *Personal Knowledge: Towards a Post-critical Philosophy* (Chicago: University Press, 1958); *Science, Faith, and Society* (Chicago: University Press, 1964); *The Study of Man* (Chicago: University Press, 1959); and *The Tacit Dimension* (Garden City, NY: Anchor, 1966).

5. Michel Foucault, *Power/Knowledge: Selected Interviews and Other Writings 1972–1977,* ed. Colin Gordon (New York: Pantheon, 1980), 78–92.

6. *Suddenly: The American Idea Abroad and at Home 1986–1990* (New York: Free Press, 1990), 372, hereinafter cited in the text as SUD.

7. The idea that inquiry involves arrests in experience is advanced in Michael Oakeshott, *Experience and Its Modes* (Cambridge: University Press, 1933).

8. In more radical moments, I have described it as Augustinian anarchy, especially in "Augustinian Anarchy: Preliminary Formulations," a paper delivered at the 1989 meeting of the Southern Political Science Association in Atlanta, Georgia. My chief inspiration for invoking Augustine to support a liberal regime is Reinhold Niebuhr. Key works in his large corpus include *The Children of Light and the Children of Darkness: A Vindication of Democracy and a Critique of Its Traditional Defense* (New York: Charles Scribner's Sons, 1944); *An Interpretation of Christian Ethics* (New York: Meridian, 1956); *The Nature and Destiny of Man*, 2 vols. (New York: Charles Scribner's Sons, 1941, 1943); and *Moral Man and Immoral Society: A Study in Ethics and Politics* (New York: Charles Scribner's Sons, 1932). Another major influence on my brand of Augustinianism is Jacques Ellul. See especially *The Political Illusion*, trans. Konrad Kellen (New York: Vintage, 1972). Stephen Holmes recognizes that there has always been an Augustinian dimension to liberal thought. See *The Anatomy of Antiliberalism* (Cambridge: Harvard University Press, 1993), 59.

9. St. Augustine, *The City of God*, trans. Marcus Dodd (New York: Modern Library, 1950), 112–13.

10. Karl Barth, the fountainhead of Protestant neoorthodoxy, used the phrase "wholly other" to designate God. Barth attempted to apply his radically transcendent conception of deity to politics in *Community, State, and Church: Three Essays*, ed. Will Herberg (Garden City, NY: Anchor, 1960). For useful commentary, consult Rene De Visme Williamson, *Politics and Protestant Theology: An Interpretation of Tillich, Barth, Bonhoeffer, and Brunner* (Baton Rouge: Louisiana State University Press, 1976).

11. *The Moral Life and the Ethical Life* (Chicago: Regnery, 1963). As should become reasonably clear, my version of liberalism draws heavily on the work of Thomas Hobbes. I consider Hobbes (along with Spinoza and Locke) a truncated Augustinian—truncated in the sense of cutting off the transcendence that permeates Augustine's work while maintaining his dim view of human possibility. As Karl Löwith notes, there is a point at which Christian thought most assuredly intersects with skepticism. See *Meaning in History*, (Chicago: University Press, 1949), vi.

12. John B. Cobb Jr., *God and the World* (Philadelphia: Westminster Press, 1969). The notion of ethics as a set of fragile intimations may not be as robust as Augustine's conception of "natural law." When axiological realism combines with radical transcendentalism, however, intimations may be as robust as one can get. I discuss the idea of natural law in chapter 3 and chapter 5.

13. Immanuel Kant, *Perpetual Peace: A Philosophical Sketch*, 1st supp.

14. See William Gaylin et al., *Doing Good: The Limits of Benevolence* (New York: Pantheon, 1978).

15. See SUD, 206, and *The Morning After: American Successes and Excesses 1981–1986* (New York: Free Press, 1986), 94–95, hereinafter cited in the text as MA.

16. (New York: Macmillan, 1990).

17. For an interesting debate on the ethical and political significance of Will's writings on baseball, see Donald Kagan, "George Will's Baseball: A Conservative Critique" and George F. Will, "The Romantic Fallacy in Baseball: A Reply," *The Public Interest* (Fall 1990), 3–27.

18. Will's prognostications about the end of the cold war hardly match the confidence of his criticisms of our lack of resolve toward the Soviets. Note his predictions about Central America and the outcome of the cold war in *The New Season: A Spectator's Guide to the 1988 Election* (New York: Simon and Schuster, 1988), 55 and 142, hereinafter cited in the text as NS.

Chapter 2

1. Louis Hartz, *The Liberal Tradition in America* (New York: Harcourt Brace Jovanovich, 1955). For a sharply contrasting view, see Rogers M. Smith, "Beyond Tocqueville, Myrdal and Hartz: The Multiple Traditions in America," *The American Political Science Review* 87, no. 3 (September 1993): 549–66.

2. Guido De Ruggiero, *The History of European Liberalism,* trans. R. G. Collingwood (London: Oxford University Press, 1927).

3. Robert Bellah et al., *Habits of the Heart: Individualism and Commitment in American Life* (New York: Harper and Row, 1985).

4. Indeed, the 1994 crop of Republican politicians, following the lead of Speaker of the House Newt Gingrich, described themselves as "revolutionaries." That was probably exaggeration, but, as James J. Kilpatrick notes, their strong penchant for constitutional amendments creates serious doubt about the appropriateness of the label "conservative."

5. Peter Viereck, *Conservatism Revisited* (New York: Free Press, 1962), 143–44; and Clinton Rossiter, *Conservatism in America: The Thankless Persuasion* (New York: Vintage, 1962).

6. *The Pursuit of Virtue and Other Tory Notions* (New York: Simon and Schuster, 1982), 31, hereinafter cited in the text as PV.

7. *Statecraft as Soulcraft: What Government Does* (New York: Simon and Schuster, 1983), 35, hereinafter cited in the text as SS.

8. Confirming that Americans lack a common conception of the good would not establish that they lack a common conception of justice. One of the most influential strands of liberal thought in recent years argues that we cannot expect consensus on the good, but we can arrive at common convictions on justice. See John Rawls, *A Theory of Justice* (Cambridge, MA.: Belknap, 1971) and *Political Liberalism* (New York: Columbia University Press, 1993); Bruce A. Ackerman, *Social Justice in the Liberal State* (New Haven: Yale University Press, 1980); Charles E. Larmore, *Patterns of Moral Complexity* (Cambridge: University Press, 1987); and Stuart Hampshire, *Innocence and Experience* (Cambridge: Harvard University Press, 1989). A major challenge to the priority of the right over the good is Michael J. Sandel, *Liberalism and the Limits of Justice* (Cambridge: University Press, 1982). Recent liberal thought has reaffirmed the connection

between liberalism and the good. See especially William Galston, *Liberal Purposes: Goods, Virtues, and Diversity in the Liberal State* (Cambridge: University Press, 1991).

9. *The Pursuit of Happiness and Other Sobering Thoughts* (New York: Harper, 1979), 180–81, hereinafter cited in the text as PH.

10. *Restoration: Congress, Term Limits, and the Recovery of Deliberative Democracy* (New York: Free Press, 1992), 163, hereinafter cited in the text as RES.

11. Forming personality also depends on traditions and national character. Will appeals to these on many occasions. We do not know how malleable national character and traditions are, and Will offers no general theory of how traditions change or end.

12. For instance, Michael Sandel's *Liberalism and the Limits of Justice* is virtually devoid of reference to policy issues. Sandel does address contemporary issues in "Moral Argument and Liberal Toleration: Abortion and Homosexuality," *California Law Review* 77 (1989): 521–38, but he, like others who theorize about community, generally thrives on generalities.

13. Affirming the centrality of the good without defining it puts Will in the excellent company of Plato in *The Republic*, bk. 6. For an important contemporary argument that the good is real, binding, and indefinable, see Robert Pirsig, *Zen and the Art of Motorcycle Maintenance* (New York: Bantam, 1974). For recent attempts to develop communitarian conceptions of the good, see Amitai Etzioni, ed., *Rights and the Common Good: The Communitarian Perspective* (New York: St. Martin's Press, 1995).

14. Ludwig Wittgenstein, in his later writings, develops the idea that meaning is embodied in use. For good explorations of Wittgenstein's political significance, see John W. Danford, *Wittgenstein and Political Philosophy* (Chicago: University Press, 1978) and Hannah F. Pitkin, *Wittgenstein and Justice* (Berkeley: University of California Press, 1972). Michael Oakeshott lays bare the conservative implications of the view that meaning is embodied in linguistic and cultural practices. He argues that overreliance on "theory" savages vital ways of living. See especially his *Rationalism in Politics and Other Essays*, 2d ed. (Indianapolis: Liberty Press, 1991).

15. Compare Alasdair MacIntyre's statement of a "provisional conclusion about the good life for man: the good life for man is the life spent seeking for the good life for man, and the virtues necessary for the seeking are those which will enable us to understand what more and what else the good life for man is." *After Virtue* (Notre Dame: University Press, 1981). Like MacIntyre, Will stresses that the search for the good begins with a discussion that holds forth the possibility of meaningful conclusions. Unlike MacIntyre, Will seems to believe that "nature" offers a potential resting point for moral conclusions. MacIntyre wants to compare stories across cultures to determine which is (are?) best. "Science," for him, is one narrative structure among others needing comparison for justification. Will is much more prone to appeal directly to our common scientific standards to establish the naturalness and consequent rightness

of behavior. The propriety of affirming a unicultural norm is a subject to which I return in chapter 5.

16.   The literature on community and communitarianism is large and diffuse, and many authors conscripted to the communitarian cause deny that they belong. Some good texts to start a reader through the maze of this literature include Daniel Bell, *Communitarianism and its Critics* (Oxford: Clarendon, 1993); Robert N. Bellah et al., *Habits of the Heart* and *The Good Society* (New York: Vintage, 1992); Markate Daly, ed., *Communitarianism: A New Public Ethics* (Belmont, CA: Wadsworth, 1994); Amitai Etzioni, *The Spirit of Community* (New York: Touchstone, 1993); Robert Booth Fowler, *The Dance With Community: The Contemporary Debate in American Political Thought* (Lawrence: University of Kansas Press, 1991); Donald L. Gelpi, ed., *Beyond Individualism* (Notre Dame: University Press, 1989); Daniel Kemmis, *Community and the Politics of Place* (Norman: University of Oklahoma Press, 1990); Stephen Mulhall and Adam Swift, *Liberals and Communitarians* (Oxford: Blackwell, 1992); Robert A. Nisbet, *The Quest for Community* (Oxford: University Press, 1953); and Charles Taylor, *Sources of the Self: The Making of the Modern Identity* (Cambridge: Harvard University Press, 1989).

17.   The notion of essentially contested concepts was developed in W. B. Gallie, *Philosophy and the Historical Understanding,* 2d ed. (New York: Schocken, 1968), 157–91. For an important elaboration of Gallie's theme, see William E. Connolly, *The Terms of Political Discourse,* 2d ed. (Princeton: University Press, 1983), 9–44.

18.   Two books that illustrate senses of community while remaining concrete are Philip Abbott, *Seeking Many Inventions: The Idea of Community in America* (Knoxville: University of Tennessee Press, 1987) and Howard Rhiengold, *The Virtual Community: Homesteading on the Electronic Frontier* (Reading, MA: Addison-Wesley, 1993).

19.   The best overview of the debate is Mulhall and Swift, *Communitarians and Liberals.*

20.   Kallen, *Cultural Pluralism and the American Idea* (Philadelphia: University of Pennsylvania Press, 1956) and *Culture and Democracy in the United States* (New York: Boni and Liveright, 1924).

21.   Thick and thin are common metaphors in contemporary philosophical discourse. John Rawls, for instance, distinguishes his "thin theory of the good" from the versions advocated by writers such as Will. See *A Theory of Justice,* 395–452. A fascinating use of the metaphor that takes it to the heart of moral reasoning is Michael Walzer, *Thick and Thin: Moral Argument at Home and Abroad* (Notre Dame: University Press, 1994). Walzer uses the metaphor to argue that there are moral universals, but that these are largely subordinate to thicker local moralities. His usage and argument are quite consistent with the sort of federal liberalism I am defending, in which the national morality is thin while local morals are thick. It is quite possible to contend for a localism more radical than Walzer's. See, for example, Clifford Geertz, *Local Knowledge*

(New York: Basic Books, 1983). It is also possible to move closer to affirming moral universals without denying the reality and desirability for wide local variations. See James Q. Wilson, *The Moral Sense* (New York: Free Press, 1993). Will's position is quite close to that of Wilson, to whom Will has acknowledged a continuing intellectual debt.

22. See Rawls, *Political Liberalism,* 320–23.

23. A good introduction to the contemporary philosophical debates about virtue is John W. Chapman and William A. Galston, eds., *Virtue* (New York: New York University Press, 1992). Will's recent thinking on virtue is heavily influenced by James Q. Wilson, *The Moral Sense* and *On Character,* (Washington, DC: American Enterprise Institute, 1991).

24. "Beyond the Reach of Majorities: Closed Questions in the Open Society" (Ph.D. diss., Princeton University, 1968), 46–70, hereinafter cited in the text as BM.

25. Will correctly understands that Hobbes lowers the aims of political philosophy by comparison with the ancients. For classical and Christian thought, politics aims for the highest good (*summum bonum*). Hobbes doubts that we can agree on the highest good. Instead, we should orient ourselves by resisting the greatest evil (*summum malum*) and striving to avoid our worst fears (*De Homine,* ch. 11). See Leo Strauss, *The Political Philosophy of Hobbes: Its Basis and Genesis,* trans. Elsa M. Sinclair (Chicago: University Press, 1952), 6–29 and Eric Voegelin, *The New Science of Politics* (Chicago: University Press, 1952), 182–84. Hobbes understands that we cannot eradicate enthusiastic visions of the good and the fearless disruptions of public order that frequently ensue, but we can minimize them. Liberalism minimizes enthusiasm by privatizing visions of the good. Judith Shklar analyzes the philosophical psychology of classical liberalism in "The Liberalism of Fear," in *Liberalism and the Moral Life,* ed. Nancy Rosenblum (Cambridge: Harvard University Press, 1989). For an interesting criticism of Shklar, see Thomas L. Dumm, *united states* (Ithaca: Cornell University Press, 1994).

26. Hobbes was sensitive to the need for cultivating virtues as well. See R. E. Ewin, *Virtues and Rights: The Moral Philosophy of Thomas Hobbes* (Boulder, CO: Westview, 1991).

27. Thomas Hobbes, *Leviathan,* ch. 30; John Locke, *A Letter Concerning Toleration* (Indianapolis: Hackett, 1983); John Locke, *On the Reasonableness of Christianity As Delivered in the Scriptures* (Chicago: Regnery, 1964); John Milton, *Areopagitica* (London: 1644); Benedict Spinoza, *Tractatus Theologico-Politicus,* ch. 14; Roger Williams, *The Bloody Tenet of Persecution for Cause of Conscience* (London: 1644). The literature on civil religion is large and growing. Helpful studies include Robert N. Bellah, *The Broken Covenant* (New York: Seabury, 1975); David Chidester, *Patterns of Power* (Englewood Cliffs, NJ: Prentice Hall, 1988), 81–109; Sanford Levinson, *Constitutional Faith* (Princeton: University Press, 1988); Leroy S. Rouner, ed., *Civil Religion and Political Theory* (Notre Dame: University Press, 1986); Ellis Sandoz, *A Government of Laws* (Baton Rouge:

Louisiana State University Press, 1990), 51–82; and Eric Voegelin, *The New Science of Politics,* 76–106.

28.   Early modern liberals frequently directed their fire at "enthusiasm" understood as the conviction that God had infused a special understanding into the soul of someone obligated to act on God's will. Enthusiasm was one of Hobbes's regular targets.

29.   See William A. Galston, *Liberal Purposes;* Stephen Macedo, *Liberal Virtues* (Oxford: University Press, 1990); Judith Shklar, *Ordinary Vices* (Cambridge: Harvard University Press, 1984).

30.   Aristotle contends that the moral virtues aim at correctness rather than truth. Teaching virtue requires inculcating good habits rather than sound understanding (*Nicomachean Ethics,* bk. 6, ch. 9).

31.   I discuss Will's approach to legal tolerance in chapter 3.

32.   For a good discussion of modern conceptions of interest, consult Albert O. Hirschman, *The Passions and the Interests: Political Arguments for Capitalism before its Triumph* (Princeton: University Press, 1977).

33.   James Q. Wilson stresses the centrality of self-control for good character in *The Moral Sense,* 79–98.

34.   For good discussions of neutrality in liberal thought, see R. Bruce Douglass et al., eds., *Liberalism and the Good* (New York: Routledge, 1990). Part of the problem with cultivating bourgeois virtues lies in their inadequacy for a fully satisfying life. A wholly bourgeois society would be insufferable— lacking in the graces brought by art, philosophy, and spirituality. The genius of liberalism (when it works well) is that it allows for, even encourages, expression of temperaments fundamentally at odds with itself.

35.   The problem of maintaining the virtues necessary for a complex, modern economy is addressed in Francis Fukuyama, *Trust: The Social Virtues and the Creation of Prosperity* (New York: Free Press, 1995).

36.   For an excellent critique of the reading of Aristotle as a strong communitarian thinker, see Bernard Yack, *The Problems of a Political Animal: Community, Justice, and Conflict in Aristotelian Political Thought* (Berkeley: University of California Press, 1993). Yack observes that those who build an ethic of community obligation on Aristotle's notion of "political friendship" forget that he classifies it as friendship of advantage rather than complete friendship. Aristotle, like Hobbes, views the community as a source of private advantage more than as an entity worthy of allegiances independent of the services it performs. Were Aristotle's bedrock allegiance to the community, he would probably not have fled Athens.

37.   The literature on classical republicanism is vast. Most of it stems from J. G. A. Pocock's classic study *The Machiavellian Moment* (Princeton: University Press, 1969). I explore Will's contribution to republican discourse in chapter 6.

38.   One can construe patriotism in such a way as to make it seem incompatible with a liberal regime. Much of the attempt to distance liberalism

from patriotic feelings and actions relies on claiming that liberals are so committed to universalism and individualism that they cannot support the collective will to act that patriotism requires. Liberalism may indeed conflict with some types of patriotism, and some extreme liberal theories may exclude all forms of communal loyalty, but we can hardly ignore the effective nationalism and war-making capacity of actual liberal regimes. For observations concerning the tension between liberalism and loyalty, see Alasdair MacIntyre, "Is Patriotism a Virtue," in *Communitarianism: A New Public Ethics,* ed. Markate Daly, 307–18.

39. Josiah Royce's *The Philosophy of Loyalty* (New York: Macmillan, 1920) remains one of the finest attempts to formulate a notion of loyalty not confined by the parochial fervor of patriotism. Will has some appreciative remarks on Royce in BM, 348–49. The sort of loyalty I seek is captured well by Jean Bethke Elshtain: "We can be patriots. . . . But it is a *chastened* patriot I have in mind, men and women who have learned from the past. Rejecting the counsels of cynicism, they modulate the rhetoric of high patriotic purpose by keeping alive the distancing voice of ironic remembrance and recognition of the way patriotism can shade into the excesses of nationalism; recognition of the fact that patriotism in the form of armed civic virtue is a dangerous chimera. The chastened patriot is committed *and* detached: enough apart so that she and he can be reflective about patriotic ties and loyalties, cherishing many loyalties rather than valorizing one alone" *Women and War* (New York: Basic Books, 1987), 252–53. Rob Waters suggested that Russell Kirk provides a better distinction between patriotism (a virtue) and nationalism (a vice). I find the distinction appealing but resist it for two reasons. First, I prefer a nongendered word. Second, I, along with Will, want to recommend the much neglected writings of Josiah Royce, and the term "loyalty" allows that. Third, Americans who practice nationalistic excesses are the people most likely to describe themselves as patriots.

40. See Rawls, *Political Liberalism,* 205–6.

41. "Good Will," *American Spectator,* February 1994, 64–65.

42. For a more recent assessment, see *The Leveling Wind: Politics, the Culture, and Other News, 1990–1994* (New York: Viking, 1994), 265–82, hereinafter cited in the text as LW.

43. *Demosclerosis,* (New York: Random House, 1994); *Dead Right* (New York: Basic Books, 1994).

44. John C. Calhoun, *A Disquisition on Government* (Indianapolis: Bobbs-Merrill, 1953).

45. Bennett expresses his views on the connection between government and morals in *The Devaluing of America: The Fight for Our Culture and Our Children* (New York: Summit, 1992). A more interesting, less government-centered work is his edited volume *The Book of Virtues: A Treasury of Great Moral Stories* (New York: Simon and Schuster, 1993).

46. There is quite a distance between "values," which denote subjective attitudes and beliefs, and "virtues," which are habits and dispositions known to

contribute to a good life. It is difficult indeed to see how a government could inculcate values that would somehow improve lives, especially while denying their binding character. See Gertrude Himmelfarb, *The Demoralization of Society: From Victorian Virtues to Modern Values* (New York: Knopf, 1995), 3–20.

Chapter 3

1. For useful perspectives on the philosophy of constitutionalism, see Edward S. Corwin, *Corwin on the Constitution,* vol. 1, ed. Richard Loss (Ithaca, NY: Cornell University Press, 1981), 45–230; Carl J. Friedrich, *Constitutional Government and Democracy: Theory and Practice in Europe and America,* 4th ed. (Waltham, MA: Blaisdell, 1968); and Charles H. McIlwain, *Constitutionalism, Ancient and Modern* (Ithaca, NY: Cornell University Press, 1940).

2. Contrast Will's view with that of Bruce Ackerman, who thinks everything in the Constitution is amendable by both formal amendment and by the consensus of informal supermajorities. See Ackerman, *We the People,* vol. 1, *Foundations* (Cambridge, MA: Belknap, 1991).

3. Edmund Burke, "Speech on the Representation of the Commons in Parliament," *Selected Writings and Speeches,* ed. Peter J. Stanlis (Chicago: Regnery, 1964), 330.

4. The most famous appeal to popular sovereignty by an American occurs in Stephen Douglas's defense of slavery in his debates with Lincoln. See Harold Holzer, ed., *The Lincoln-Douglas Debates* (New York: Harper, 1993).

5. Edward S. Corwin, *Corwin on the Constitution,* 79–139 and 195–212; Carl J. Friedrich, *Transcendent Justice: The Religious Dimension of Constitutionalism* (Durham, NC: Duke University Press, 1964).

6. Cicero, *On the Commonwealth,* trans. George H. Sabine and Stanley B. Smith (Indianapolis: Bobbs-Merrill, n.d.), 215–16.

7. St. Augustine, *On Free Will,* bk. I, sec. 5, in *Augustine: Earlier Writings,* ed. and trans. John H. S. Burleigh (Philadelphia: Westminster, 1953), 118. See also St. Thomas Aquinas, *Summa Theologica,* I–II, q. 95, 2d art.

8. See Edgar Bodenheimer, *Jurisprudence: The Philosophy and Method of the Law,* 2d ed. (Cambridge: Harvard University Press, 1974), 31–170; Carl J. Friedrich, *The Philosophy of Law in Historical Perspective,* 2d ed. (Chicago: University Press, 1963), 57–188; Martin P. Golding, *Philosophy of Law* (Englewood Cliffs, NJ: Prentice Hall, 1975), 24–51; and Edmund L. Pincoffs, *Philosophy of Law: A Brief Introduction* (Belmont, CA: Wadsworth, 1991), 89–141.

9. The phrase "a government of laws, not of men" captures the spirit of constitutionalism. The phrase comes from James Harrington, who adapted the phrase from Aristotle's *Politics.* See Ellis Sandoz, *A Government of Laws: Political Theory, Religion, and the American Founding* (Baton Rouge: Louisiana State University Press, 1990), 228–31.

10. Robert Bork, *The Tempting of America: The Political Seduction of the Law* (New York: Touchstone, 1991). Will's comments on the controversy surrounding Bork's nomination to the Supreme Court are in SUD, 335–58.

11. The fifth Amendment also contains a Due Process Clause, but little litigation has centered on it.

12. The double standard on property rights and other civil liberties in the post–1937 Court is analyzed in Henry J. Abraham and Barbara A. Perry, *Freedom and the Court,* 6th ed. (New York: Oxford University Press, 1994), 9–29.

13. Ronald Dworkin, *Taking Rights Seriously* (Cambridge: Harvard University Press, 1978).

14. Eric Voegelin, *The Nature of Law and Related Legal Writings* (Baton Rouge: Louisiana State University Press, 1991).

15. Stephen L. Carter, *The Confirmation Mess: Cleaning Up the Federal Appointments Process* (New York: Basic Books: 1994), 228–29.

16. Actually, the "rule of thumb" originally was rather precise within a tolerance narrower than, say, using a "stone" as a measure of weight. The rule of thumb forbade a husband from beating his wife with a stick thicker than his thumb. Fortunately, the phrase has been entirely severed, and I emphasize "severed" and "entirely," from its original intention.

17. Theories of original meaning (to which Will appears to subscribe) are frequently lumped with theories of original intent, but they differ. Original meaning refers to the way words were commonly understood at the time of the founding, which can differ from the way the drafters, signatories, or ratifiers wanted the words understood.

18. See Lief Carter, *An Introduction to Constitutional Interpretation: Cases in Law and Religion* (New York: Longman, 1991) and *Reason in Law,* 3d ed. (Glenview, IL: Scott, Foresman, 1988).

19. Patrick Devlin, *The Enforcement of Morals* (London: Oxford University Press, 1965); Walter Berns, *For Capital Punishment: Crime and the Morality of the Death Penalty* (New York: Basic Books, 1974).

20. James Q. Wilson concludes that early punishment of juveniles, even if it is mild, will serve to rehabilitate, but that severe punishments later in a criminal career do not appear to affect rates of recidivism. See *Thinking about Crime,* 2d ed. (New York: Vintage, 1985), 162–77.

21. The seamier side of a punitive legal culture is explored in Stuart A. Scheingold, *The Politics of Street Crime: Criminal Process and Cultural Obsession* (Philadelphia: Temple University Press, 1991) and *The Politics of Law and Order: Street Crime and Public Policy* (New York: Longman, 1984).

22. Wilson, *Thinking About Crime,* 75–89; *On Character,* 25–39.

23. Wilson, *Thinking about Crime,* 117–44; James Q. Wilson and Richard J. Herrnstein, *Crime and Human Nature* (New York: Touchstone, 1985), 489–507.

24. *Dennis v. U.S.,* 341 U.S. 494, 71 S. Ct. 857, 95 L. Ed. 1137 (1951).

25. Upon reading this, Rob Waters noted correctly that the Germans have kept extremists out of government, which is, of course, a major achievement. Whether this result is more attributable to repression or to other cultural and institutional factors is difficult to ascertain.

Chapter 4

1. Some important contributions to the literature on abortion include Barbara Hinkson Craig and David M. O'Brien, *Abortion and American Politics* (Chatham, NJ: Chatham House, 1993); Ronald Dworkin, *Life's Dominion: An Argument about Abortion, Euthanasia, and Individual Freedom* (New York: Vintage, 1994); John T. Noonan Jr., *A Private Choice: Abortion in America in the Seventies* (New York: Life Cycle, 1979); and Laurence H. Tribe, *Abortion: The Clash of Absolutes* (New York: Norton, 1992).

2. For defenses of the view that liberal regimes ought take issues out of the public arena, see Bruce Ackerman, "Why Dialogue?" *Journal of Philosophy* 86 (1989): 5–22; Stephen Holmes, *Passions and Constraint: On the Theory of Liberal Democracy* (Chicago: University Press, 1995), 202–35.

3. Mary Ann Glendon, *Abortion and Divorce in Western Law: American Failures and European Challenges* (Cambridge: Harvard University Press, 1987) and James Davison Hunter, *Before the Shooting Begins: Searching for Democracy in America's Culture War* (New York: Free Press, 1994).

4. Glendon generalizes this argument beyond the issues of abortion and divorce in *Rights Talk,* (New York: Free Press, 1991).

5. For a broad analysis of our "culture wars," see James Davison Hunter, *Culture Wars: The Struggle to Define America* (New York: Basic Books, 1991).

6. For a more detailed analysis of public opinion on abortion, consult Elizabeth Adell Cook et al., *Between Two Absolutes: Public Opinion and the Politics of Abortion* (Boulder, CO: Westview, 1992).

7. Sandel, "Moral Argument and Liberal Toleration," 522.

8. I recall a pro-life cartoon that sarcastically portrayed Lincoln temporizing on the issue of slavery, thereby creating an invidious comparison with our current leaders. The trouble with the cartoon was this: Compromise on slavery was consistently Lincoln's policy. See Garry Wills, *Certain Trumpets: The Call of Leaders* (New York: Simon and Schuster, 1994), 13–17.

9. Glendon agrees that rights talk is endemic to American discourse. What we should do, she argues, is to resist extending it. Consequently, she contends that we should not add the language of "welfare rights" to our constitutional repertoire even though such language has had few deleterious consequences in Europe. Here we would likely take the rights claims more seriously than the Europeans. See "Rights in Twentieth Century Constitutions," in *Rights and the Common Good,* ed. Amitai Etzioni, 27–36.

10. Elizabeth Mensch and Alan Freeman argue that abortion is more discussible than we had thought, especially if we reintroduce theological issues into the debate. I am more skeptical. Most of their best arguments show that theologically sophisticated people can have civil moral debates. I do not doubt that, but I do doubt that these arguments can occur in a large-scale political arena. See *The Politics of Virtue: Is Abortion Debatable?* (Durham, NC: Duke University Press, 1993).

11. *Why Americans Hate Politics* (New York: Simon and Schuster, 1991), 343.

12. Whatever Will's doubts about the legal theories guiding the courts, our judges have never acceded to the view that there is, *simpliciter,* a right to pornographic expression. The main issue has been whether we can regulate pornography without endangering protected expression.

13. See Joseph Campbell, *The Inner Reaches of Outer Space* (New York: Harper and Row, 1986) and Joseph Campbell with Bill Moyers, *The Power of Myth* (New York: Doubleday, 1988), 3–35.

14. Carle Jackson reminded me that people raised on westerns are people who have celebrated the virtues of genocide.

15. Walker Percy, America's finest physician, envisioned an end to the world when "conservatives have begun to fall victim to unseasonable rages, delusions of conspiracies, high blood pressure, and large-bowel complaints. Liberals are more apt to contract sexual impotence, morning terror, and a feeling of abstraction of the self from itself" (*Love in the Ruins: The Adventures of a Bad Catholic at a Time near the End of the World* [New York: Dell, 1971], 19).

16. Indeed, Will has cited data that refute claims concerning the deleterious effects of pornography (LW, 30).

17. Gordon Hawkins and Francis E. Zimring, *Pornography in a Free Society* (Cambridge: University Press, 1988).

18. For a critique of Will's view of pornography as violence against women, see Kimberle Williams Crenshaw, "Beyond Racism and Misogyny: Black Feminism and 2 Live Crew," in *Words that Wound: Critical Race Theory, Assaultive Speech, and the First Amendment,* by Charles Lawrence et al. (Boulder, CO: Westview, 1993), 111–32.

19. The Supreme Court struck down a St. Paul "hate crime" statute partially on the ground that it constituted an unconstitutional regulation of content and partially because the statute was vague and overbroad. Justice Scalia rejected the statute because it was underbroad; i.e., it selectively punished some hate crimes while allowing other expressions of hate to go unpunished. See *R.A.V. v. City of St. Paul,* 112 S. Ct. 2538; 120 L. Ed. 2d 305 (1992). The United States Court of Appeals for the Seventh Circuit struck down an ordinance punishing "pornography" as a practice that discriminates against women declaring, per Easterbrook, "the Constitution forbids the state to declare one perspective right and silence opponents." See *American Booksellers Association, Inc. v. Hudnut,* 771 F. 2d 323 (7th Cir. 1985).

20. Banning misogyny would mean censoring figures like Aristotle, Machiavelli, Nietzsche, Rousseau, and Schopenhauer—a step I doubt Will would undertake. Restricting the ban to violent misogyny would still set the scissors to passages in Machiavelli and Nietzsche.

21. The Supreme Court felt compelled to overturn a local finding that the film *Carnal Knowledge* is obscene (*Jenkins v. Ga,* 418 U.S. 153 [1974]). By both trusting our censors (local prosecutors and juries) and (thankfully) not

trusting them fully, we ensure litigation. Of course, the argument from mistrust can be too dogmatic. Eventually, we say no even as we are aware of the danger. Consequently, we just say no to child pornography. Even here the danger is real. We punish people for possessing material involving children even if the material is not pornographic.

22. "Everything which is bad in morality is also bad in politics. But the preacher stops at personal evil, the magistrate sees only the public consequences; the former has as his object only man's perfection, to which man never attains; the latter, only the good of the state insofar as it can be attained; thus all that is right to blame from the pulpit ought not to be punished by the laws" (Jean-Jacques Rousseau, *Politics and the Arts: Letter to M. D'Alembert on the Theater*, ed. and trans. Allan Bloom [New York: Cornell University Press, 1960], 109). In explaining why divine law is needed to supplement natural law, St. Thomas Aquinas observes that "as Augustine says, human law cannot punish or forbid all evil deeds, since, while aiming at doing away with all evils, it would do away with many good things, and would hinder the advance of the common good, which is necessary for human intercourse" (*Summa Theologica*, I–II, q. 91, art. 4., from St. Thomas Aquinas, *On Law, Morality, and Politics*, ed. William P. Baumgarth and Richard J. Regan [Indianapolis: Hackett, 1988], 24). St. Augustine feared that the absence of prostitutes would lead men to rape and other repulsive behavior.

23. *Politics and the Arts,* 64–65.

24. *Pensées,* 139, 140, 141, 142, 143, 168, 170.

25. For compelling arguments about the distorting effects of modern media on our civic consciousness, see Neil Postman, *Amusing Ourselves to Death: Public Discourse in the Age of Show Business* (New York: Penguin, 1986). For celebrations of the dislocating effects of mass media as well as media's roots in cultural archetypes, see Camille Paglia, *Sexual Personae: Art and Decadence from Nefertiti to Emily Dickinson* (New Haven: Yale University Press, 1990); *Sex, Art, and American Culture* (New York: Vintage, 1992); and *Vamps and Tramps* (New York: Vintage, 1994). Will certainly understands that the principle aim of television is to entertain—and how that impulse drives every aspect including televised news (PH, 84–86).

26. Trans. Michael Henry Heim (New York: Penguin, 1980), 228.

27. For an excellent history of the affirmative action controversy, see John David Skrentny, *The Ironies of Affirmative Action* (Chicago: University Press, 1996). For an introduction to the key arguments in the debate, consult Barbara R. Bergmann, *In Defense of Affirmative Action* (New York: Basic Books, 1996); Carl Cohen, *Naked Racial Preference: The Case Against Affirmative Action* (New York: Madison, 1995); Gertrude Ezorsky, *Racism and Justice: The Case for Affirmative Action* (Ithaca, NY: Cornell University Press, 1991); and Nicolaus Mills, ed., *Debating Affirmative Action: Race, Gender, Ethnicity, and the Politics of Inclusion* (New York: Delta, 1994).

28. Amy Gutmann, *Democratic Education* (Princeton: University Press, 1987), 179–80.

29. *Regents of the University of California v. Bakke*, 438 U.S. 265 (1978).

30. During most of the latter half of the 20th century, the role of genetics in racial differences has been absent from policy debates. That changed dramatically with the publication of Richard J. Herrnstein and Charles Murray, *The Bell Curve: Intelligence and Class Structure in American Life* (New York: Simon and Schuster, 1995).

31. The literature on the "underclass" is vast. Some works worth consulting are Ken Auletta, *The Underclass* (New York: Vintage, 1983); Christopher Jencks and Paul E. Peterson, eds., *The Urban Underclass* (Washington, DC: Brookings, 1991); Michael B. Katz, *The Undeserving Poor: From the War on Poverty to the War on Welfare* (New York: Pantheon, 1989); Lawrence M. Mead, *The New Politics of Poverty: The Nonworking Poor in America* (New York: Basic Books, 1992); Charles Murray, *Losing Ground: American Social Policy 1950–1980* (New York: Basic Books, 1984); and William Julius Wilson, *The Truly Disadvantaged: The Inner City, the Underclass, and Public Policy* (Chicago: University Press, 1987).

32. That concept explains the fatuousness of the argument that asking for an ordinance against discrimination against gay people is asking for "special rights." No one deserves protection against discrimination unless there has been discrimination. If there has been discrimination, it will necessarily involve reference to group status. The issues then become: Can we prove the discrimination? If so, was the discrimination reasonable? Is there a suitable remedy for the discrimination?

33. Many critics and defenders of affirmative action believe that it only can apply as a remedy for past discrimination. In criticizing Ron Brown's statement that affirmative action addresses current discrimination, Richard Kahlenberg retorts that "this is a relatively new theory, which conveniently elides the fact that preferences were supposed to be temporary. It also stands logic on its head. While discrimination undoubtedly still exists, the Civil Rights Act of 1964 was meant to address prospective discrimination. Affirmative action— discrimination in itself—makes sense only to the extent that there is a current day legacy of *past* discrimination which new prospective laws cannot reach back and remedy." See "Class Not Race," *New Republic* (3 April 1995): 24. This argument is not correct because it assumes that the legal remedy is for an individual against whom discrimination has occurred. Rather, the remedy gives relief to a group against whom discrimination has continued. The relief should indeed be temporary. When the pattern has ceased, the remedy should lapse (although it may be reinvoked). Many affirmative action programs should be reviewed and suspended on this ground. The currently popular idea that class is a good "marker" for race is not particularly convincing. Discrimination in, for instance, the selection of receptionists for some industries, is well documented. Even among people of color who "succeed," the insults of discrimination are hardly foreign. See Lois Benjamin, *The Black Elite: Facing the Color Line in the Twilight of the Twentieth Century* (Chicago: Nelson Hall, 1992); Ellis Cose, *The Rage of a Privileged Class* (New York: Harper, 1993); and Jake Lamar, *Bourgeois Blues: An*

American Memoir (New York: Plume, 1991). For general assessments of the continuing presence of race in American life, see Thomas Byrne Edsal and Mary Edsal, *Chain Reaction: The Impact of Race, Rights, and Taxes on American Politics* (New York: Norton, 1992); William W. Goldsmith and Edward J. Blakely, *Separate Societies: Poverty and Inequality in U.S. Cities* (Philadelphia: Temple, 1992); and Andrew Hacker, *Two Nations: Black and White, Separate, Hostile, Unequal* (New York: Charles Scribner's Sons, 1992).

34. In many cases the government creates patterns of behavior that stifle opportunity. For instance, the governmental policies regulating native American populations have created a way of life much inferior to the one supplanted. Carle Jackson called this point to my attention.

35. Bill Bryson, *The Mother Tongue: English and How It Got That Way* (New York: Morrow, 1990); Robert McCrum et al., *The Story of English* (New York: Viking, 1986).

36. Harold Bloom defends the thesis that western literature is aesthetically great without affirming that it is morally uplifting. See *The Western Canon: The Books and the School of the Ages* (New York: Harcourt Brace and Company, 1994). For the argument that an artist ought to take moral responsibility in creating a work of art, see John Gardner, *On Moral Fiction* (New York: Basic Books, 1977). I think that art can enrich our moral lives by enlarging our imaginations, but there is no necessary connection between imagination and virtue. Some grand aesthetes are dreadful people; some simple folk are sublimely good.

37. For the argument that acceptance of discord is the genius of liberal living, see Isaiah Berlin, *Four Essays on Liberty* (Oxford: University Press, 1969).

38. For a valuable exploration of the role of dissimulation in philosophy, see Leo Strauss, *Persecution and the Art of Writing* (Chicago: University Press, 1952).

39. "Comment," in *Multiculturalism: Examining the Politics of Recognition*, 2d ed., ed. Amy Gutmann (Princeton: University Press, 1994), 81. This book provides a good introduction to key philosophical issues concerning multiculturalism. Other works worth consulting are John Arthur and Amy Shapiro, eds., *Campus Wars: Multi-culturalism and the Politics of Difference* (Boulder, CO: Westview Press, 1995); Mark Edmundson, ed., *Wild Orchids and Trotsky* (New York: Penguin, 1993); Robert Hughes, *Culture of Complaint: The Fraying of America* (New York: Oxford University, 1993); Mark Poster, ed., *Politics, Theory, and Contemporary Culture* (New York: Columbia University Press, 1993); Edward W. Said, *Culture and Imperialism* (New York: Vintage, 1993); and Arthur M. Schlesinger, *The Disuniting of America: Reflections on a Multicultural Society* (New York: Norton, 1992). It is not clear in what sense "we" have "a" culture. In any event, no useful purpose comes from assuming that culture is an impermeable block isolated from other cultures. Western culture today would be without Aristotle if Arabic scholars had not preserved his work.

40. Matthew Arnold, *Culture and Anarchy,* ed. J. Dover Wilson (Cambridge: University Press, 1960), 70.

41. *The Sociological Imagination* (Oxford: University Press, 1959), 199. I have had success teaching B. F. Skinner's *Walden Two* and Ayn Rand's *The Virtue of Selfishness.*

42. *The Revolt of the Elites and the Betrayal of Democracy* (New York: Norton, 1995), 176. See also Russell Jacoby, *Dogmatic Wisdom: How the Culture Wars Divert Education and Distract America* (New York: Anchor, 1994), 21–28. For generally sound critiques of the research culture that dominates our universities, see Russell Jacoby, *The Last Intellectuals: American Culture in the Age of Academe* (New York: Noonday, 1987); Charles Sykes, *ProfScam: Professors and the Demise of Higher Education* (New York: St. Martin's Press, 1988).

43. Russell Jacoby, *Dogmatic Wisdom,* 105.

44. The most perceptive commentator on manners in contemporary society is Miss Manners (the pen name for Judith Martin). See *Miss Manners' Guide to Excruciatingly Correct Behavior* (New York: Warner, 1982) and *Miss Manners' Guide to Rearing Perfect Children* (New York: Atheneum, 1984). For Will's appreciative comments on Miss Manners, see MA, 62–64 and 386–87; SUD, 382–83.

45. See John Stuart Mill, "The Utility of Religion," in *Nature and the Utility of Religion,* ed. George Nakhnikan (Indianapolis: Bobbs-Merrill, 1958), 45–80.

46. For an analysis of our culture of victimization, see Charles J. Sykes, *A Nation of Victims: The Decay of the American Character* (New York: St. Martin's Press, 1992).

47. William F. Buckley, *God and Man at Yale: The Superstitions of Academic Freedom* (South Bend, IN: Gateway, 1951, 1977).

48. *Chaplinsky v. New Hampshire,* 315 U.S. 568 (1942).

49. Russell Kirk, *A Program for Conservatives,* 2d ed. (Chicago: Regnery, 1962), 20–50.

50. Christopher Lasch, *The True and Only Heaven: Progress and its Critics* (New York: Norton, 1991). Lasch understood quite well that progress can both promote authoritarian purposes and justify an unrestrained market. He groped, in his last years, toward a populist alternative to both. His stress on equality led him to stress restraints on our passions that resonated well with many cultural conservatives. See especially *The Culture of Narcissism* (New York: Norton, 1978) and *Haven in a Heartless World: The Family Besieged* (New York: Basic Books, 1975).

51. *Illiberal Education: The Politics of Race and Sex on Campus* (New York: Free Press, 1991). D'Souza is a poor role model for conservatives who wish to defend high standards of scholarship in the academy. Many of D'Souza's factual errors are exposed in John K. Wilson, *The Myth of Political Correctness: The Conservative Attack on Higher Education* (Durham, NC: Duke University Press, 1995).

52. The examples that Will cites do not clarify whether the professors with whom he commiserates were badgered out of teaching preferred courses by mere protests or by formal charges (LW, 119–21).

53. Eric Voegelin, *Autobiographical Reflections,* ed. Ellis Sandoz (Baton Rouge: Louisiana State University Press, 1989), 57–58.

54. Plato, *The Laws,* bk. 4, 718–23.

55. "She Stumbles (Elegantly) upon Good P.C.," *Jackson (MS) Clarion Ledger,* 25 June 1995, 7(E).

Chapter 5

1. For good reviews on the current (highly inconclusive) research on the genetic basis of homosexuality, see Chandler Burr, "Homosexuality and Biology," *Atlantic Monthly* (March 1993): 47–65; and Richard Horton, "Is Homosexuality Inherited?" *New York Review of Books* (13 July 1995): 36–41.

2. *Bowers v. Hardwick,* 478 U.S. 186 (1986).

3. The rhetoric of localism is popular in Republican circles. Why do conservative intellectuals consistently fail to notice the inconsistency between the rhetoric and these antigay initiatives?

4. Devlin, *The Enforcement of Morals,* 1–25. Devlin admits that the purported harms from changing these laws are unproved. For a critique of Devlin, see H. L. A. Hart, *Law, Liberty, and Morality* (Stanford: University Press, 1963).

5. I know of almost no one who seriously believes that all forms of sexual behavior are equally valuable or equally acceptable. There are those who claim that all consensual sex acts among adults should be allowed, but that hardly robs a libertarian of the capacity to condemn some sexual behavior. Again, liberal societies distinguish between legality and morality.

6. For good introductions to the theory of natural law, consult A. P. Entreves, *Natural Law: An Introduction to Legal Philosophy,* 2d ed. (London: Hutchinson, 1970) and Paul E. Sigmund, *Natural Law in Political Thought* (Cambridge, MA: Winthrop Press, 1971). For a sophisticated defense of natural law, see John Finnis, *Natural Law and Natural Rights* (Oxford: University Press, 1980).

7. Aristotle explores whether justice is natural or conventional. He concludes that it is partly natural and partly conventional. Nowhere does Aristotle claim that the standard of natural justice forms a law, however (*Rhetoric,* 1373b).

8. See St. Thomas Aquinas, *Summa Theologica,* II–II, 154. St. Augustine contends that the men of Sodom acquired a taste for one another through the force of habit and customary approval. He anticipated God's judgment on all who follow their example (*The City of God,* bk. 16, ch. 30) John Boswell has argued that Christian intolerance of homosexuality has not always dominated Christian thought. See his *Christianity, Social Tolerance, and Homosexuality: Gay People in Western Europe from the Beginning of the Christian Era to the Fourteenth Century* (Chicago: University Press, 1980). In any case, antigay themes have

been present in major strands of the tradition. These themes are quite consistent with the strong strain of asceticism in Christian thought. For good reviews of the interaction between asceticism and Christian thought on sexuality, see Peter Brown, *The Body and Society: Men, Women, and Sexual Renunciation in Early Christianity* (New York: Columbia University Press, 1988) and Elaine Pagels, *Adam, Eve, and the Serpent* (New York: Random House, 1988).

9. The triumph of antiteleology and the mechanist versions of biology that have frequently accompanied it has not been universal. See Theodosius Dobzhansky, *The Biological Basis of Human Freedom* (New York: Columbia University Press, 1956); Floyd Matson, *The Broken Image: Man, Science, and Society* (New York: Braziller, 1964); Ronald Munson, ed., *Man and Nature: Philosophical Issues in Biology* (New York: Delta, 1971); Hans Jonas, *The Phenomenon of Life: Toward a Philosophical Biology* (New York: Harper and Row, 1966); and Hans Jonas, *Philosophical Essays: From Ancient Creed to Technological Man* (Chicago: University Press, 1974).

10. *Nicomachean Ethics,* 1148b. For commentary, consult K. J. Dover, *Greek Homosexuality,* 2d ed. (Cambridge: Harvard University Press, 1989), 167–70.

11. Aristotle's cosmology includes perversions of nature—things that do not live up to their true essence. These things may be condemned, but the condemnation is not moral since ethics concerns choices. Because the defining essence of humanity is reason, there would be no plausible basis for claiming that desire for members of the same sex perverts our telos. Aristotle knew too many reasonable men exhibiting this desire to allow this conclusion.

12. J. S. Mill, "Nature," reprinted in *The Essential Works of John Stuart Mill,* ed. Max Lerner (New York: Bantam, 1961), 365–401.

13. *Man in the Modern World,* (New York: Mentor, 1948), 7–28.

14. For a thorough critique of naturalistic ethics, see Eliseo Vivas, *The Moral Life and the Ethical Life.* For essays that question the existence of any common and intelligible notion of nature, see Jane Bennett and William Chaloupka, eds., *In the Nature of Things: Language, Politics, and the Environment* (Minneapolis: University of Minnesota Press, 1993).

15. Whitehead, *Process and Reality,* corr. ed., ed. David Ray Griffin and Donald Sherburne, (New York: Free Press, 1978), 7–8; *Science and the Modern World* (Cambridge: University Press, 1925), 64–72.

16. Interview by Rodney Clapp and Beth Spring, "The Opinions of America's Most Respected Newspaper Columnist," *Christianity Today* (13 July 1984):26.

17. *Science and the Modern World,* 59.

18. See Jonathan Ned Katz, *The Invention of Heterosexuality* (New York: Dutton, 1995); and Michel Foucault, *The History of Sexuality,* 3 vols., trans. Robert Hurley (New York: Vintage, 1980, 1986, 1988).

19. The older term "sodomite" was, of course, used as a predicate—a term of derision and persecution. By emphasizing the "congenital" basis (to use

Will's term) of much same-sex attraction, the psychologists diminished the element of moral blame, thereby protesting cruelty. They also instituted a new regime emphasizing "illness" that could be quite cruel. See Martin Duberman, *Cures: A Gay Man's Odyssey* (New York: Plume, 1991).

20. For some scholars even (ex)friendship is not enough to escape the belief that sexual orientation wrecks scholarship. See Harry V. Jaffa, "Humanizing Certitudes and Impoverishing Doubts: A Critique of *The Closing of the American Mind*," in *Essays on "The Closing of the American Mind*," ed. Herbert L. Stone (Chicago: Chicago Review Press, 1989), 129–57.

21. The nastiest comments from the left are in Eric Alterman, *Sound and Fury: The Washington Punditocracy and the Collapse of American Politics* (New York: Harper, 1992), 96. Caveat emptor. A book that competently covers much the same territory as the Alterman book without personal invective is Alan Hirsch, *Talking Heads: Political Talk Shows and Their Star Pundits* (New York: St. Martin's Press, 1991).

22. *Character and Cops*, 2d ed. (Washington, DC: AEI Press, 1994), 241–42.

23. There seems to be sentiment among some conservatives that the deinstitutionalization of people with mental disabilities was simply the mistake of a group of wrong-headed liberals and radicals. These social commentators urge a return to the warm and welcoming places we fashioned before the fall. These conservative critiques usually rely on a false option. Either we must dump on the streets people who need some help or we must send them to large, impersonal institutions. We can (and sometimes do) help them find ways to live in the community. The classic critique of "total institutions" has lost none of its power: Erving Goffman, *Asylums: Essays on the Social Situation of Mental Patients and Other Inmates* (Garden City, NY: Anchor, 1961).

24. David Frum, in a mistaken reading of Isaiah Berlin, argues that laws against discrimination may serve the interests of equality or toleration, but that we misuse the term "liberty" when we describe these laws as enhancing freedom (*Dead Right*, 159–64). Frum's confusion, and his inability to understand Berlin, derive from an odd notion that only governments can restrict freedom. Somehow, if government tells someone not to go into a restaurant, freedom suffers, but if a private individual keeps you out, it is merely an exercise of property rights. What Frum does not grasp (as Berlin did) is that protecting one person's freedom may restrict another's. The most important case where religious freedom conflicted with freedom against discrimination involved denying Bob Jones University tax exemption because it practiced racial discrimination (*Bob Jones University v. U.S.*, 461 U.S. 574 [1983]). Berlin distinguishes between negative freedom, involving restrictions on the liberty of an individual to choose, and positive freedom, concerning the self-mastery of persons—their ability to make the right decisions for themselves. Positive freedom asks us to find our true selves and frequently justifies coercion on behalf of "true" freedom (Berlin, *Four Essays*, 118–72). Prohibiting an employer from fir-

ing me because he has pried into my sex life limits his negative freedom and enhances mine. Enforcing the law would require no appeal to positive freedom.

25. Sandel, "Moral Argument and Liberal Toleration," 521–22.

26. 387 U.S. 479 (1965).

27. For an important critique of Sandel, see Bonnie Honig, *Political Theory and the Displacement of Politics* (Ithaca, NY: Cornell University Press, 1993), 162–99.

28. Michael Ignatieff, *Blood and Belonging: Journeys into the New Nationalism* (New York: Farrar, Straus, and Giroux, 1993).

29. *Wisconsin v. Yoder,* 406 U.S. 205 (1972). For a bitter critique of *Yoder* as a threat to the integrity of liberal culture, see Walter Berns, *In Denfense of Liberal Democracy* (Chicago: Gateway, 1984), 299–307.

30. *Mozert v. Hawkins County Board of Education,* 827 F. 2d 1058 (6th Cir. 1987).

31. J. L. Dillard, *Black English: Its History and Usage in the United States* (New York: Vintage, 1972); Geneva Smitherman, *Talkin and Testifyin: The Language of Black America* (Detroit: Wayne State University Press, 1977).

32. *Liberalism, Community, and Culture* (Oxford: Clarendon, 1989).

33. Christopher Lasch argues that the notion of upward mobility that dominates our current ethos is a fairly late addition to our basic beliefs. *The Revolt of the Elites,* 25–79.

34. Michael Sandel is a very effective critic of some strands of liberalism that would make justice the central value that trumps all others. See *Liberalism and the Limits of Justice,* 133–74.

35. A powerful indictment of deifying art is a story by Flannery O'Connor, "The Enduring Chill," *The Complete Stories* (New York: Farrar, Straus, and Giroux, 1971), 357–82. Judith Shklar argues that snobbery is a grave vice in a liberal society (*Ordinary Vices,* 87–137).

36. The distinction between self-respect and self-esteem is explored in Charles Murray, *The Pursuit of Happiness and Good Government* (New York: Touchstone, 1988), 113–19.

37. For an important critique of the prohibition against curiosity, see Hans Blumenberg, *The Legitimacy of the Modern Age,* trans. Robert M. Wallace (Cambridge, MA: MIT Press, 1983), 229–453. Blumenberg argues that releasing curiosity bestows real benefits, among them the possibility of modern science. That may be true, but pedagogy requires structure. If we direct students to learn, we must instruct them on what is important and what we can profitably ignore. Of course, we should allow our students to learn in ways different from those we teach.

38. Clifford Geertz, *Works and Lives: The Anthropologist as Author* (Stanford: University Press, 1988); Tzvetan Todorov, *The Morals of History,* trans. Alyson Waters (Minneapolis: University of Minnesota Press, 1995).

39. See William E. Connolly, *Identity/Difference: Democratic Negotiations of Political Paradox* (Ithaca, NY: Cornell University Press, 1991) and *The Augus-*

tinian Imperative: A Reflection on the Politics of Morality (Newbury Park, CA: Sage, 1993).

Chapter 6

1. For a critique of the notion that any single paradigm can capture a political tradition as rich as ours, see Isaac Kramnick, *Republicanism and Bourgeois Radicalism: Political Ideology in Late Eighteenth Century England and America* (Ithaca, NY: Cornell University Press, 1990). Will's account of republican thought leans heavily on Garrett Ward Sheldon, *The Political Philosophy of Thomas Jefferson* (Baltimore: Johns Hopkins University Press, 1991).

2. Gordon S. Wood, *The Creation of the American Republic 1776–1787* (New York: Norton, 1969), 519–64.

3. The substitution of "family resemblance" for essential identity originates with Ludwig Wittgenstein, *Philosophical Investigations,* 3d ed., trans. G. E. M. Anscombe (New York: Macmillan, 1958), secs. 67, 77, 108, 164, and 179.

4. *Republics Ancient and Modern: Classical Republicanism and the American Revolution* (Chapel Hill: University of North Carolina Press, 1992), 139.

5. Orlando Patterson, *Freedom,* vol. 1, *Freedom in the Making of Western Culture* (New York: Basic Books, 1991), 1–199.

6. *The Politics,* bk. 5, 1310a. Jowett translation rev., Johnathan Barnes, ed. Stephen Everson (Cambridge: University Press, 1988).

7. Peter Riesenberg, *Citizenship in the Western Tradition: Plato to Rousseau* (Chapel Hill: University of North Carolina Press, 1992).

8. The notion of voice has been explored in managerial and political contexts by Albert O. Hirschman in *Exit, Voice, and Loyalty: Responses to Decline in Firms, Organizations, and States* (Cambridge: Harvard University Press, 1970) and in *Rival Views of Market Society and Other Recent Essays* (New York: Viking, 1986), 77–101.

9. There is extensive literature on populism. Studies worth consulting include John D. Hicks, *The Populist Revolt: A History of the Farmers' Alliance and the People's Party* (Lincoln: University of Nebraska Press, 1961); Simon Lazarus, *The Genteel Populists* (New York: McGraw Hill, 1974); Norman Pollack, *The Just Polity: Populism, Law, and Human Welfare* (Chicago: University Press, 1987); Norman Pollack, *The Populist Response to Industrial America: Midwestern Populist Thought* (New York: Norton, 1962); and C. Vann Woodward, *Tom Watson, Agrarian Rebel* (New York: Macmillan, 1938). Christopher Lasch in his last writings attempted to extract from populism a vision of a society composed of small freeholders devoted to productive exchange uncorrupted by large, corporate markets. Can we transform ourselves into such a society? Is it desirable? Even if we answer these questions yes, we still must find ways to divorce populist politics from the xenophobia, racism, and plebiscitary mentality that soils its history. The most likely leaders of a new populism come from the right. See Lasch, *The True and Only Heaven,* 476–532. On the possibility for a right-wing populist revolt, readers would still do well to consult Richard Hofstadter, *The*

Paranoid Style in American Politics and Other Essays (New York: Vintage, 1967). For a critique of Lasch's populism, see Stephen Holmes, *The Anatomy of Antiliberalism*, 122–40.

10. Introduction to *Running in Place: Inside the Senate*, by James A. Miller (New York: Touchstone, 1986), 10.

11. Joseph A. Schumpeter, *Capitalism, Socialism, and Democracy*, 3d ed. (New York: Harper Torchbooks, 1962), 232–302.

12. John Stuart Mill, *Considerations on Representative Government* (London: Parker, Son, and Bourn, 1861), ch. 3. For commentary, consult Dennis F. Thompson, *John Stuart Mill and Representative Government* (Princeton: University Press, 1976), 28–53.

13. For an excellent introduction to the theoretical issues concerning representation, see Hannah Pitkin, *The Concept of Representation* (Berkeley: University of California Press, 1972).

14. Edmund Burke, "Speech to the Electors of Bristol on October 13, 1774," *Burke's Politics: Selected Writings and Speeches of Edmund Burke on Reform, Revolution, and War,* eds. Ross J. S. Hoffman and Paul Levack (New York: Knopf, 1949), 114–17.

15. Defenses of pluralism worth examining include Robert A. Dahl, *A Preface to Democratic Theory* (Chicago: University Press, 1956) and Robert A. Dahl, *Dilemmas of Pluralist Democracy: Autonomy vs. Control* (New Haven: Yale University Press, 1982).

16. A critic worth consulting is E. E. Schattschneider, *The Semisovereign People: A Realist's View of Democracy in America* (New York: Holt, Rinehart, and Winston, 1969).

17. For the classic argument that political organizations preclude democratic decision making, see Robert Michels, *Political Parties: A Sociological Study of the Oligarchical Tendencies of Modern Democracy,* trans. Eden and Cedar Paul (New York: Free Press, 1962). For a case study providing a contrast to Michels's "iron law of oligarchy," see Seymour Martin Lipset et al., *Union Democracy* (Garden City, NY: Anchor, 1956).

18. Pluralists do not have to abandon the notion of a common interest. Some pluralists reintroduce it by discussing "public goods." Public goods are those provisions we cannot divide. If we provide to one; we provide to all. Someone will benefit even if no contribution is forthcoming. (This is known as the "free rider" problem.) Public goods must be provided through compulsory contribution or they will not be provided at all. The classic example of a public good is national defense. Everyone benefits regardless of who pays. Some provisions are close enough to count as public goods, but they do not exactly fit. We all have an interest in clean air and water, but polluters have more incentive to maintain these "negative externalities" than others. We even ask polluters to bear more of the costs of cleanup. In cases like these we must appeal to a notion of the common good that trumps the mere process of competition.

19. Will takes the phrase and much of his analysis of the presidency from Jeffrey K. Tullis, *The Rhetorical Presidency* (Princeton: University Press, 1987).

20. Some students of public opinion and American elections have affirmed the rationality of voters. See V. O. Key Jr., *The Responsible Electorate: Rationality in Presidential Voting 1936–1960* (New York: Vintage, 1966); Benjamin I. Page, *Choices and Echoes in Presidential Elections: Rational Man and Electoral Democracy* (Chicago: University Press, 1978); and Gerald Pomper, *Elections in America: Control and Influence in Democratic Politics* (New York: Dodd, Mead, and Company, 1971). Most students of opinion have rated party affiliation, socioeconomic status, and the personal appeal of candidates above ideology and issues in determining voter behavior. See Paul Abramson et al., *Change and Continuity in the 1988 Elections* (Washington, DC: CQ Press, 1990); Herbert Asher, *Presidential Elections and American Politics: Voters, Candidates, and Campaigns Since 1952* (Homewood, IL: Dorsey, 1976); and Angus Campbell et al., *The American Voter* (New York: Wiley, 1964).

21. *The Emerging Republican Majority* (Garden City, NY: Anchor, 1970).

22. Compare with Murray Edelman, *Political Language: Words That Succeed and Policies That Fail* (New York: Academic Press, 1977) and *The Symbolic Uses of Politics* (Urbana: University of Illinois Press, 1980).

23. Will has expressed support on *This Week with David Brinkley* for replacing the income tax with a consumption tax on the theory that it would simplify taxation and improve rates of saving and investment. Whether these benefits would accrue is a complex and contentious matter that I cannot pursue here. A national sales tax would be, like any unmodified sales tax, highly regressive. Here the issue of fairness is, well, fair. Unfortunately, a sales tax sensitive to income differentials runs the risk of being politicized.

24. For a good introduction to the debates on term limits, see Gerald Benjamin and Michael Malbin, eds., *Limiting Legislative Terms* (Washington, DC: CQ Press, 1992).

25. For a good discussion of some controversies surrounding Aristotle's claim, see David Wiggins, "Deliberation and Practical Reason," in *Essays on Aristotle's Ethics,* ed. Amelie O. Rorty (Berkeley: University of California Press, 1980), 221–40.

26. R. G. Mulgan, *Aristotle's Political Theory: An Introduction for Students of Political Theory* (Oxford: Clarendon Press, 1977), 559. The stress on law finding rather than lawmaking is even more marked in medieval political theory where only God truly authors laws.

27. Jürgen Habermas, *Communication and the Evolution of Society* (Boston: Beacon, 1979); *The Theory of Communicative Action,* 2 vols. (Boston: Beacon, 1984 and 1988).

28. For Locke's views on education, see *Some Thoughts Concerning Education,* ed. John W. and Jean S. Yolton (Oxford: Clarendon, 1989) and *Of the Conduct of the Understanding,* ed. Francis W. Garforth (New York: Teacher's College Press, 1966).

29.   Compare Will's brief discussion of delegation with the considerably more extensive work of Theodore Lowi whom, unfortunately, Will does not cite. See *The End of Liberalism,* 2d ed. (New York: Norton, 1979). See also Lowi, "Toward a Legislature of the First Kind" in *Knowledge, Power, and the Congress,* ed. William H. Robinson and Clay H. Wellborn (Washington, DC: Congressional Quarterly, 1991), 9–36. Lowi has argued that conservatives have been just as ineffective as liberals in dealing with the problem of delegation. See *The End of the Republican Era* (Norman: University of Oklahoma Press, 1995).

30.   Bernard Bray first pointed out to me that Will's questions about political scientists constitute a foray into the sociology of knowledge.

31.   Lani Guinier, *The Tyranny of the Majority: Fundamental Fairness in Representative Democracy* (New York: Free Press, 1994). Cumulative voting involves giving each voter several votes that can be given to one candidate or distributed among several candidates in a multimember district.

32.   A claim of discrimination in voting must establish that the discrimination is "invidious." It is not enough to show discrimination; a plaintiff must show that the discrimination is against a group, not merely for a group. I do not think white plaintiffs have met this standard in major redistricting cases. A five-person majority on the court has disagreed. See *Shaw v. Reno,* 509 U.S. 113 S. Ct. 2816 (1993).

33.   *The Concept of Representation,* 168–89.

34.   478 U.S. 30, 106 S. Ct. 2752 (1986).

35.   "The Voting Rights Act at 30," *Newsweek* (10 July 1995):64.

36.   Many scholars doubt that our rough categories for classifying races have any biological basis. Of course, race is a cultural and political reality that cannot be gainsaid. The best history of how the idea of race infected our culture remains Jacques Barzun, *Race: A Study in Superstition,* 2d ed. (New York: Harper Torchbooks, 1965).

37.   The evidence for a lack of self-respect among African Americans is less compelling than at the time Will wrote his dissertation. For a devastating review of the empirical evidence supporting the thesis that African Americans suffer from debilitating self-hatred, see William E. Cross Jr., *Shades of Black: Diversity in African American Identity* (Philadelphia: Temple University Press, 1991).

Chapter 7

1.   *The Genealogy of Morals,* second essay, sec. 13.

2.   William F. Buckley, "Notes Toward an Empirical Definition of Conservatism," in *What Is Conservatism?* ed. Frank S. Meyer (New York: Holt, Rinehart, and Winston, 1964), 211.

3.   "Notes," 211–12. Many years ago I heard Buckley's brother, Reid, describe this definition as "quite precise." Many in the audience did not share his standards of precision. Beyond the many clarifications the definition demands (e.g., exactly how is he using the word "phenomenology"?), the defin-

ition is perplexing. How does one conserve a paradigm of essences? Presumably the paradigm is eternal. Weaver seems to be hinting at some Neo-Platonic notion of participation in an eternal order, but the definition allows little more than guesses.

4. *Ideas Have Consequences* (Chicago: University Press, 1948).

5. Weaver's tracing of our political ills to nominalism is mirrored in Karl Popper's argument that totalitarianism stems from "the spell of Plato," or essentialism. Popper creates a Manichaean divide between totalitarians who believe in essences and defenders of "the open society" who do not. See *The Open Society and Its Enemies,* 2 vols. (London: Routledge, 1945). Weaver and Popper are about equally convincing.

6. For useful perspectives on the history of conservatism, consult William F. Buckley Jr., ed., *Did You Ever See a Dream Walking? American Conservative Thought in the Twentieth Century* (Indianapolis: Bobbs-Merrill, 1970); William F. Buckley Jr. and Charles R. Kesler, eds., *Keeping the Tablets: Modern American Conservative Thought* (New York: Harper and Row, 1987); Charles W. Dunn and J. David Woodard, *American Conservatism from Burke to Bush: An Introduction* (Lanham, MD: Madison Books, 1991); John P. East, *The American Conservative Movement: The Philosophical Founders* (Chicago: Regnery, 1986); Paul Gottfried and Thomas Fleming, *The Conservative Movement* (New York: Twayne, 1988); Russell Kirk, *The Conservative Mind: From Burke to Elliot* (New York: Regnery, 1953); Russell Kirk, ed., *The Portable Conservative Reader* (New York: Penguin, 1982); George H. Nash, *The Conservative Intellectual Movement in America since 1945* (New York: Basic Books, 1976); Robert Nisbet, *Conservatism* (Minneapolis: University of Minnesota Press, 1986); Peter Steinfels, *The NeoConservatives* (New York: Simon and Schuster, 1979); Peter Viereck, *Conservatism: From John Adams to Churchill* (Princeton: Van Nostrand, 1956); and Mark Royden Winchell, *Neo-Conservative Criticism* (New York: Twayne, 1991).

7. Samuel T. Coleridge, "Table Talk of February 24, 1832," in *Conservatism,* by Peter Viereck, 127.

8. Daniel Bell, *The End of Ideology: On the Exhaustion of Political Ideas in the Fifties* (New York: Collier, 1962); Seymour Martin Lipset, *Political Man* (New York: Doubleday, 1960); Robert E. Lane, *Political Ideology: Why the American Common Man Believes What He Does* (New York: Free Press, 1962); Robert E. Lane, *Political Man* (New York: Free Press, 1972).

9. Thomas R. Dye and L. Harmon Zeigler, *The Irony of Democracy: An Uncommon Introduction to American Politics,* 7th ed. (Belmont, CA: Wadsworth, 1987); Harry Holloway and John George, *Public Opinion: Coalitions, Elites, and Masses,* 2d ed. (New York: St. Martin's Press, 1986); Robert Lane, *Political Ideology;* Herbert McClosky and Alida Brill, *Dimensions of Tolerance: What Americans Believe about Civil Liberties* (New York: Russell Sage Foundation, 1983); Samuel Stouffer, *Civil Liberties, Communism, and Conformity* (New York: Doubleday, 1955).

10. Dan T. Carter, *The Politics of Rage: George Wallace, the Origins of the New Conservatism, and the Transformation of American Politics* (New York: Simon and Schuster, 1995).

11. *The Conservative Affirmation* (Chicago: Gateway, 1985).

12. Strategically, Buchanan mistakes the reality that most Americans are not particularly liberal with the fantasy that we are illiberal about the same things. Madison was right. Our factions do tend to cancel one another. On another level, Buchanan misreads the intensity of our illiberalism. Most Americans would restrict freedom of speech for some "undesirable" speakers, but we will not go out of our way to make these restrictions because we do not hold our views with much intensity. Furthermore, most Americans are quite liberal about our own rights. It is these other guys we must watch. We tend to make common cause with libertarians when our rights are at stake, and we become intense about our own rights as well. For Will's critique of Buchanan, see LW, 287–89.

13. Russell Kirk, *Enemies of the Permanent Things: Observations of Abnormity in Literature and Politics* (New Rochelle, NY: Arlington House, 1969).

14. Burleigh Taylor Wilkins, *The Problem of Burke's Political Philosophy* (Oxford: Clarendon Press, 1967).

15. See Francis P. Canavan, *The Political Reason of Edmund Burke* (Durham, NC: Duke University Press, 1960); Charles Parkin, *The Moral Basis of Burke's Political Thought* (Cambridge: University Press, 1956); Peter J. Stanlis, *Edmund Burke and the Natural Law* (Ann Arbor: University of Michigan Press, 1958).

16. Perhaps the most thoroughgoing attempt to cope with the problem of criticizing tradition from within tradition comes from a writer who is scarcely regarded as a conservative, Michael Walzer. See *The Company of Critics: Social Criticism and Political Commitment in the Twentieth Century* (New York: Basic Books, 1988); and *Interpretation and Social Criticism* (Cambridge: Harvard University Press, 1987).

17. Michael Walzer, *Just and Unjust War: A Moral Argument with Historical Illustrations,* 2d ed. (New York: Basic Books, 1992).

18. Alasdair MacIntyre, *After Virtue,* 1–34.

19. Alasdair MacIntyre, *Three Rival Versions of Moral Inquiry: Encyclopedia, Genealogy, and Tradition* (Notre Dame: University Press, 1990); and *Whose Justice? Which Rationality?* (Notre Dame: University Press, 1988).

20. For Burke's views on the French and American revolutions, consult Edmund Burke, *Reflections on the Revolution in France* (Indianapolis: Bobbs-Merrill, 1955); *Further Reflections on the Revolution in France,* ed. Daniel E. Ritchie (Indianapolis: Liberty Fund, 1992); and *Selected Writings and Speeches on America,* ed. Thomas H. D. Mahoney (Indianapolis: Bobbs-Merrill, 1964).

21. *The Life of the Mind,* vol. 2, *Willing* (New York: Harcourt Brace Jovanovich, 1978), 195–217.

22. *The Life of the Mind,* 207.

23. Voegelin, *The New Science of Politics,* 56–58.

24. See Eric Voegelin, "On Debate and Existence," in *Published Essays 1966–1985*, ed. Ellis Sandoz (Baton Rouge: Louisiana State University Press, 1990), 36–51.

25. *Conservatism Revisited*, 150.

26. *Conservatism in America*, 222.

27. The analogy is limited since we usually know the rules with a fairly high exactitude in card games. "The rules of the game" in politics is a metaphor, albeit a useful one. The trump metaphor is frequently deployed in the work of Ronald Dworkin. Dworkin rather consistently calls trumps in the same suit—equality.

28. *Schenck v. U.S.*, 249 U.S. 47, 39 S. Ct. 247, 63 L. Ed. 470 (1919).

29. The idea that right order involves maintaining tensions is a major theme in Eric Voegelin's work. A good source for exploring this motif is *What is History? and Other Late Unpublished Writings* (Baton Rouge: Louisiana State University Press, 1990). The idea that the human condition is an in-between existence is also central to Voegelin's philosophical anthropology and political ethics.

Chapter 8

1. Michael Ignatieff, *The Needs of Strangers: An Essay on Privacy, Solidarity, and the Politics of Being Human* (New York: Viking, 1984), 138–40.

2. Ignatieff, *The Needs of Strangers*, 140.

3. Peter L. Berger and Richard John Neuhaus, *To Empower People: The Role of Mediating Structures in Public Policy* (Washington DC: American Enterprise Institute, 1977); Robert Nisbet, *The Twilight of Authority* (New York: Oxford University Press, 1975), 230–87.

4. For an interesting use of the notion of communal freedom, see Benjamin R. Barber, *The Death of Communal Liberty: A History of Freedom in a Swiss Mountain Canton* (Princeton: University Press, 1974).

5. (New York: Farrar, Straus, and Giroux, 1971), 57.

6. I have explored the issue of letting go more fully in "Letting Go: On Looking Without Watching," presented at the 1992 meeting of the Midwest Political Science Association in Chicago, Illinois. I will develop my thoughts at greater length with my coauthors, Bernard Bray and Carle L. Jackson, in a book tentatively entitled *No Continuing City: Essays and Dialogues on Bondage and Freedom*.

7. *The Politics of Law and Order*, 203–23.

8. Quoted in Scheingold, *The Politics of Law and Order*, 117.

9. Gertrude Himmelfarb discusses Thatcher's views in *The Demoralization of Society*, 3–23.

10. *The Spirit of Community*, 170–73.

11. John Stuart Mill, *On Bentham and Coleridge*, ed. F. R. Leavis (New York: Harper, 1950).

12. *Rationalism in Politics*, 488–541.

Selected Bibliography

PRIMARY SOURCES

"Beyond the Reach of Majorities: Closed Questions in the Open Society." Ph.D. diss., Princeton University, 1968.

The Leveling Wind: Politics, the Culture, and Other News 1990–1994. New York: Viking, 1994.

Men at Work: The Craft of Baseball. New York: Macmillan, 1990.

The Morning After: American Successes and Excesses 1981–1986. New York: Free Press, 1986.

The New Season: A Spectator's Guide to the 1988 Election. New York: Simon and Schuster, 1988.

"The Opinions of America's Most Respected Newspaper Columnist. Interview by Rodney Clapp and Beth Spring." *Christianity Today,* 13 July 1984, 26.

The Pursuit of Happiness and Other Sobering Thoughts. New York: Harper and Row, 1978.

The Pursuit of Virtue and Other Tory Notions. New York: Touchstone, 1983.

Restoration: Congress, Term Limits, and the Recovery of Deliberative Democracy. New York: Free Press, 1992.

Statecraft as Soulcraft: What Government Does. New York: Simon and Schuster, 1983.

Suddenly: The American Idea at Home and Abroad 1986–1990. New York: Free Press, 1990.

Will, George F. Interview by author. 10 June 1994.

SECONDARY SOURCES

What follows is a selection of some of the more interesting commentaries on aspects of George Will's writings. This is the first comprehensive study of Will's ethical and political thought.

Eric Alterman. *Sound and Fury: The Washington Punditocracy and the Collapse of American Politics.* New York: HarperPerennial, 1993. George Will says he has not read this book. Perhaps he should. In its own way the book is flattering since it attributes extraordinary power to Will and a few other journalists. Then again, he would have to plod through a dull and implausible book to appreciate the flattery.

David Bromwich. "Moral Education in the Age of Reagan: On Some Recent Proposals for a Culture Without Criticism." *Dissent,* Fall 1986, 447–69. Critiques George Will and William Bennett from a social democratic perspective. One of the most thoughtful critiques of Will from the left.

Larry W. Chappell. Review of *Restoration,* by George F. Will. *The American Review of Politics,* Autumn 1993, 420–22. Provides the starting point for many of my observations in chapter 6.

Kimberle Williams Crenshaw. "Beyond Racism and Misogyny: Black Feminism and 2 Live Crew." In *Words That Wound: Critical Race Theory, Assaultive Speech, and the First Amendment,* 111–32. Boulder, CO: Westview, 1993. Questions Will's sincerity in sympathizing with feminist critiques of pornography. Crenshaw and other critical race theorists are not as distant as she imagines from Will's position—especially the position he took in his dissertation.

Benjamin DeMott. "The Pursuit of . . . Charm." *Nation,* 27 March 1982, 371–79. A scorched-earth critique of *The Pursuit of Virtue and Other Tory Notions* that argues that Will is palatable to some liberals because his work is vague.

Samuel T. Francis. "The Case of George Will." *Modern Age,* Spring 1986, 141–47. Argues that Will correctly articulates conservative principles while mistakenly using them to justify liberal policies.

Tim Ferguson. "Good Will." *American Spectator,* February 1994, 64–65. Analyzes the movement in Will's thought away from "big government conservatism" toward a growing mistrust of government.

Judith Frank. "In the Waiting Room: Canons, Communities, 'Political Correctness.' " In *Wild Orchids and Trotsky: Messages from American Universities,* edited by Mark Edmundson, 125–49. New York: Penguin, 1993. Takes sharp issue with Will's views on the canon debates and political correctness.

William A. Henry III. "George Will among the Polysyllables." *Esquire,* January 1987, 87–92. Enters the controversy over the authenticity of Will's erudition stirred by some "Doonesbury" comic strips concluding that Will's learning is genuine and his conservatism unusual and interesting.

Alan Hirsch. *Talking Heads: Political Talk Shows and Their Star Pundits.* New York: St. Martin's Press, 1991. Thoughtful and well-informed reflections on the tension between Will's writing career and his broadcast journalism.

Donald Kagan. "George Will's Baseball: A Conservative Critique." With George F. Will, "The Romantic Fallacy in Baseball: A Reply." *The Public Interest,* Fall 1990, 3–27. An interesting and acerbic debate on the ethical and political significance of Will's writings on baseball.

James Nuechterlein. "George Will and American Conservatism." *Commentary,* November 1983, 35–43. A generally appreciative reading of Will's work stressing the importance of his short essays rather than *Statecraft as Soulcraft.* The author thinks that Will's philosophical forays actually undermine an otherwise strong defense of democratic capitalism.

Garry Wills. "Undemocratic Vistas." *New York Review of Books,* 19 November 1992, 28–34. A sharply critical review of *Restoration.*

Index

Buckley, William F., 66, 116, 117, 151, 159, 160
Burke, Edmund, 12, 30, 72, 94, 112, 117, 122, 123, 124, 144, 157, 160, 161
Burr, Chandler, 152
Bush, George, 119

Cahn, Edmond, 38
Calhoun, John C., 26, 143
Campbell, Angus, 158
Campbell, Joseph, 146
Canavan, Francis P., 161
canons, 60–63
Carnal Knowledge, 54, 147
Carter, Dan T., 161
Carter, Jimmy, 98
Carter, Lief, 145
Carter, Stephen, 37, 145
censorship, 52
Cervantes, 60
Chaloupka, William, 153
Chaplinsky v. New Hampshire, 151
Chapman, John W., 141
Chappell's laws of constitutional interpretation, 9
Chappell's theorem on the circulation of elites, 66
Chidester, David, 141
Christ, 7
Christian fundamentalists, 81–82; philosophers, 32; thought, 153
Christianity, 14
Cicero, 12, 144
citizenship, 24, 85, 88, 90, 107; Fourteenth Amendment's definition of, 91
civic education, 89, 92
Civil Rights Act of 1964, 149
civil theology, 20: liberal 20
classical republicanism, 24, 25; 90, 92 102, 106, 124, 129
Clinton, Bill, 12, 77
coarsening, 52, 53
Cobb, John, Jr., 8, 137
Cohen, Carl, 148
cold war, 96, 138
Coleridge, Samuel Taylor, 88, 118, 160
Communist Party of America, 44

communitarians, 16, 80, 82, 140; conservative, 86
community, 13, 16–18, 75, 80, 81, 86, 128, 140; thick, 129, 130
compactness, 112
Congress, 109; culture of spending in, 110; delegation by, 110, 159; and the presidency, 110; professionalism in, 109, 110–11
Connolly, William E., 140, 155
consent, 32
consequentialism, 40, 43, 44
conservatism, 10, 99, 116, 118, 126, 161
conservatives, 5, 10, 12, 66, 116, 131, 133
constitutional interpretation, 33–40
constitutionalism, 29–33, 46
constructive repression, 22, 42–45; for totalitarian or racist causes, 44, 55
conversation, 127, 135
Cook, Elizabeth Adell, 146
core curriculum, 60–61
corruption, 106, 107, 124
Corwin, Edward, 144
Cose, Ellis, 149
Craig, Barbara Hinkson, 146
critical race theorists, 55
criticism, 5–6
Cross, William E. Jr., 159
cuisinart theory of justice, 13, 94
cultural identity, 83, 85
culture wars, 146

Daly, Markate, 140
Danford, John W., 139
decay, 107
Declaration of Independence, 95
Deep Throat, 54
Delattre, Edwin J., 77
deliberation, 103, 104, 110
deliberative democracy, 102
democracy, 30; and constitutionalism, 30–31
Democratic Party, 98, 99–101, 113
Dennis v. U. S., 145
De Tocqueville, Alexis, 23, 129, 138
Devlin, Patrick, 40, 72, 83, 145, 152
Dillard, J. L., 155

Hacker, Andrew, 150
Hampshire, Stuart, 15, 138
handicapped, 68
Hand, Learned, 43
Harrington, James, 88, 144
Hart, H. L. A., 152
Hartz, Louis, 11, 138
hate crime, 147
Hawkins, Gordon, 147
Hegel, G. W. F., 12
Helms, Jesse, 66
Heraclitus, 48
Herrnstein, Richard J., 145, 149
Hicks, John D., 156
hierarchy, 67
higher law, 30, 31; tradition in American
    constitutionalism, 31. *See also* natural
    law
Hill, Paul, 50
Himmelfarb, Gertrude, 143, 162
Hirsh, Alan, 154
Hirschman, Albert O., 142, 156
Hobbes, Thomas, 142
Hofstadter, Richard, 156–57
Holloway, Harry, 160
Holmes, Oliver Wendell, Jr., 19
Holmes, Stephen, 137, 146, 157
Homer, 21
homosexuality, 70, 71, 73, 76, 77, 78,
    79, 115, 139
Honig, Bonnie, 155
Hooker, Richard, 12, 135
Horton, Richard, 152
Hughes, Robert, 150
Hunter, James Davison, 49, 50, 146
Huxley, Aldous, 56
Huxley, Julian, 75

Ignatieff, Michael, 46, 128, 155, 162
Indians, 68. *See also* Native Americans
intermediary institutions, 129
international relations, 10
intervention, 130

Jackson, Carle, 147, 150, 162
Jacoby, Russell, 63, 151
Jaffa, Harry, 154
Jefferson Airplane, 56

Jefferson, Thomas, 20, 95, 124, 129, 156
Jencks, Christopher, 149
Jenkins v. Ga., 147
Jonas, Hans, 153
journalism, 1–5, 14
judicial restraint, 34, 47

Kagan, Donald, 138
Kahlenberg, Richard, 149
Kahn, Genghis, 125
Kahn, Kuyuk, 125
Kallen, Horace, 16, 140
Kant, Immanuel, 8, 40, 137
Katz, Jonathan Ned, 153
Katz, Michael B., 149
Kemmis, Daniel, 140
Kemp, Jack, 27, 131
Kendall, Willmoore, 119, 121, 125
Kennedy, Ted, 12
Kesler, Charles R., 160
Key, V. O. Jr., 158
Kilpatrick, James J., 138
King, Martin Luther Jr., 95
Kirk, Russell, 125, 151, 160, 161
Kramnick, Isaac, 156
Kundera, Milan, 56–57
Kymlicka, Will, 82–84, 130

laissez faire, 12, 119
Lamar, Jake, 149
Lane, Robert E., 160
Larmore, Charles E., 138
Lasch, Christopher, 63, 151, 155, 156
Last Temptation of Christ, The, 54
Lazarus, Simon, 156
leadership, 103
letting go, 130–31
Levinson, Sanford, 141
liberalism, 11, 12, 18, 50, 51, 92, 118,
    119, 141; American, 11, 14; classical,
    11–12, 67; of fear, 141; of mistrust,
    65; welfare state, 118, 143
liberals, 12, 16, 19, 24, 47, 66, 80, 90,
    105, 135; jurists, 35, 42
liberal societies, 16, 17, 23, 26, 55, 79,
    86
libertarians, 121, 161
liberty, 42, 78, 80,

Sigmund, Paul E., 152
Silence of the Lambs, The, 54
Skinner, B. F., 151
Skokie, 65
Skrentny, John David, 148
slavery, 47
Smith, Adam, 12, 22
Smitherman, Geneva, 155
Smith, Rogers M., 138
sobriety check points, 134–35
social pathologies, 58
sociology of knowledge, 111, 115
Socrates, 90
Solzhenitsyn, Alexander, 12
Sparta, 14, 89–90
special rights, 149
Spencer, Herbert, 12
Spielberg, Stephen, 52–53
Spinoza, Benedict, 11, 48, 137, 141
Springsteen, Bruce, 11
Stanlis, Peter J., 161
Star Wars, 21, 52
statecraft as soulcraft, 14, 28, 41
Steinfels, Peter, 160
Stouffer, Samuel, 160
Strauss, Leo, 141, 150
strict construction, 34
Swift, Adam, 140
Sykes, Charles, 151

Taylor, Charles, 61, 140
teleology, 73, 104 ;Christian sexual, 73
tension, 10, 20, 127, 128, 134
term limits, 102, 103, 107, 109,110, 111
Thatcher, Margaret, 132
thickness, 17, 18, 140
thinness, 17, 140; of liberal civil theology, 20
This Week With David Brinkley, 53, 96, 158
Thomas, Clarence, 115
Three's Company, 53, 54
Todorov, Tzvetan, 155
tolerance, 20, 21, 22, 66, 80, 86, 154; legal, 142; versus acceptance, 76, 78
tradition, 30
traditionalism, 32, 125

traditionalists in education, 81, 84–85
Tribe, Laurence H., 146
trumps, 126
Tullis, Jeffrey K., 158

underclass, 58, 149
unity, 88, 89

values, 51, 143
Viereck, Peter, 46, 125, 138
virtual representation, 94
virtucrats, 65, 66
virtue, 9, 13, 18–19, 22, 23, 26, 139, 143; civic, 10, 13, 18, 23, 88, 90, 109; commercial, 23–24; liberal, 24; private, 18, 23; republican, 25, 133
Vivas, Eliseo, 7, 153
Voegelin, Eric, 37, 68, 125, 135, 141, 142, 145, 152, 161, 162
voice, 91
voter rationality, 96
Voting Rights Act of 1965, 113
vulgar, 53

Wallace, George, 119, 120, 161
Walzer, Michael, 123, 140, 161
Warren Court, 37
Waters, Rob, 143, 145
Wayne, John, 56
Weaver, Richard, 116, 117, 160
Weld, William, 12
welfare state, 12, 132, 133
Wesley, John, 56
West, Cornell, 136
Whitehead, Alfred North, 76–77, 116, 153
Wiggins, David, 158
Wildmon, Donald, 53, 54
Wilkins, Burleigh Taylor, 122, 161
William of Ockham, 117
Williams, Kimberle Crenshaw, 147
Williamson, Rene De Visme, 137
Williams, Roger, 141
Wills, Garry, 13–17, 146
Wilson, James Q., 41, 133, 145
Wilson, John K., 151
Wilson, William Julius, 149

Winchell, Mark Royden, 160
Wisconsin v. Yoder, 155
Wittgenstein, Ludwig, 139, 156
Wolf, Susan, 61–62
Woodard, J. David, 160
Woodward, C. Vann, 156

Yack, Bernard, 142

Zeigler, L. Harmon, 160
Zimring, Francis E., 146

WIDENER UNIVERSITY
WOLFGRAM
LIBRARY
CHESTER, PA.

The Author

Larry W. Chappell is Associate Professor of Political Science at Mississippi Valley State University. He received a Ph.D. from Louisiana State University in 1982. His teaching and research specializations are in political philosophy and constitutional law. He was elected president of the Mississippi Political Science Association at the 1995 meeting. He serves as associate editor of *The Southeastern Political Review.* He has delivered papers at the American Political Science Association and the Northeast, Southwest, Southern, Midwest, Western, Arkansas, and Mississippi Political Science Associations. He served on a roundtable at the national meeting of the Modern Language Association. He serves on the lecture bureau of the Mississippi Humanities Council, delivering public lectures on "Death and Politics" and on "What Good Is Freedom? Reconsidering John Stuart Mill's *On Liberty.*" He has contributed articles and book reviews to a variety of journals, including the *Journal of Politics,* the *Review of Politics,* the *American Journal of Political Science,* the *Southeastern Political Science Review,* and the *South Carolina Review.* He has received several fellowship awards from the National Endowment for the Humanities. Professor Chappell resides in Itta Bena, Mississippi.

The Editor

Frank Day is a professor of English and head of the English Department at Clemson University. He is the author of *Sir William Empson: An Annotated Bibliography* (1984) and *Arthur Koestler: A Guide to Research* (1985). He was a Fulbright lecturer in American literature in Romania (1980–81) and in Bangladesh (1986–87).